D0853097

# GEISHA · HARLOT · STRANGLER · STAR

Asia Perspectives

# GEISHA · HARLOT ·

**Asia Perspectives**

HISTORY, SOCIETY, AND CULTURE

A series of the East Asian Institute, Columbia University, published by
Columbia University Press

Carol Gluck, Editor

*Comfort Women: Sexual Slavery in the Japanese Military During World War II*,
by Yoshimi Yoshiaki, tr. Suzanne O'Brien

*The World Turned Upside Down: Medieval Japanese Society*,
by Pierre François Souyri, tr. Käthe Roth

*Yoshimasa and the Silver Pavilion: The Creation of the Soul of Japan*,
by Donald Keene

# STRANGLER · STAR

## A WOMAN, SEX, AND MORALITY IN MODERN JAPAN

## WILLIAM JOHNSTON

COLUMBIA UNIVERSITY PRESS ★ NEW YORK

Columbia University Press
*Publishers Since 1893*
New York Chichester, West Sussex
Copyright © 2005 Columbia University Press
All rights reserved

Library of Congress Cataloging-in-Publication Data
Johnston, William, 1955–
Geisha, harlot, strangler, star : a woman, sex, and
moral values in modern Japan /
William Johnston.
    p.   cm.
Includes bibliographical references and index.

1. Abe, Sada, 1905–   . 2. Murder—Japan—
Tokyo—History—Case Studies. 3. Sex crimes—
Japan—Tokyo—History—Case studies.
4. Women murderers—Japan—Tokyo—Biography.
5. Prostitutes—Japan—Tokyo—Biography. I. Title.
HV6535.J33T63   2005
364.152'3'0952135—dc22            2004043882

Columbia University Press books are printed
on permanent and durable acid-free paper.
Printed in the United States of America
c 10 9 8 7 6 5 4

# CONTENTS

Everything happens for the first time, but in a way that is eternal.
Whoever reads my words is inventing them.

—Jorge Luis Borges, "Happiness"

This book is about a modern Japanese woman named Abe Sada who first worked as a geisha and later became a prostitute. After she left prostitution, she committed a murder in 1936 that made her an improbable and reluctant celebrity not only in Japanese society but also throughout the world. Yet this is, above all, an enduring story about love and one woman's quest to find and hold on to it.

Abe herself would probably agree that love remains mysterious to us all, eternally surprising, no matter how intimate we might be with its whims and twists. As she discovered, it takes us to places that we cannot predict but that appear when we surrender ourselves to love's direction. Those places can be shocking but enticing, with an allure that spurs repeated visitations. The story at the center of this book is one that I could not forget or resist passing along, just as others have retold it innumerable times before. What I hope readers might discover in it is a basic humanity that helps them reflect on both their own and that of the people around them. To retell this story is to reinvent it, and in the process to examine something as mysterious as love itself: our ability, as humans, to communicate with other humans.

A number of people communicated with me in ways that made this book a reality. Carol Gluck encouraged me to pursue a project that until then remained just another pot on one of my stove's uncountable back burners. Without her encouragement, it probably would still be simmering there. At Columbia University Press, Jennifer Crewe helped turn an idea into a book with helpful suggestions of ingredients to add and others to delete. In Kyoto, Yamada Keiji and Inoue Shôichi, among others, brought some vital ingredients to my attention just as I started, while in Nagoya, Haga Shôji and Takahashi Kimiaki added more just as I was finishing. Several people, including Ikumi Kaminishi, Gaye Rowley, Ellen Widmer, four anonymous readers for Columbia University Press, and all of my senior colleagues in the History Department at Wesleyan University read the entire manuscript and made helpful suggestions. Long before there was a book manuscript, Kay Poursine read the translations that started this project and kindly pointed out passages that remained muddled. Leslie Kriesel at Columbia University Press patiently transformed my words into prose. Librarians at several institutions, including Wesleyan University, the Harvard-Yenching Library at Harvard University, Nagoya University, Kyoto University, and the National Diet Library in Tokyo provided raw materials with which I worked. Among other things, to love is to care, and these individuals have been very caring indeed. I am grateful to all.

Perhaps most important, something that my parents taught me by example is that one does not always need to understand in order to love. Although they might not understand this book, it is to my mother and the memory of my father that I dedicate it.

# INTRODUCTION

Some crimes achieve notoriety far out of proportion to the events themselves, and often they are crimes by women. Examples abound. Most schoolchildren in the United States learn a nursery rhyme about an ax murder committed in 1893, allegedly by a woman named Lizzy Borden.[1] Although the evidence against her was only circumstantial, her story has inspired books, films, an opera, a ballet, and an eponymous heavy metal rock band. Another renowned example is that of Bonnie Parker, half of the murder-and-robbery duo Bonnie and Clyde, who remains an icon in American culture despite her mean spirit and petty ruthlessness. But the criminal women most likely to attract attention are those whose transgressions involve sex. In part, this is because of the novelty:more men than women commit sex-related crimes. But this is not all. Thesewomen's stories combine vulnerability and violence, a contrast that perennially fascinates. Lorena Bobbitt's name remains nearly as familiar today as it was in June 1993, when she severed her husband's penis—which physicians later reattached—as revenge for domestic abuse. In Japan, the name of one woman remains similarly persistent: Abe Sada has never faded from memory since May 1936, when she murdered her lover, severed his genitals, and briefly disappeared into the streets of Tokyo.

It was in 1975, during my first stay in Japan, that I initially heard of Abe Sada. Japanese friends talked about her in tones of horror-tinged fascination. During my second sojourn there, from 1978, I saw the government-censored version of Ôshima Nagisa's film *In the Realm of the Senses* (1976), which was based on Abe Sada's relationship with the lover who became her victim. At that time neither the incident nor the film seemed to be more than odd curiosities. Yet after an intervening decade of researching the history of medicine and public health in modern Japan, I found the woman named Abe Sada, the forces that pushed her to commit the crime for which she became famous, and her place in the history of women, gender, and sexuality in modern Japan subjects of compelling interest.

The leap from the history of public health to the history of sexuality is not far: both have social and cultural values, not to mention medical issues, at their center. Both also raise questions concerning the movement of culture across national and state boundaries. They demonstrate how Japanese people have absorbed elements of western—shorthand for mainstream European and North American—culture because they have fulfilled pre-existing needs. Parallel intellectual, cultural, and social developments have, over time, made some western ideas and practices seem both familiar and useful. In addition, an important issue in both categories of history is the intersection of Japanese and western ideas and cultural norms concerning the human body.

By the late nineteenth century, western sexual discourse and practices had become useful to several groups in Japanese society, including the political oligarchy and the social classes, consisting primarily of former samurai and others of aristocratic descent, from which it arose; the scientific community; and a number of socially influential intellectuals including writers, university professors, and some feminists. Part of that usefulness arose from Japan's need to mirror the West in order to regain international recognition as an equal. The more western, civilized, and enlightened the Japanese appeared, the more difficult it became for the western powers to justify extraterritoriality and other provisions in unequal treaties. In addition, western ideas and practices fulfilled a practical need for those who wished to reconfigure the economic and social rights of Japanese women.

The most powerful men in Japan after the Meiji Restoration of 1868 were former samurai, descendants of a centuries-old patrilineal culture. One of their goals was to replicate that culture, at least in part, throughout the populace. As this book discusses in some detail, most of the other social classes, which constituted between approximately 93 and 95 percent of the people, did not live by the same values as the former samurai class. Certain contemporary western ideas concerning gender and sexuality supported the values that the former samurai wished to impose on the rest of Japanese society, and as a consequence were politically useful. A central theme of this book is how these values of gender and sexuality intersected across national, gender, and class lines. Instead of approaching these issues from a broad perspective, I have used the case of Abe Sada to provide a sharply focused view.[2] It is well documented, which makes it helpful in mapping the boundaries of socially, legally, and medically acceptable sexual behavior for many and perhaps most female-male relationships in Japan before World War II.

Until recently, the subject of sexual values and behaviors, both inside and outside the family, has rarely been taken seriously among Japanese scholars in general, and even more rarely among historians.[3] Many considered it, as some still do, a topic unworthy or inappropriate for serious thought or historical research.[4] Yet the times have been changing, and in 1992 I had the opportunity to join a small group of scholars of both Japanese and other nationalities who gathered in Kyoto to read and discuss both primary sources and one another's work concerning the history of sex and sexuality in Japan.[5] That was when I discovered the published transcript of Abe Sada's police interrogations and the report of the police investigation of the murder she had committed in 1936.[6]

Although in Japan Abe Sada was as well known in the early 1990s as at any time before, these documents made it clear that few people were familiar with many details of her life or with the circumstances behind the murder she committed. For most people, her name conjured up only a lurid crime and prurient fiction and films. Few thought about her as a person, somebody who could be the woman next door, and not simply an icon of extreme concupiscence. After reading her own description of her early life, I came to think of her as a complex individual. She had grown up in a traditional and comfortable, if not wealthy, Tokyo family, not the background one would expect of a prostitute and murderer whose life manifested a collision of traditional and modern sexual values during the early twentieth century. This was no simple conflict of "traditional Japanese" and "modern western" categories; both contained contradictory elements of their own. As the split between the values of the ex-samurai and aristocratic classes and the rest of society suggests, "traditional" sexual values in Japan were hardly homogeneous. Customs varied widely by region as well as social class, some being quite liberal in their allowances for contact between young men and women. "Modern" sexual values in the West ranged from the religiously sanctioned chastity of Protestant fundamentalists to the free love of radical intellectuals. Abe Sada's life unfolded under the influence of traditional Edo customs in her family, household, and neighborhood environment, combined with a binary "good girl–bad girl" categorization of women that was reinforced by both the values of the former samurai class and imported Victorian ideas.

In part, her story is valuable because it allows a focus primarily, if not exclusively, upon sexual practices instead of discourse. It is, of course, impossible to separate the two completely. Yet as others have argued convincingly, neither can they be equated.[7] There are varied and numerous texts available to examine sexual discourse in early twentieth-century Japan, but relatively few sources allow a close look at the lives of ordinary women who worked as prostitutes.[8]

The result of my research is a narrative account of Abe Sada's life that includes brief discussions of the cultural context in which she lived. The English translation of her police interrogations is appended. This book places the events of her life, rather than an interpretive or analytical apparatus, at the forefront.[9] Abe Sada's life invites interpretation, but my goal is to present a narrative that incorporates, as much as possible, her own voice. It would be naïve to assume that the police interrogations and investigation that form the documentary basis for this account provide a transparent window on Abe's life. They have their own internal logic, one of criminal discovery, that in many ways provided the structure by which Abe told her own life story. Yet because there are no substantial alternative sources on which to base her biography, the official documents reveal a story that otherwise would not exist at all. What I have added to them is there to help the reader understand the society, culture, and values that made up her world. In part, the form of this book was inspired by other narrative microhistories based primarily on legal and other contemporary documents.[10] Some of the interpretive issues that this account raises, especially those best addressed through works by other writers, receive attention in the notes.

Nevertheless, this book does have issues at its center that reach far beyond the narrative itself. Broadly speaking, it is about changes in boundaries of sexual moralities and behaviors, of gender roles, and of love attachments between women and men in modern Japan. Four questions are at the core: What determined the boundaries between permissible and forbidden sexual behaviors between women and men? How were those boundaries changing in Japan during the early twentieth century? In what ways were they different for women and for men? Indeed, do the simple terms "women" and "men" by themselves best describe gender definitions at that time, or might other terms better convey how the categories related to sex determined the social status of individuals? This last question places the term "gender" closer to its original but now generally obsolete meanings of "genus," "sort," or "class."[11] The life of Abe Sada and the story of the murder she committed provide, in microcosm, at least some answers to these questions, which suggest conclusions reaching far beyond this specific case.

Central to this book is the observation that the categories of sex and gender are cultural constructions.[12] Some skeptics still scoff at this idea with the commonsensical "I know one when I see one" argument of sexual difference. This is akin to commenting on the world as seen through one particular lens while remaining unaware that other lenses provide alternative views and understandings. Only by switching lenses do we become aware of how our previous view was limited. The "I know one when I see one" perspective equates sex with anatomical structure and gender with sex.

In reality, anatomy by itself is silent.[13] The physical differences that we use to distinguish between sexual categories of human beings and other animals exist outside of language, yet we depend on language to conceptualize and understand those differences. What becomes apparent in the space between the silence of anatomy and the articulation of culture are variations in the ways people construct the concept of sex and consequently of gender. Once we apply language to biological differences, we introduce the values of human culture into the matrix of understanding both bodies and sexual behavior. Along with the expression of anatomical difference that appears when making a sexual distinction are all the other associations that people make with "sex," especially regarding what we call sexuality. They include activities that have nothing whatsoever to do with reproductive anatomy or male-female physical differences. Importantly, erotic desire and sexual activity do not depend on anatomical difference. In sex, maybe more than anyplace else in human life, things are not always what they seem.

This is especially true when thinking historically. It is easy to forget that the concept of sex with all its nuances, in both the contemporary West and Japan today, is itself a recent construction. Before the eighteenth century, "sex" in the English language implied little more than the difference between males and females. Similarly, in the Japanese language before the nineteenth century there was no word with the meanings that "sex" had in European languages. The modern term for sex in Japanese, *sei*, originally meant "inherent qualities" or "essence" and had a broad range of uses. It came to mean sex among intellectuals in the late nineteenth century and that meaning achieved common currency only in the twentieth.[14]

The modern terms for "sexual desire" (*seiyoku*) and "sexual intercourse" (*seikô*) appeared in the Japanese language for the first time in the early years of the twentieth century.[15] This paralleled practices in the English language: the first citation of the term "sex act" in the *Oxford English Dictionary* dates to 1918. By contrast, the verb "to touch," meaning "to have sexual intercourse," is older by centuries but obsolete today. Japanese terms equivalent to the English word "sexuality" are of even more recent vintage. The western ideas that menstruation and masturbation were pathological were completely foreign to the Japanese—although they had the notion that menstruation was a source of ritual pollution—and had to be argued repeatedly by medical writers and social commentators from the late nineteenth century before they entered the pantheon of common sense.

Another accepted western idea, that women were sexually passive, was more or less difficult to implant in Japan depending on the social class. Aristocratic ex-samurai women tended to be passive in many respects, but women of other classes, depending on the region and other circumstances, often were sexually active. An even larger gap existed between the Victorian concept that women embodied both savage and childlike characteristics, and as a result required special treatment in society, and the practice in Japanese farming and other working classes, where women and men usually worked shoulder to shoulder.[16] In short, the sexual common sense of Japan before 1900, including that expressed in medical and other discourse, had little in common with that of the West.

It is also important to note that the concept of love, the emotion most often associated with sexuality, is subject to historical change and depends on cultural circumstances. In terms of romantic attractions and attachments, love stories have been central to Japanese culture since ancient times. A founding myth of the Japanese islands was based on an attraction between two gods, Izanami and Izanagi, that was both physical and emotional. The most common term for "love" in premodern Japan, *koi*, included both of these elements. Most usages of that word assumed that an emotional attraction included a physical element.

Human culture and the boundaries that determine its categories and symbols are in a constant state of flux. The boundaries that people of one time take for granted might be totally different or even absent in other times and places. The boundaries of sex and gender, if those categories exist at all in a society, can be positioned in innumerable ways, yet only understood through specific instances. Theory can suggest useful perspectives, but understanding a place requires going there, or at least getting as close as possible. The case of Abe Sada provides an entry point into the lives and culture of many other people in early twentieth-century Japan. One goal of this book is to facilitate a better understanding of how Abe Sada, and as a consequence many other Japanese women and men of her time, understood sexuality and its expression. It attempts to provide readers with an alternative lens through which to see not only this woman and her time but also themselves and their own milieu.

# A MURDER GRIPS THE NATION

On the morning of May 19, 1936, Tokyo awoke to a sensational news story. In a red-light district, a beautiful woman had murdered her lover and mutilated his corpse. It was a jarring account, but also a welcome respite from long-standing political and economic tensions. The unfolding newspaper account was like an erotic thriller that had improbably slipped past government censors, bringing relief from more troubling current events. Yet unlike incidents that garnered furious but only momentary media attention, this left an indelible mark on twentieth-century Japan. The events and the personalities related to the murder fascinated people at the time and have continued to do so ever since.

Political turmoil, civil strife, and disaster had dominated the news all spring. Only three months before, on February 26, a radical group of ostensibly pro-emperor army officers attempted a coup d'etat. They murdered several prominent politicians and other leaders whom they considered corrupt and seized the prime minister's residence, National Diet (Parliament) building, army ministry, and other key points in Tokyo. The government immediately declared martial law. Emperor Hirohito himself found the coup attempt profoundly disturbing and declared the offending officers—who had murdered several of his good friends—rebels. Two officers immediately committed suicide; the rest were soon apprehended and put on trial before secret military tribunals. The affair spread unease over not only Tokyo but also the entire country. As if this were not enough to set the nation on edge, before the spring was out a major arson incident occurred in Yokohama and a big, long-standing business scandal continued to embroil political and financial leaders. All of this occurred against a backdrop of smoldering war in China, sporadic yet sometimes violent resistance among the colonial subjects in Korea, and the increasingly egregious usurpation of political and human rights at home. People were ready for a diversion.

It came that morning when headlines in the *Tokyo Asahi shinbun*, a leading newspaper, read: GROTESQUE MURDER IN OGU RED-LIGHT DISTRICT. BLOOD CHARACTERS CARVED IN MASTER'S CORPSE. BEAUTIFUL MAID DISAPPEARS FOLLOWING LOVE TRYST. The following story depicted Abe Sada as an ex-geisha from Nagoya with ties to a prominent politician and educator from that city. Other newspapers carried similar and sometimes even more lurid headlines and stories. None put the story on its front page—crime stories rarely appeared there—but its splash could hardly have been bigger. Newspapers and then magazines competed in their coverage of the event. Some, such as the *Yomiuri* and the *Hôchi*, were sensationalistic and emphasized the erotic and grotesque aspects. Others, such as the *Asahi*, were more straightforward and restrained in their reporting. For several days they gave the murder many inches of column space over multiple pages. The incident was shocking, but many people responded with laughter and ribald jokes.[1] It resonated with the stereotypes of *ero-guro*, the erotic and the grotesque, that already had captured contemporary imaginations as part of the aesthetic troika of *ero-guro-nansensu*, or erotic, grotesque, and nonsense. Indeed, this incident came to represent *ero-guro* for years to come. And not a few also found it nonsensical.

In pursuit of the details, the *Asahi* interviewed the owner of Masaki, the teahouse (a euphemism for a small inn that specialized in renting rooms for sexual liaisons, the forerunner of the love hotel) where the murder had occurred. She explained how during the previous week a "professional-looking" woman of about age 31 or 32 had checked in with a "dapper-looking playboy type" of approximately age 50. They spent most of the week in bed. The woman left early in the morning of May 18, but well into the afternoon the man still failed to show his face. Just before three o'clock a maid looked into the couple's room and found the man dead inside the futon. He had been strangled and his genitals removed with a knife. Written on the futon in blood were words that translate roughly as "Sada Kichi together forever." On his thigh was written "Sada Kichi together."[2] And carved into his left arm was the single character that read "Sada."

Police investigators soon discovered the victim's identity. He was Ishida Kichizô—also known as "Kichi"—age 42, owner of a small restaurant named Yoshidaya, which he had opened in 1920 in Tokyo's Nakano Ward, generally a middle-class district. His killer's identity was also clear. She was Abe Sada, age 32, who had worked as a maid at Yoshidaya. Although the police quickly identified the murderer, they were slower in catching her. By the time they knew Abe was the killer, she had escaped into Tokyo's labyrinthine streets. News reports described a sexually and criminally dangerous woman on the loose, triggering a nationwide "Abe Sada panic" the following day. Journalists followed her footsteps through the city, but she had managed to shake police and reporters alike. Police received reports of sightings not only in Tokyo but also in Yokohama, Osaka, and other cities. A supposed sighting in Ginza created a mad rush of people trying to catch a glimpse, resulting in a large traffic jam. All these were false alarms. Yet officers did find Abe just in time to keep her from taking her own life.

Newspapers on May 21 reported her arrest the day before at an ordinary inn near Tokyo's Shinagawa Station, the main departure site for all points west and south along the coast. People had awaited news of Abe's capture with an expectant tension. Members of the Diet interrupted a regularly scheduled committee meeting to read the newspaper extras on the day of her arrest. They reported that after the murder she had done her best to remain inconspicuous, changing costumes more than once. She had planned to leave the next morning for Osaka, where she intended to commit suicide, but with the police present everywhere she looked, she had decided to hang herself in her room at the Shinagawa inn instead. Despite the momentary panic she had inspired, it was immediately obvious that she endangered nobody but herself.

The gruesome story of murder and mutilation initially captured the public's gaze, but the killer's photographs, taken just after her arrest and printed in the newspapers the next day, revealed a diminutive and strikingly attractive woman with an odd smile that approached nothing less than a sheepish grin. The police were grinning along with her. When asked why she had committed the murder to which she freely confessed, she answered, "Because I loved him." Most of her contemporaries would immediately have seen both the logic and the terror in this answer. She had killed not out of hatred or simple jealousy—although jealousy played its part—but out of love and a desire to control her beloved forever. Her explanation struck a chord throughout society. "Because I loved him" made Abe Sada a focus of fascination while tapping a current of subterranean fear, especially among men.

For many, Abe was an archetypical manifestation of the "dangerous woman," representing a female sexuality that threatened the stability of the nuclear household or *ie*.[3] Women and men alike, especially those of the elite in a self-consciously hierarchical society, found this most disturbing.

Abe's actions also raised questions about love itself and its proper role both in female-male relationships and in society as a whole. One thread in her life story recalled the hoary theme of lovers who could not be joined in life and so pursued unity in death. However, Abe's lover did not wish to die,

**FIGURE 1.** Abe Sada immediately following her arrest, surrounded by police officers at Takanawa Police Station in Tokyo, May 20, 1936. Photo: The Mainichi Newspapers

so she resolved to murder him and to kill herself later. Superficially, the enormity of Abe's desire to dominate her lover explains her crime. But it does little to help us understand her as a woman in the world in which she lived. Arguably few Japanese women in modern times have done more to raise awareness of the issues of sexual and gender inequality. Yet unlike most of the other women who argued for equality in one form or another, she had neither the explicit ideology of a political radical nor the refined discourse of an educated writer. Rather, she represented a common and less discursive side of contemporary culture, one that included most of the Japanese people but has generally been overlooked.

The existing evidence allows us to follow a number of threads through Abe's life. One particularly revealing thread is her difficulty accepting social boundaries. She remained forever on the margins of society. From adolescence she lived outside the boundaries of "normal" women, but for her the "abnormal" became the ordinary. Eventually she lost her bearings so completely that murder and mutilation, which to her made a kind of logical sense, became acceptable.

Most acts of violence have multiple causes, and this one is no exception. There is no single reason Abe Sada murdered and mutilated her lover, despite her statement that she did it because she loved him. Individuals certainly commit crimes, but social circumstances make those crimes possible and must be considered contributing causes. In Abe Sada's case, contemporary sexual politics established circumstances that pushed her toward murder. How that happened is in part what makes her historically important as more than just the perpetrator of a colorful crime.

Although as a working prostitute Abe had had sex with innumerable men, she testified in court that her victim, Ishida Kichizô, was her first true love. She had become obsessed with controlling him in the same way a man could control a woman. She concluded that only through murder could a woman "monopolize"—to translate her Japanese literally—a man as completely as a man could legally "monopolize" a woman. Her argument had an undeniable logic. The legal system gave little or no means of redressing social and legal inequalities between the sexes. It was obvious to her contemporaries how Abe's response to this system reflected an inescapable asymmetry of power.

Yet ever since she committed murder in 1936, Abe Sada has not been remembered primarily because of her opposition to women's social, legal, and sexual oppression. Rather, she fits the popular and enduring tropes of the "poisonous woman" (dokufu) and the "evil woman" (akujo), long-standing categories with much overlap.[4] These women are attractive yet dangerous, erotically charged and murderous. They are objects of desire to be feared, for they can squander a fortune, debilitate a man's body, disqualify him as a family man. An example of the "evil woman" is the classical poet Ono no Komachi, who, legend has it, used her femininity to manipulate the men who desired her. Her willfulness led to a man's death, though not at her own hands. The "poisonous woman" also has roots in Chinese literature and history. In most cases she usurps male power, usually causing at least one man's death. Most retellings of Abe Sada's story in the theater, fiction, film, and other media make her into some version of the "evil woman," a type rather than a complex, living human being. Arguably, these accounts of Abe Sada tell more about their creators—usually men—and their times than about the woman herself. She becomes a locus of male fantasy in which a sexually desirable woman assumes complete control over the phallus. Making the dangerous woman a type and consequently the subject of fantasy makes it possible to take control of her. Any semblance to a living, breathing, and complex person disappears.

This book turns away from these constructions of Abe Sada. It presents her and the people surrounding her as unique yet not uncommon individuals, and describes some of the circumstances in which they all lived. Like most real-life stories, it contains ambiguities and many shades of gray, some very dark indeed. It is a tale of indulgent, middle-class parents, the consequences of acquaintance rape, life as a prostitute, and an obsessive desire to shatter a taboo on sexual equality.

Abe Sada's historical importance is independent from her immortality in fiction and other representations. Even if she had been forgotten from the time she committed murder until the present, even if she had never entered the pantheon of seductive yet poisonous and evil women, her story would still be valuable for what it reveals about contemporary culture and society. Most important, the available documents related to her crime allow us to hear her own voice. Once apprehended, she hid little, if anything, from the police while avoiding unnecessary embellishments. The police interrogation of Abe Sada gives her own view both of her life up to the time of the crime and of the crime itself. This does not, of course, mean that the record is free of deletions or distortion. At some points she seems to give the police what she thinks they want. For example, she emphasizes repeatedly how she did her best to be a filial daughter. At other points she seems to strive toward self-creation rather than accurate recall from memory. Nevertheless, the interrogation record does give the closest approximation of Abe's own voice telling much of her life story.

Abe's interrogation record and the report of the police investigation document not only a crime but also the perpetrator: a woman who grew up in middle-class circumstances in Tokyo, became a prostitute, and worked in several locations at different kinds of establishments during the course of her career. In the report of the police investigation we hear the voices of procurers, brothel owners, prostitutes, patrons, relatives, neighbors, and others whose lives intersected with Abe's. This report also includes some of Abe's statements that are not in the interrogation. This is curious, and suggests the existence of records that have not survived, or at least have not become public. At no point do the existing records explain this discrepancy, which raises the question what other evidence remains that has not yet seen the light of day. Yet the available information is rich and detailed, creating a clear image of this woman and the people around her, including her colleagues in the sex industry.

Thousands of women worked as prostitutes in twentieth-century Japan, but we know little about them as people or the concrete circumstances of their everyday lives. One important facet that remains somewhat unclear is what motivated them. A vast number became licensed prostitutes for economic reasons, whether poverty or the needs of a family member such as a sick parent or sibling. Government policy and rhetoric allowed no other reason for entry into prostitution, and alternative job opportunities, especially for women with little education, were scarce.[5] Factory work was one, but some women who had worked in factories quit to become prostitutes; it would be difficult to say which business was harder on its employees. Yet there were reasons for entering the sex industry other than poverty. Abe's case is an example; she did not become a prostitute because of personal or familial penury. Economics did, however, keep women in the industry who might have started there for other reasons. Confined first to the geisha houses and later to the brothels, Abe soon detested her job and her living conditions but had no other means of self-support.

After several years of work as a registered prostitute, she attempted to escape on multiple occasions, only to be arrested by the police and, as the law required, returned to the brothels. When a woman attempted escape, owners invariably sold her contract to another brothel. Because any such woman was a dangerous investment, her contract's value fell and her working and living conditions deteriorated. Consequently, Abe experienced life in a sequence of ever-seedier establishments and increasingly worse conditions. Her explanations of these episodes spoke for many others who faced similar and often worse fates.

While the circumstances of Abe Sada's life before she committed murder reveal much about the sex industry, sexuality, and gender relations in early twentieth-century Japan, the legal consequences of that murder say even more about government policy regarding all of these areas. The links between science, law, and gender relations are vividly clear. Her punishment for premeditated murder was six years of imprisonment; for good behavior, her sentence was commuted after she had completed five. The government's reasons for this mild response illuminate its attitudes regarding gender relations and sexual mores at that time.

The following chapters explore the world of Abe Sada, in part as described in her own voice, in part in the voices of others around her. It is a story that must be told from various perspectives to make it possible to grasp the many layers of meaning. Specifically, it is the story of a relationship that unfolded in a few short weeks, during which a newly hired maid and a restaurant owner became partners in an affair that locked them together in love to the death. More generally, it is the history of many more lives and their social and cultural milieu. There certainly are many more layers of meaning than the ones I have tried to illuminate here. I encourage readers to read the complete translation of the police interrogation to become even more intimate with Abe and how she saw her world.

# 1. AN UNREMARKABLE FAMILY HISTORY

Abe Sada's family and ancestors were quite ordinary, like innumerable other families then living in Tokyo and throughout the country. The ancestors of both her mother and her father had been stable and hard working, if not illustrious. Most had moved to Tokyo from outside the city during the previous century. Little more is known about them except that none left a criminal record. Yet in 1936 many people would have expected otherwise. Common sense dictated that criminal behavior had a hereditary taint. In premodern times, entire families had been extinguished for the felonious behavior of one member, partly because of this belief. So behind any heinous crime police would look for a criminal history, at least of repeated petty offenses, in the accused's family. A major felon in the family tree helped explain a crime as the outcome of a person's natural tendencies. Faced with explaining Abe Sada's deed but finding no sign of inherited criminality, the police attempted to tie it to aberrant behavior related to sexuality, alcohol, mental and physical disease, and gender roles.

The police described her father, Abe Shigeyoshi, as "an honest and upright man, highly circumspect in his dealings with women." In other words, if he had any affairs outside marriage, he did not allow them to become a legal problem. Serious financial difficulties also would have come to the attention of the police, so their failure to mention anything of the kind suggests that he was always financially stable. The testimony of those who had known him certainly supports that view. There was nothing remarkable about his family, which was from Chiba prefecture, just east of Tokyo. As a young man he had been adopted into the Abe family in the city and successfully headed its tatami-making business. Because the enterprise dated back three generations, one can assume that the Abe family had adopted him because he showed promise. As far as the business went, they were correct. He did not consume alcohol. Contemporary Victorian values current among many Japanese reinforced long-standing Confucian prejudices against inebriation, so this stood in his favor. When choosing a successor to head his business, Abe gave it to his daughter, Sada's older sister, because her husband showed more promise than did his own son, who in his early twenties had gotten himself disowned by running off with a prostitute and saying he wanted nothing to do with the enterprise. Despite this inauspicious start, he later become a tatami maker himself and protested his father's decision to give the business to his sister, whose husband then carried on the Abe line. The police saw Abe Shigeyoshi as morally untarnished. In terms of Confucian as well as "modern" Victorian values, he was consistently upstanding. There was no reason to think that his daughter's criminal tendencies stemmed from his family.

The family of Katsu, Abe Sada's mother, was equally without trace of moral turpitude, although many who knew her said she had a somewhat unwholesome patina. Katsu's father had run a moneylending business in the Ueno part of Tokyo. Although a civilian, he had somehow been slashed to death in the Battle of Ueno in 1868, one of the few fiercely violent confrontations of the Meiji Restoration. Although she remained a single parent, Katsu's mother had, according to the police report, strictly raised her four daughters.[1] The report does not explain how Katsu herself had come to marry Abe Shigeyoshi or if she had otherwise entered the Abe family. It is possible that the family was entirely childless and so adopted both a daughter and a son, who then as a couple continued both the family line and the tatami-making business. This would not have been an unusual arrangement; for centuries, it had been common for families to adopt capable heirs when a living, but incapable, one already existed. Although the police found Katsu's family unassailable, they also described her as a self-centered woman who liked gaudy things—a characteristic that gave her a faintly degenerate hue. The police reported no signs of hysteria, an observation that carried the weight of medical diagnosis. She had been faithful to her husband and did not drink alcohol, so despite her peccadilloes she was in all respects morally unblemished. The police concluded that neither parent's family line suggested criminality.

Among Abe Sada's siblings, however, the police caught a whiff of moral decay. She was the seventh of eight children, only four of whom lived to adulthood. Of those who did not survive, one was stillborn, one died of beriberi, one died of meningitis, and the last ended in a miscarriage. None of these deaths was unusual. Her oldest brother, Shintarô, was a womanizer. His former sister-in-law accused him of being somewhat abnormal. At the time that Abe Sada committed murder he worked as a tatami maker in Kobe and had no children. Toku, Abe Sada's eldest sister, had married into a merchant's family and raised eight children herself. She had never had a brush with the law, and the police described her as "successful." Teruko, the fifth child in the family, shared a certain characteristic with her youngest sister: both were sexually precocious. At a relatively early age she had an affair with a local craftsman; later, she had three lovers at the same time. Her father then sold her into a brothel, but friends and family soon persuaded him to buy her back. Soon after that Teruko married a tatami merchant and apparently lived a quiet life; her sexual history was no obstacle to marriage for somebody of her natal family's social class.

To the police, these mild aberrations from contemporary ideals in Abe Sada's family history did not suggest a hereditary cause for her actions. The main deviations then considered suspect—mental disease, nervous disease, leprosy, hysteria, and alcoholism—were absent. There was, in other words, nothing remarkable about her background to suggest it might produce a woman who would commit murder and mutilation.

# 2. EARLY CHILDHOOD

Tokyo before the great earthquake of 1923 was still much as it had existed in previous centuries, although modernity had already brought many changes. Many of the oldest buildings dated back to the mid-1850s, constructed after the great earthquake of 1855. Only a few were from before that. After the Meiji Restoration in 1868, the shogun's castle became the emperor's palace and the city of Edo, which literally meant "entry to the estuary," received the new name of Tokyo, which meant "eastern capital." By 1900 there had appeared rows of brick buildings, as innovative as steam locomotives and constitutional government. In some neighborhoods traditionally built wooden row houses sprawled next to baroque creations of an imagined or replicated Europe. Few of these buildings survived the great earthquake of 1923; far fewer also survived the firebombings of the Pacific War.

At the beginning of the twentieth century the city was changing from the military and political center of a semifeudal state to the political and business capital of an internationally recognized modern country. Tokyo had lost a large percentage of its population in the mid-nineteenth century when the *daimyo*, or feudal lords, had moved out during the 1870s. When they left, so did their retainers and support staffs. Many of the townspeople left behind went elsewhere in search of work. Parts of the city remained desolate. In the late nineteenth century, city residents considered the area around what is now Tokyo Station as a home to foxes and badgers. By 1895 Japan had become a constitutional monarchy and won a major war against China; by 1905 the country had defeated Russia in an even larger war. Tokyo was just reaching the crest of its revival, and many inhabitants could not help but feel close to these events. Despite the many changes over these years, Tokyo remained divided into the High City, where the warrior aristocrats of the previous age had lived in their mansions, and the Low City, where those who serviced the aristocracy usually lived.[1]

By the early twentieth century, people in the High City, which lived up to its name both metaphorically and literally, had generally embraced the modern. Aristocrats in tuxedos and ballgowns staged elaborate dinner parties serving haute cuisine inside luxurious western-style houses. Men of rank discussed politics and policy. At a time when few women were literate, their wives and daughters were both educated and cultured. They valued chastity highly. Men, however, had considerable contact with women outside marriage, as had been customary from earlier times. Indeed, it required considerable effort for the government to convince some men that they should be monogamous and not accept children born outside wedlock as legitimate.[2] But men's values also were changing, and by the beginning of the twentieth century the crown prince who later became the Emperor Taishô declared that he would have only one wife. This imperial pronouncement set a modern example for others, although many men, and especially those of the upper classes, continued to have mistresses, frequent brothels, or do both.

The ancient rhythms of Edo continued in many other ways. European Victorian values were certainly felt in the Low City, the geographical part of Tokyo where Abe Sada's family lived, but many centuries-old traditions also remained vibrant. The festivals that Shinto shrines sponsored frequently had the characteristics of carnival and remained highlights of the year for entire neighborhoods. Workmen in the various trades often lived close together and remained proud of their crafts. They could also be boisterously bawdy. The songs of Yoshiwara, the licensed brothel district, were sung widely and the highest ranking of the geisha and prostitutes won considerable esteem. They set fashion styles that many Tokyo women emulated.[3]

Kanda, the Tokyo neighborhood into which Abe Sada was born in 1905, was in the heart of the Low City. At that time her father, aged 52, was relatively advanced in years. He hardly appeared in Abe's own retelling of her childhood and until her teenage years seems to have shared few intimacies with his youngest daughter. Her mother, on the other hand, had a close relationship with Sada, to whom she passed on her own enjoyment of the gaudy culture that Confucian and Victorian values alike tended to disparage: bright, elaborate kimono, heavy makeup, stylish hair, and music and dance from the pleasure quarters, as the brothel district was euphemistically called.

In their search for possible explanations of Abe's later criminal behavior, the police pieced together a finely detailed picture of her birth and early childhood. Little seemed unusual. While pregnant with Sada her mother experienced no difficulties. The birth was normal except that the baby was slow to begin breathing. Katsu had trouble nursing and Abe was sent to a wet nurse who became her foster mother, a common practice at the time. After a year she returned to live with her birth parents. Her subsequent development was normal except that she did not acquire speech skills until age four. She experienced few childhood health problems other than an ear infection, which permanently affected her hearing in her left ear.

The police found little to fault in Abe's physical development but were quick to see problems in her upbringing. They described her early years as follows:

> Being the youngest child, however, she was badly spoiled. Her mother, who wanted to live out her desires through her child, loved her blindly and raised her so that she could have anything she wanted. According to [her older brother] Shintarô, her mother was proud of her child's beauty and often dressed her up and took her out. Following her admission to Kanda primary school she followed the custom of people living in that area and took lessons for the *shamisen*. She tended to be lazy in school and her grades invariably were poor. She mostly had Bs and Cs but few As. Her only As were in singing, and she received Cs in deportment. Naturally, she increasingly disliked school. Her teachers told her to quit taking [shamisen] lessons, but both mother and child disagreed and she continued to take lessons the entire time she was in primary school.[4]

In her police interrogation, Abe said that her parents had spoiled her. They were relatively rich, and as she was the youngest child, it seemed natural that she should be spoiled. The shamisen and singing lessons became her main focus of attention while she was in school. Today the musical skills that she learned would be considered "classical" and valued as such, but contemporary educators frowned upon them. They brought to mind the decadent worlds of geisha and prostitutes. On the other hand, Kanda had a reputation for its emphatically Low City culture, in which the geisha world with its arts of dance and shamisen-accompanied singing was still held in regard. In other words, the neighborhood where the Abe family lived retained a strong flavor of Edo with its traditional customs and values.[5]

Abe's own interests were rooted more in a romantic past than in an academic future; graduation from primary school ended her institutional education. While she continued to live at home she took sewing and calligraphy lessons from tutors who came to the house, skills considered necessary for any woman who hoped to marry a respectable husband. Apparently she became proficient in both. In addition, she continued to visit a teacher outside the house for shamisen and vocal lessons. Although these were hardly skills expected of a respectable wife, they were by no means unusual subjects of study for any young woman with her background.

As a young girl, Abe was strong-willed and brave. When she argued with other children, even if her opponent was an older boy who struck her, she never cried and always held her ground. As an older child, she took a liking to going to the public baths although her family had a bath at home. People considered her wasteful for doing so. She also had a way of provoking her young friends. Once, while she was at the public bath, a boy of her own age had challenged her to come over to the men's side, saying that he would put his hands together in apology and eat soap if she was brave enough to do so. With neither hesitation nor a stitch on her body she charged over to the men's side and told her friend to apologize and eat soap.[6] While this behavior was by no means criminal or even decadent, it did reflect a lack of respect for what many at the time considered proper decorum for a girl.

At this point in time, Abe Sada's older brother Shintarô was once again the focus of domestic troubles that had an effect on her life. Her graduation from primary school occurred when the family was continuing its long-standing argument over whether he or his sister, Teruko, should inherit the Kanda property and the tatami-making business. This dispute itself suggests that women in the family had significant economic and decision-making power. In any event, Abe's parents thought it better that she not witness some of the bickering, so they frequently sent her out to play. This gave her the habit of staying outside the house, which was located in the middle of Tokyo, without supervision for extended periods of time.

A doting mother, selfishness, local customs, poor academic performance, little respect for a "proper" girl's social skills, a love of "decadent" music: none of these was criminal. However, when Abe became the subject of police scrutiny later in her life, they found in this combination a fitting backdrop for criminal behavior.

# 3. MAIDENS OR HARLOTS ONLY

be Sada grew up at a time when sex education and sexuality in general were subjects of intense scrutiny and debate, both in public and in private. During the nineteenth century and before, sexual customs depended on social class and region. Among the samurai and aristocratic classes, concerns of identity and loyalty made lineage an issue of prime importance. The integrity of the family line or *ie* was paramount. Hence the sexuality of women in those classes was closely controlled. Virginity until marriage and chastity thereafter ensured a pure family line, at least where patrilineage was concerned. However, among the urban working classes and rural peasantry there existed a broad range of sexual values.[1] For some commoners, wealth demanded attention to a patrilineal family that rivaled samurai rigor regarding the control of women's sexual lives. Urban working-class and farm and other rural women, on the other hand, had less money and status but often also far more freedom than women of the samurai or the more affluent classes of commoners. For many, either a patrilineal house was not an important issue until modern times, or they had ways of resolving differences by giving women household power.[2] Furthermore, in rural villages and some urban settings, sexual experience before marriage was expected for women and men alike. Indeed, if a village woman had never had a sexual encounter before marriage, prospective partners often questioned what might be wrong with her.[3]

Although it seems modern for women to have economic independence, many women in premodern Japan were much more independent than their granddaughters who lived in the early twentieth century. Until the late nineteenth century, in urban and rural locales alike many women had their own viable means of earning a living or owned substantial property, which gave them some degree of financial independence.[4] In these circumstances divorce and remarriage were not stigmatized. Able to depend on more than their reproductive abilities to support themselves, many women had considerable power over their lives, including their sexuality.

Modernity changed all that. The most powerful blow came with the promulgation of the Civil Code of 1898, which alienated women from many of their traditional legal rights.[5] For over two decades before then, the promoters of "Civilization and Enlightenment," as one of the most important reform movements that followed the fall of the military government in 1868 was called, pressed for the creation of a family system based primarily on that of their own social classes. In their eyes, the working classes of Tokyo's Low City provided a model of what to avoid in gender relations.[6] The reformers did advocate monogamy, or at the most only one concubine per man, but they drew the line at equal legal rights for women and men.[7] Although old attitudes and behaviors did not immediately disappear, those who yearned to make Japan "civilized" and "enlightened" did their best to rework social norms into a model they believed fit those qualifications. Women's sexuality, a cornerstone of the society they envisioned, did not fall from their gaze. By the end of the nineteenth century a new ideal for young women had appeared. This was the maiden, or *otome*, which emerged from a confluence of feminine moral codes, one based on aristocratic Confucian themes of chastity and filial piety, the other based on European—or more specifically Victorian—values. During the last three decades of the nineteenth century and into the twentieth, writers advocated the traditions both of samurai women and of "proper" western women, those who belonged to the ruling classes of the great imperial powers. This required the suppression of centuries-old common law practices that governed women's affairs outside samurai society.

For the ruling oligarchs and those who voiced their opinions, tradition had little or no value if it did not mesh with their vision of a modern society. One goal was to "raise" the cultural level of all Japanese subjects to that of the former samurai class, which meant applying codes of samurai women's behavior to all women. This refined etiquette impressed western visitors to Japan and provided an indigenous source of pride as a civilized people. Consequently, the Civil Code of 1898 supported both the state's claim to legal modernity and its efforts to strip women of their customary rights. Women suddenly found themselves unable to inherit property, assume the headship of households, or divorce husbands according to established custom. They became legal minors and were cut off completely from political activities. Because the samurai class comprised only 5 to 7 percent of the population before it was legally dissolved in the 1870s, this nationwide imposition of its values brought about an enormous transformation of Japanese society and culture.

From the late 1870s through the 1890s, there appeared in print numerous editions of moral texts for women written more than a century earlier. These included the well-known *Onna daigaku* [Greater learning for women] and similar works. Their original audience was primarily from the samurai and wealthy classes. However, by the late nineteenth century the guides were distributed throughout society.[8] The values at the center of these texts demanded absolute obedience to one's husband and in-laws to the point of severing ties with one's natal family, in addition to diligence, frugality, chastity, formal grace, not talking back, good health, a refusal to become jealous, and *politesse*. They gave men grounds for divorce based on a number of conditions over which a woman might have no control, including jealousy, disease, and an inability to conceive. These texts, like later Japanese law, provided women no grounds for divorce.

In this context, Japanese lawyers, physicians, journalists, university professors, and others were highly sensitive to western ideas of women's social and sexual place. Consequently, Victorian sexual norms and beliefs contributed to the ongoing transformation of Japanese values governing sexuality. Amid debates concerning the proper role of scientific knowledge in people's everyday affairs, there emerged a new set of notions concerning sexual mores, especially for young women.[9] These meshed well with the Confucian ideals advocated by those who saw the moral codes of the warrior class as applicable to all of society. A major goal of these codes was to make everybody into samurailike subjects loyal to the emperor. According to the Confucian model, it was necessary for the household to be in order for the state to have its proper order, so women had to follow strict rules of behavior. In addition, Japan's modernization movement required close attention to European moralists and medical scientists, who agreed on the benefits of women's chastity until marriage and their fidelity within it. They debated whether young women should receive some instruction on sexual anatomy and physiology—if delivered in a clinical tone. But all agreed that masturbation was to be avoided by young women and men alike, and that women should remain distant from sex until marriage. This required carefully traversing a narrow path between encouraging ignorance and explicitly discussing things sexual when it came to managing the onset of the menses and explaining the pregnancies of older sisters. Modern scientists (nearly all male) proved up to the task and established procedures to ensure young women's hygiene and chastity.[10]

Young women who fulfilled these modernized ideals of sexual purity, innocence, charm, and submissiveness constituted the new category of "maiden." For contemporary Japanese to understand this, however, the con-cept of virginity, as conceived in standard English usage, first had to become commonly understood and accepted. Until the late nineteenth century the modern Japanese term for virgin, *shojo*, simply meant an unmarried young girl. It implied little or nothing about sexual experience.[11] However, young women (*shojo*) of the samurai and aristocratic classes before this time could be expected to have had no sexual experience, and as a result, they were pre-sented as the ideal. Medical scientists also created a standard that envi-sioned the health of both the individual and society as dependent on women's virginity until marriage and their fidelity thereafter. This combina-tion of Confucian and Victorian ideals created the innocent, pure, and chaste maiden, promoted as the perfect marriage partner.[12] A young woman either was or was not a virgin; there was no gray zone.

Before the late nineteenth century the idea that virginity might be a pre-requisite for marriage found adherents primarily among the aristocratic classes, including the samurai, courtiers, and wealthy merchants who were dominated by a system of sexual values that reinforced patrilineal succes-sion. From the late nineteenth century, women outside the aristocratic classes needed to learn that no mistake was too small to be ignored. Conse-quently, women became morally polarized.

This polarization reflected the existence of two distinct female genders. One was the household woman, who belonged inside the *ie* and was intended to stimulate little or no erotic interest.[13] Before marriage, these were the good girls, maidens respected as worthy sisters and ideal daugh-ters; after marriage, they were the good wives, wise mothers. For them, expression of erotic desire was generally taboo. Then there was the "fallen" woman. These were the women of the erotic domain, as opposed to the household domain. A woman could fall into this category because a pre-marital sexual experience, which violated the patrilineal codes of women's sexual behavior, had stained her reputation. Consequently, the women of the erotic domain became undesirable as family members.[14] They generally remained outside the family in "proper" society, and when a "fallen" woman became a member of a household, as sometimes happened with concubines and mistresses, relatives and neighbors were—or at least feigned to be—scandalized. But contemporary men found such women desirable as objects of erotic interest, as lovers or partners in sexual adventure, in ways they did not see their household women. Objects of male desire whose existence required that they remain outside marriage, hence almost always outside the household, women of the erotic domain were simultaneously unsuitable for marriage and sexually attractive. They established their credentials with shows of sexual desire and the specific clothing, hairstyles, and other details of appearance that advertised their profession and social position.

A double sexual standard combined with economic demand created various classes of sexually professional women, from streetwalkers who serviced multiple men nightly to monogamous mistresses. Geisha fell between these two extremes. According to the new ideal, women who experienced sex outside marriage were "fallen" and, in certain classes at least, often found it difficult to marry or remain a member of a society that placed the patrilineal household (ie) at the center of private life.

Yet outside the upper classes, this dualistic view of feminine morality was generally foreign before modern times, and even later did not always hold sway. This was especially true in rural villages where, although specific customs differed by location, there was a common convention—or rather many sets of conventions—called yobai.[15] In general, yobai allowed a young woman who was living with her parents to accept clandestine lovers, either in her parents' house or elsewhere in the village. In some regions, it was the custom for young women to go to the houses of men they chose.[16] Parents, who in their youth had themselves participated in these practices, knew perfectly well what was happening but pretended to see nothing. Usually, it was assumed that the visitors would be eligible young men from the village who came during the night. Women generally retained a right of refusal if they did not wish to sleep with a man. As one might expect, some women subsequently conceived. In some communities, if she became pregnant, a woman could then choose her husband from among her partners. In any event, pregnancy before marriage tended not to be a problem but rather an indication of a woman's fertility—an asset in itself. In some places where pregnancy did not lead to marriage it was the custom for an unmarried woman's mother to accept her daughter's child as her own; there was no stigma attached.[17] This occurred where *yobai* provided a socially recognized chance for premarital sexual play, since in many regions parents chose their children's marriage partners. *Yobai* started to disappear in the late nineteenth and early twentieth centuries for a number of reasons; two of the most important were streetlights, which greatly reduced privacy, and the spread of venereal diseases.

Further reinforcing the regional and class differences regarding sexual values were attitudes regarding the open discussion of sex and sexuality. In "proper society," sexuality tended not to be discussed and increasingly became the focus of government censorship in print and other media. However, unfettered conversation about sex was not uncommon among many in the working urban and rural farming classes.[18] By an early age, country girls had already learned the facts of nature, with horses, oxen, dogs, and other animals often providing examples. For urban girls, the sights and sounds of crowded living conditions made the sex lives of family and neighbors virtually unavoidable. As previously mentioned, during Shinto festivals—Japanese manifestations of carnival—the normal rules of behavior often collapsed or were inverted. In most villages, these festival times and places created opportunities for sexual experimentation outside marriage. But by no means did licentiousness hold sway. Strict lines of taboo tended to fall around village communities. Outsiders were not eligible for the same privileges as residents; cases were recorded in which outsiders were either beaten up or killed for having violated village rules governing sexuality.[19] Organized prostitution, however, was generally an urban activity. Before modern times there was little need or economic means to support brothels in most rural communities, especially when *yobai* remained a common practice.

Modernity, which promoted a cash economy, a mobile workforce, and a double standard for sexual morality, also spread prostitution throughout the country, to communities where it had not existed before. Indeed, it was access to prostitution and the spread of venereal diseases that in some areasbrought about the demise of *yobai* and similar customs.[20] For good reason, parents became afraid that if they allowed their daughters to practice these age-old traditions they might become infected with syphilis or gonorrhea. However, where the practice survived both disease and identity-revealing streetlights, the police did their best to eliminate opportunities for young women and men to meet without supervision because it resulted in "moral corruption" (literally the "corruption of customs," or *fûzoku kairan*).[21] This disdain for ancient traditions followed by the vast majority of the Japanese people reflects attitudes of the Meiji ruling class, which saw most commoners—and consequently much of the population—as the "stupid people" (*gumin*). In this way, from the late nineteenth century, the ruling class used the customs of the former samurai class and of the aristocracy, in addition to Victorian values, to mold the everyday lives of the populace through the multivalent rhetoric of "tradition" and "modernity."

When prostitution became licensed by the state during the late nineteenth century, local police assumed responsibilities for enforcing hygienic measures aimed at reducing the spread of venereal diseases. The emergent system made sex with professional workers—all of whom were women—a legal and common practice among men. However, the state made it illegal for married women to have sex outside marriage and promoted an abstinence-only policy for unmarried women. The only legally acceptable reason for becoming a prostitute was economic duress: a chaste young woman could do so to save a parent or sibling in need or otherwise help her family. For example, from a perspective informed by Confucian ethics, a woman could sell her body so that her parents could buy medicine without which they would die. In reality this official boundary created a blind spot.[22] The state simply refused to perceive the diversity of reasons women entered the sex industry. For example, it could not begin to measure the romantic appeal that the music and costumes of the pleasure quarters had on some young women, including Abe Sada. The art and fashions of the highest-ranking geisha were imitated both among many of Tokyo's residents and throughout the country.

Indeed, it was at her mother's urging that Abe Sada studied styles of music, dress, and make-up that were inspired by the geisha and women of the brothel districts. Consequently, it is hardly surprising that she did not clearly understand what women in these professions really did or the differences between them. Those differences were sometimes enormous but sometimes slight, depending on location and status.

# 4. GEISHA AND PROSTITUTE

Even before she had graduated from primary school, Abe Sada seemed to embrace the image of the geisha profession as a romantic occupation. She had skipped school in favor of shamisen and singing lessons and had already started to wear stylish make-up. Abe was hardly alone in her attraction to the geisha ideal, which stood at the peak of style and fashion, at least in some parts of society if not among the women of established families and the upper class. Leading geisha were, in a sense, equivalent to supermodels, popular singers, and screen actresses all rolled into one. Yet they did not merely strike poses and parade fashions; the well-trained geisha—unlike most prostitutes—also embodied genuine artistic accomplishment and social sophistication. This was the goal to which the young Abe Sada aspired, even if somewhat vaguely. Importantly, the geisha ideal did not contradict the ethos of the "maiden" since it involved no sexual activity.

Geisha had a history that reached back to the earliest kabuki performers of the late sixteenth and early seventeenth centuries.[1] At that time, geisha included both men and women who not only performed on stage but also freely sold sexual favors. Literally, the term means "arts" or "skills" (*gei*) "person" (*sha*). From medieval times, *gei* suggested a broad range of skills, including many crafts and fine arts. It was not until the late eighteenth century that "geisha" came to signify the female performers from whom today's geisha directly evolved. By then, these women were known primarily for their performing skills, especially in singing and dancing, rather than sexual skills. They were allowed into the government-controlled brothel district under agreements that kept them from competing for customers with the house professionals. The role of geisha was to provide an artistic interlude in an evening's entertainment that otherwise inclined toward more carnal activities. With the support of a licensing system, geisha thereafter maintained reputations as performing artists, although before modern times the boundaries between them and the higher-ranking prostitutes were not always clear.

From the seventeenth century the government had restricted the legal sex industry in most cities to controlled districts referred to in English as the "pleasure quarters."[2] In premodern times these districts were quite literally gated communities. All prostitutes, called *yûjo*, were required to live and work within their confines. In large cities, at least, a private, illegal sex industry also existed, but private prostitutes and their support staff of pimps and keepers faced frequent and sometimes rather arbitrary legal sanctions. Sometimes the women who worked in the private sex industry were forced to serve in the pleasure quarters for extended periods without pay.

*Yûjo* is a category that included a long list of specific titles for women, depending upon rank. The highest ranking were called *tayû*. These women had great authority within the pleasure quarters and considerable autonomy. Despite their status, however, they remained legally bound to a brothel. Geisha, on the other hand, as singers and dancers who came and went freely through the gates of the pleasure quarters, remained outside those ranks. During the nineteenth century the geisha grew rapidly in popularity and stature until they became more highly regarded by the male clientele than the previously prestigious ranks of *yūjo* from the district itself.

Following the founding of a new government in 1868, overhauls of the country's legal system changed the conduct of legal prostitution. In 1872 the government liberated all prostitutes and geisha from their debts and allowed them to return to their homes. Many did just that, but a significant number chose to stay in the sex industry, which remained under the control of the prefectures rather than the state until 1900.[3]

Before long, the question of government regulation for health reasons arose, and geisha and prostitutes were required to obtain separate licenses. A few women held both licenses simultaneously. Under the new laws, revised in 1900, licensed prostitutes were required to undergo medical examinations for syphilis. A physician would periodically visit brothels and check each of the women working there. Based on a simple, visual examination, if the doctor found a syphilitic lesion on a woman, she was required to go to a special hospital for infected prostitutes until she had recovered. The women who had contracted venereal diseases were kept together under close watch to lessen their chances of escape.[4]

Requirements for medical examinations were one way the line between geisha and legal prostitutes was kept distinct. As artistic performing women, geisha were not expected to engage in sex; therefore, they were not required to undergo medical exams. In addition, while both were subject to systems of contractually based indentured servitude, the law made specific provisions for prostitutes that it did not make for geisha. At the end of the nineteenth century a "genuine" geisha was a highly skilled woman trained in music, dance, and other arts and a range of social skills. The proudest traditions existed in Tokyo and Kyoto; others also existed in regional cities. For the geisha who were serious artistic performers in Kyoto and Tokyo, a willingness to have sex with clients was necessary almost only when, following extended negotiations with the geisha's manager, the man offered to become a long-standing patron with a marriagelike commitment. For women who worked under the generic title of "geisha" in other places, which could but did not necessarily include those who were called *maiko*, *geigi*, *geiko*, and *odoriko*, circumstances could differ. Men tended to be less respectful toward geisha who charged low rates, which implied that their main skill was sexual.

By the beginning of the twentieth century, "geisha" also had become a generic term that included any number of women who entertained men for a living. Some knew barely a smattering of the more sophisticated skills but could perhaps play a few lines on the shamisen and sing a little. They were the lowest rank of geisha, frequently were little more than prostitutes. Others were women who lived and worked in rural hot springs resorts. They served their customers food and drinks, sang, danced, and frequently, but by no means always, performed sexual favors. Before World War II, most cities and many towns had women who called themselves geisha and had some if not all of the abilities practiced by their sisters in Tokyo and Kyoto. Most broadly speaking, the minimal requirements were skills at applying make-up and wearing a certain style of kimono, usually some degree of vocal and shamisen competence, and a willingness to serve men food and drink while engaging in more or less subtle erotic banter and word play.

Just as the category of women called geisha included both stylish sophisticates and relatively untrained country women, among brothel workers there also existed a broad hierarchy. At the top were chic women who modeled the latest kimono fashions and worked in elegant houses. Those in the worst circumstances wore whatever they could afford and occupied basic rooms, although their workload was not necessarily heavy, with an average of between 1.2 and 2.5 customers per day.[5] Most brothels gave their women few holidays, but at the time, the vast majority of workers in most industries were treated this way. Women working in the lowest-ranking brothels suffered disease more frequently because their clients were more likely to be infected. They also had longer working hours, poorer living conditions, and barely adequate diets.

As might be expected, women attempting escape from the brothels were a constant problem for owners and managers. Like the textile mills and dormitories in which factory women worked and lived, brothels required a high level of security. Because prostitution involved a legal obligation between brothel owners and a woman's guarantor—women were still legal minors—escape constituted a breach of contract. A woman was legally obligated to repay the owner a sum of money that she or her guarantor, often but not always a family member, received when she entered a house. Frequently these advances involved considerable sums, as much as two or almost three thousand yen in Abe's case, at a time when one thousand yen would easily buy a new house in Tokyo.

After a woman went to work for a brothel, she also had to pay for her room, board, clothing, and incidentals out of her daily earnings. In order to maximize their own profit, some owners charged inflated prices for these necessities. This system made it possible for a woman to go into greater debt the longer she worked, especially if she bought new clothes or had to borrow even petty sums. When this happened, the possibility of paying off her obligation and regaining her freedom could become increasingly distant. A considerable number of women did manage to settle their debts themselves or with the help of lovers or family members. Many women stayed in the business until they could no longer work because of poor health. Death, often from syphilis, was common. Obviously, there was reason for desperation.[6]

Nevertheless, the legal structure of this system allowed brothel owners to call the police for help in tracking and capturing women who fled. The owner would notify the police and inform them of all the possible locations, including the addresses of the woman's parents, other family members, and friends, where she might be found. Police then kept close watch to see if the woman appeared. To escape, a woman had to have the resources to avoid a police watch; returning to her family was virtually impossible. Should she succeed, her guarantors were legally obligated to repay her outstanding debts. This in itself was a strong deterrent to escape, and a good reason guarantors would help police find an escaped prostitute for whom they might be responsible.

The state justified this system with the rationale that women who worked as prostitutes did so only to support their families economically. This was based on the idea, rooted in Confucian ethics, that women sacrificed themselves as prostitutes for the sake of their parents and the rest of their families. Consequently, economic duress was the only legitimate reason they could become prostitutes. Of course, many women did so for other reasons. The events that eventually led Abe Sada to enter the profession reflected one such reason.

# 5. ACQUAINTANCE RAPE

Young women of a craftsman's household in Tokyo would have heard a good deal about sex, whether directly or indirectly, from older sisters and brothers, workmen employed in the home, and others in the neighborhood. It was generally taboo for a young woman to make overt expressions of sexual desire, but sexual banter was common among young men working in the Low City. So it was hardly surprising when Abe declared that by age ten she knew quite well what, to paraphrase her only slightly, women and men do together.[1] She was not particularly precocious; she had older siblings and numerous young men worked inside her household. In addition, her older brother had brought his mistress into the house, demonstrating to Abe that not all adult women were simply good wives and wise mothers. By her early teens she had seen a broad spectrum of women's sexuality. But it would have been made clear to her, as to most young women at that time, that she should pretend to know little or nothing about sex. Like many young people, however, Abe was curious. She was supposed to ignore all that she had observed but found that impossible. She did not know how to be curious and still navigate safely between the two extremes of maiden and harlot. And Abe, probably like many other young women, did not fall but rather tripped.

Because domestic arguments over inheritance issues were becoming increasingly violent, Abe's parents encouraged her to spend longer stretches of time away from her house. She made friends with neighborhood girls who were equally independent. They frequently spent whole afternoons and longer together on their own. They had the freedom to explore both forbidden neighborhoods and dangerous play. One afternoon, Abe's precociousness caught up with her. She recounted that day's events:

At that time, I went out with Fukuda Minako almost every day. This was when I was fifteen. At her place I got to know a Keiô University student named Sakuragi Ken who was a friend of Minako's older brother. I acted a little older than my age and we started to get intimate. While we were playing around on the second floor he forced himself into me. Because it hurt horribly and I bled for two days after that, I was frightened and felt that I had to tell my mother about it, so I did. Some time later I met that student again at Minako's house. We went out for a walk together and I told him that because I had told my mother what had happened between us I wanted him to tell his parents, too. After that he quit showing up around Minako's. My mother then went to his parents' house, but they wouldn't even talk with her. I just stayed in my bed and cried. At that time I didn't think that I wanted to marry that student, but I couldn't stand to think that he was making a fool out of me the whole time. When I realized that I was no longer a virgin [shojo] I hated [that I had] to hide the fact so that I could get married. It was worse to think of discussing the facts concerning my virginity [with a prospective marriage partner] before I could get married. Because [now] it was impossible for me to get married, I wondered what I would do with myself and got really angry about it.[2]

Abe's first sexual experience fits the definition of acquaintance rape, which is forced intercourse by somebody the victim knows. Neither violence nor the threat of violence is necessary, but intercourse without a person's consent is. According to Abe herself, she was not hoping to have sexual intercourse at the time and had thought that remaining a virgin until marriage was important for a woman. She explicitly stated this both in her interrogation and in her trial. There, she testified that the first time she had sexual intercourse it had been forced.[3] At no point did she say the student had threatened her; he simply took advantage of the place, his gender, and his social station. It is also possible that he did not perceive the incident as rape, just as many American males later in the century would be reported as not perceiving the use of force when their partners did.[4]

Elements of a repeated scenario in Abe's life appear here: a man fails to live up to his implicit obligations; she finds his duplicity intolerable; an impossible situation stokes her anger. Abe herself at this point was honest, but she wanted others, including the men in her life, to be also. The fact that neither she nor her mother contemplated legal pursuit of this incident is suggestive of contemporary attitudes toward rape among the police, who, in Japan as in many other countries, have never been known to be particularly sensitive to the issue. Consequently, this incident gave rise to a crushing sense of injustice. By age fifteen, experience had taught Abe that women and men lived by different moral standards. Her main reaction was anger.

She made this clear herself when on another occasion she described the events of that day as follows: "in the summer of my fifteenth year because I was raped by a student at a friend's house, my attitude immediately changed and I started to go around Asakusa [the Low City's main entertainment district] with a bunch of delinquents. . . . What had happened drove me to desperation."[5] It seems to have been a desperation that grew quietly yet inexorably. Abe's feelings and actions following this event fit a common profile of women's responses to sexual assault. The way Abe sometimes downplayed this incident is a common reaction of women who have been assaulted by someone they know well. Other typical responses include anger, in Abe's case so strong that it came to interfere with her life, and social problems, especially in establishing trusting relationships. These are distinct signs of post-traumatic stress disorder, a frequent result of rape.[6]

Although the police investigation reported this statement, the police did not take into consideration the effects on her life of the feelings resulting from the incident. Sexual assaults of any kind were rarely reported at that time, since the victim usually faced social stigma worse than the pain of concealing the crime. Reporting a rape to the police required that a woman inform her family of the incident. Husbands, rather than reacting with sympathy, often found their wives suddenly undesirable. In addition, police sometimes—and perhaps often—failed to treat rape as a serious offense and tended not to be sympathetic with the victim. Acquaintance rape, like other forms of sexual assault, was something to be hushed up, not reported.

In the end, it was not losing her virginity that seemed to bother Abe the most, but rather that her boyfriend had returned her trust with disdain. Abe had hoped he would be as frank with his family as she had been with hers. Instead, he fled, and her mother could not elicit any response from his family. For Abe, it was a quick lesson in contemporary differences between both the sexes and the social classes: since her family was of the artisan class, her boyfriend's family would have nothing to do with Sada or her mother. The lesson also was traumatic in that it shook the foundations of her beliefs about the world. She had met somebody on what she thought was a level playing field, only to find it wildly tilted against her. Unfortunately, her desperation found no listeners. Nobody sensed her despair at having been driven into the "bad girl" camp on a moral battlefield that allowed only two extremes.

One alternative was to lie. Her mother told her that if she were to stay quiet about the whole affair, it would not amount to anything. Were the subject of her sexual history to arise with a prospective marriage partner, she and her mother could simply avoid mention of this incident. After that, they would have to hope that her prospect would not investigate her past and discover the truth. Abe seemed to fear that if she did marry, she would have to hope that her husband never would discover her previous sexual experience; both it and her duplicitiousness would be sufficient grounds for divorce. Being a liar carried its own weight as a moral transgression. It was a burden that Abe refused to take on, because it seemed just that the student should have made her his fiancée. Then she would never have had to worry about the possible consequences of lying. But he refused responsibility for their sexual encounter and she refused to lie about it. She knew that by refusing to pretend she was still a virgin she had little chance of finding an ideal marriage partner, a man of higher social standing than Abe herself who had not been married before. The ideal marriage was for "good girls." Abe became increasingly angry since marriage as she implicitly desired it had become impossible.

Her mother recognized Abe's turmoil, and to mollify her daughter she bought her a new *koto*, a zitherlike instrument played either solo or to accompany vocals But her anger was not quelled. Before long she stole fifteen yen, a sizable sum, from her parents to see how it might empower her in a social context where money created new possibilities.

The rape and its aftermath blurred Abe's sense of social boundaries beyond what had resulted from being "spoiled" by her family. It became difficult for her to live by the definitions of right and wrong that a young woman of her station was expected to follow. Although she was hardly subject to the strict rules of deportment imposed upon a young woman of the upper classes, she constantly challenged even the more relaxed standards of an artisan's household in the Low City.

It is, of course, impossible to guess exactly what Abe felt and thought aside from what she later said or wrote herself. And it's possible that she misremembered her emotions and thoughts during the weeks and months after she had lost her virginity, not to mention what she thought about it years later. Nevertheless, we do know that many, perhaps one third or more, of the women who experience acquaintance rape later develop some symptoms of psychic trauma. It is not my intention to diagnose Abe. Responses to trauma are, after all, culturally dependent; symptoms manifest themselves depending on where and how a person lives. Yet the combined evidence of her experience and knowledge about other women in similar situations suggests strongly that the way she lost her virginity had a powerful influence on how she saw herself—and hence dealt with the world around her—afterward. At her trial, Abe stated that she thought all the men in her life, with the exception of Ishida Kichizô, were liars. The man to whom she lost her virginity certainly helped give her this attitude.

Ultimately, Abe Sada's first sexual experience put her on the fast track to moral marginality. As a child she did not, of course, aspire to become a social misfit. She gained that status because she lost her virginity in a manner that the governors of Japan's new sexual morality found unacceptable. It did not matter that an upper-class man was largely responsible. Suddenly, she fell into the category of unmarried women commonly called "damaged goods."

For men whose families aspired to the social respectability of the professional if not aristocratic classes—aspirations certainly expressed by sending a son to college—a sexually experienced woman was an undesirable marriage partner. Any respectable man's family could be expected to have a private investigator research the family and personal background of a prospective marriage partner and in the process find out about any previous sexual experience. It made no difference whether that experience arose from rape or from precociousness. If a woman had lied about her virginity, her deflowered status and the fact of the lie would be embarrassments to herself and her family and probably prevent the marriage from happening, unless the prospective husband had something in his own past that would create a kind of equality of blemishes.

Abe Sada believed there was no use trying to hide what had happened. She recognized the reality that her gender and her class made her powerless against the man who had taken advantage of her situation. So rather than trying to cover up her victimization or consigning herself passively to the category of "damaged goods," she actively pursued the role of misfit: first as a runaway, then as a geisha, later as a prostitute, and finally as a runaway prostitute. Then she unknowingly crowned herself as the ultimate misfit, a woman who through murder and mutilation attempted to gain sexual equality with men.

# 6. ACTING UP

A s Abe realized later and quite probably knew at the time, losing her virginity and then refusing to deny it was a turning point in her life. She had started down a path from which, in retrospect, there clearly was no return.

Before that summer, Abe had found the geisha fascinating, but implicitly, at least, she also had thoughts of becoming a housewife and mother, conventional roles for a woman of her social and economic background. This required several steps. Graduation from primary school ensured a knowledge of basic reading, writing, and arithmetic. After that, additional calligraphy studies enabled a young woman to write an elegant letter, a definite sign of superior social abilities and standing. While taking calligraphy lessons at home, a young woman could also study sewing and a number of other skills. From the end of the nineteenth century, the tea ceremony, for example, became more popular among middle-class women than aristocratic, middle-aged men.

After two or three years of tutorials and work at home following graduation from primary school, many a young woman became a live-in domestic in another, preferably socially superior household. There, she learned the strict rules of etiquette in dealing with guests, customers—assuming she was from a merchant, craft, or peasant household—and social superiors. Such employment increased a young woman's chances for finding a desirable marriage partner, ideally one who would raise her social station. Marriage itself started the next stage in her education. Her mother-in-law trained the new wife in the ways of the household. When she later became the household manager herself, she would know the accepted methods of doing things.

Throughout her education, a young woman was expected to subordinate herself completely, first to her parents, then to the family for which she worked, and finally to her husband and in-laws. According to the expectations of the "Greater Learning for Women," upon marriage a woman surrendered any right to intimacy with her natal family. This male-centered ethos established home as a space where men protected good girls and proper women and restricted fallen women to other spaces; common sense mandated that they should not appear in the home. Maintaining this sexual division of space helped men to keep the women in their home lives from possibly being influenced by females who survived by their sexuality rather than by their chastity. The styles and airs of the pleasure quarters had an allure not just to men but often to women as well. The life of the fallen woman could beckon as an alternative to homebound domesticity.

Before she was fifteen Abe Sada had gone far toward understanding the powers of feminine allure. At her mother's urging she had already learned to wear make-up and the most chic of kimono. Both required considerable training and attention to detail lest they become tawdry. Also at her mother's insistence, she had studied the shamisen and the songs of the pleasure quarters. It seems reasonable to speculate that Abe's mother was living out her own fantasies through her daughter. In any event, she did keep her daughter from better focusing on learning how to be an orthodox wife. For Abe, this training in the arts of music and dance helped set the direction for her life after that initial sexual encounter. Never again did she seriously cultivate a self-image as a maiden or devote herself to becoming a middle-class wife.

Instead, Abe headed to the street with its alternative social rules. There, she assumed a sense of control, looking for a radical solution to what, for her, was a radical situation. This meant that she spent unsupervised free time with other young people in Asakusa and the neighboring entertainment districts. Money opened the door to local street life. In the police interrogation she recounted her experiences following the episode, beginning with her habit of taking money from her house to distribute on the street:

> One day I took fifteen yen from the house and went out to have a good time. At that time, there were a lot of no-goods in the neighborhood. When I walked by they always teased me by calling out my name, but I would never turn around and look at them. But that time I called out to them and told them that because I was in a bad mood that day I wanted them to take me someplace where we could have a good time. Two or three of them came along and we went together to Asakusa, where we had fun until evening. I thought that if I took any money home with me I would get caught, so I divided it among them and let them have it.
>
> I'm sure that was around the time when my older sister Teruko and her husband were in the process of leaving our house and everything was a mass of confusion. My parents increasingly ignored me. My mother said that I was very late and so I told her that I had been to the hills around Ueno. It was absolutely splendid when I could give money to the no-goods in my bunch and buy them meals and drinks. They would all boisterously call me "Saachan, Saachan" [an endearing and diminutive form of "Sada"]. It was fine with me that my parents didn't

say anything, so I became increasingly contemptuous. Even if I was awakened in the morning I wouldn't get up. I got very lazy. Once I had awakened I would make somebody bring me my breakfast in bed. After eating I got up, dressed, and immediately went to Asakusa. There, I went to the Kinryûkan [a fashionable restaurant] and mainly three other establishments where I would stay all day long, refusing to go home until after nine at night.

Once, I grabbed a handful of money from my parents. When I went out and counted it I got scared because I had twenty yen. I went to return some of it but there were too many craftsmen around [who might notice what I was doing], so I just went out and spent it all. I hung around with this group of no-goods for about a year. That was the year my sister Teruko ran away from the house and left her husband. After she had returned home she took a craftsman as her lover and had illicit relations with him. I knew about this and my parents started to scold me for it but I yelled, "It's Teruko who did it, not me," and they shut up.

When I think about it now, my father didn't mind my going out. For instance, he spoiled me by ignoring me when I went out all dressed up. And my mother spoiled me by letting me back in quietly when I returned home late at night. This made me more and more contemptuous of them.[1]

She was especially contemptuous not of her parents themselves but of the principles that they enforced only half-heartedly. Abe actively pursued a free and arguably libertine life. After these incidents of theft and staying out late, her father locked her in her room at night, but to no avail. She sneaked out through her window and went out on the town. Although she spent considerable time on the street, she seems to have had few sexual partners at this time. She did admit to having an affair with one man, the son of a dried-foods merchant, when she was sixteen.[2]

At least in part, that could have been what spurred her family to make her into a live-in domestic; they had other reasons also. Abe did not take well to the situation, which she described as follows:

In April of my sixteenth year arrangements were being made for my older sister Teruko to get married. Maybe it was because they had gotten their fill of my being a no-good, but I think it is more likely that they were afraid that I would tell people about my sister's misdeeds and become an obstacle to her getting married. My mother was afraid that I might cause the negotiations to miscarry and so she said, "So that we can get your sister out of the way, you are going to have to stay quiet for a while. You have to go be a housemaid." She then put me into service in a mansion across from Seishin Academy in Shiba Ward. I was maid to the young daughter. But because I had been completely spoiled until that time, I felt horribly constrained. Not only that, but I had to eat in the kitchen, which was the worst. I felt so lonely that I wept at every meal. It was impossible for me to forget my good times playing around Asakusa. Just about a month after I had started there I put on the daughter's best kimono and ring, rather naïvely thinking it would be all right if I put them back after I returned, and I went to the Kinryûkan in Asakusa. My older sister came looking for me there and took me back. That was the first time I was taken to the police.[3]

By that time in her life, conventional social boundaries meant little to Abe. She seems to have rationalized taking her mistress's property by behaving as though they were social equals and her mistress were one of the gang from Asakusa, or at least a sister. This misjudgment terminated her employment and created yet another blot on her personal history that would best be kept from any prospective marriage partner—whether a social superior or somebody of the same social class, tatami makers and similar craft or tradespeople. If Abe's family was worried that she might spill the beans with regard to her older sister's behavior, they must have been appalled at the thought of finding Abe herself a husband. She had not only lost her virginity and become streetwise but also established a police record.

Abe's first encounter with the police left a definite impression on her. It should have, since in many ways she was still a child. For a considerable time she did her best to stay out of trouble. In addition, although she was hardly

an innocent, Abe's life story to this point and for a while after was not especially remarkable compared to that of other unruly teenage girls both in
Japan and in other times and places. Most people know of somebody who
had trouble at that age because she was having sex, going to the "wrong"
neighborhoods, and hanging out with the "wrong" friends. Many have overcome early brushes with the law to gain social respectability. As her older sister's example had shown, premarital sexual experience by itself did not
make marriage impossible. A police record was detrimental but not insur-
mountable. While in many respects she was directly responsible for her situation, the ways Abe's family dealt with her actions determined much of what
she did later.

It is impossible to fathom their intentions, but her older brother Shintarô
and his mistress encouraged Abe to become a geisha, telling her that she
then could wear beautiful kimono and live in luxury. The report of the police
investigation quoted Abe as saying, "Shintarô wanted to make me into a
geisha for three hundred yen"; she did not say what he planned to do with
the money.[4] Although her brother's gesture seems primarily manipulative,
with his own financial benefit in mind, Abe also had a juvenile infatuation
with the idea of being a geisha. She based this on her own fantasy of beautiful women in make-up who played shamisen, sang, danced, and lived in
luxury, rather than on an understanding of how geisha actually lived. This
romantic vision led her to run away one night to a geisha house in Asakusa.
Homesickness drove her back to her parents the same night, yet despite this
she retained a romantic vision of geisha life.[5] Before long, she faced the fate
of one who got what she wanted.

# 7. BECOMING PROFESSIONAL

$\mathbf{S}$ oon, family affairs changed Abe Sada's life yet again. Not long after she ran away to the geisha house for a night, her older brother Shintarô brought to an end the argument over inheritance rights when he ran off with a woman and took along the family's savings. This devastated her father, who sold his tatami business and retired to the community where Sada's older sister Toku lived, the village of Sakaishi in Saitama prefecture, just north of Tokyo. Abe accompanied her parents there and bade Tokyo farewell.

After spending her days wandering freely with her gang in Asakusa, Abe did not find rural Sakaishi to her liking. She started shamisen lessons again, but that was not enough to keep her occupied. Before long she was wearing make-up and kimono, and frequenting western-style restaurants by herself. Abe soon become sexually involved with a man who lived in her neighborhood. She started to visit even less reputable establishments, and the proprietor of a local teahouse introduced her to a newspaper reporter with whom she then ran off to an inn in Kawasaki, south of Tokyo. Her parents tracked her down and brought her home.

Although in their investigations the police did not seem to find the fact significant, Abe Sada was not the first woman in her family to challenge current bourgeois sexual norms or to be reprimanded by her parents for having done so. Her older sister Teruko had several lovers after she left her first husband. Their father reacted aggressively and sold Teruko into prostitution, as was his legal right. This reaction was not particularly unusual and actually had a long tradition behind it. Nearly three centuries before, warrior-class household heads were recorded as having disciplined sexually active daughters and sisters by selling them into prostitution for fixed three- or five-year terms.[1] In 1905, a writer speculated that probably only about one third of all women prostitutes had ended up in the sex industry because of financial circumstances; a significant number of the rest were from middle- and upper-class families and had become "overly" interested in sex.[2] There were cases in which fathers sold their daughters into prostitution for other reasons, including cupidity.[3] By no means did prostitution necessarily imply permanent marginalization: many former prostitutes later became respected housewives. Thus what Abe Shigeyoshi did to his daughter Teruko was not especially aberrant. Nevertheless, family members and a close friend of the family were shocked and immediately persuaded him to buy her back. Not long after that, Teruko married again and, at least until the police investigated her sister in 1936, she did not in any way come to the state's attention. Obviously even "fallen" girls had a chance at marriage, if not to the scions of socially and economically consequential families. So for Sada there was little reason for despair or panic, provided she would accept a social equal as a partner. Indeed, it seems that her anger was far deeper and more complex.

If Abe's father thought that having sold Teruko into prostitution had scared her into becoming serious, it would hardly be surprising if he believed the same method would work with Sada. Yet when he did indenture her as an apprentice geisha, his motivations remained ambiguous. Toku, Sada's eldest sister, testified that it was her own wish to become a geisha, not their father's design as a punishment or disciplinary tactic. The text of the police investigation illuminates this point:

> According to the testimony of Sada's older sister Toku, "From this time Sada said that she wanted to become a geisha more than anything else. Our parents kept her from doing this, but finally gave in, saying there was nothing they could do about it ... [ellipses in original] Our father said that because Sada probably had some sort of sexual dementia [*seiteki ni byôki*], if she were left to her own devices, some no-good probably would sell her off to some faraway place, so she probably would be safer if she were made a geisha [*shôgi*] from the beginning. So at the time she was 18, in July 1922, he made arrangements to have Sada become a geisha through introductions made by Inaba Masatake, a woodcarver residing at the time in Yokohama who was married to Kurokawa Nao, the younger sister of our brother Shintarô's former wife, Kurokawa Ume." With regard to the way she felt about this time in her life, Sada stated, "At first I was put to work by my older brother and his friends, and I really didn't know what being a geisha was all about. I certainly wanted to become a geisha, but when they took me to Yokohama and I knew what it was all about I hated it. At the same time I was resigned to it and thought that something would come of it in the end."[4]

The claim that Abe herself wanted to become a geisha is completely consistent with she said at an earlier time. Nevertheless, that desire was puerile, and it is questionable whether consistency should be expected of a juvenile. In any event, Toku's testimony depicts Abe's father as simply giving in to her wish. During her interrogation, Abe claimed the contrary and asserted that her father made her a geisha as punishment for her sexual promiscuity.

According to Abe, after moving from Tokyo to a small community the family felt the eyes of neighbors upon them:

> Since it was the countryside, rumors about me started to fly thick and fast. My father couldn't take it and got angry. He said, "If you like men all that much, I'll sell you off to a brothel." My mother and Toku were worried about me and made my father hold off. That really scared me, too, and I cried for three days and asked my father to forgive me, but he wouldn't listen. In July of 1922, when I was eighteen, he took me to a distant relative in Makita-chô, Yokohama, named Inaba Masatake, and asked him to make me into a licensed prostitute. In the train on the way there I didn't say a single word to my father. Since I had a blemished body anyhow there was nothing I could do about it, and I promised myself that I would never again live with my parents. But I was still too young to become a licensed prostitute, so I went to stay with the Inaba family for about a month. After that, Inaba went through an intermediary who had me take an advance of three hundred yen from a geisha house called Shunshin Mino in Sumiyoshi, Naka Ward [in Yokohama]. They made me into a trainee with the professional name Miyako. I soon became a full-fledged geisha.
>
> Around that time my family had five or six houses that they rented out, so it was easy to find a place to stay. Since I had plenty of money I gave some of the money I had been lent to Inaba and used some of it for the goods that I needed and for spending. I hated my father then, but later I heard that he had told my mother and sister that if I were to experience taking on temporary male companions as a business, I was certain to tire of it quickly and want to return home, in which case he would have welcomed me back. [5]

Abe made this statement following her arrest, possibly in an effort to describe herself as a victim of the circumstances under which she became a professional woman. However, either she or her sister might genuinely have forgotten how she ended up becoming a geisha. Clearly, the two accounts are contradictory regarding Abe's own role in the matter. Her retelling is mistaken in at least one detail: Abe's first employer was an establishment named Kanaya. She stayed there only a short time, and Shunshin Mino was her second employer. Either her memory or her desire for accuracy lacked integrity; it is impossible to tell which.

In any event, once she had arrived at the Inaba house, not much time passed before her age ceased to be a problem. It seems that Inaba persuaded a client that she was of legal age to become a working geisha, if only a trainee at first. Since girls under eighteen often were sold into geisha houses or brothels, she was by no means exceptional. Abe's ability to establish herself as a full-fledged geisha soon after she became employed suggests that she had developed the appearance of a mature woman. It also suggests that she entered the profession at a time when it was booming, making it easier for women like her to become geisha without the years of training usually required. In short, the ranks of geisha were quickly becoming filled with women who were more like prostitutes than highly cultivated professional entertainers.

Whatever the reasons Abe's father sold her into servitude in a geisha house, it had the opposite effect of that on her sister. Afterward, except for several short if meaningful visits, Abe never did return home.

# 8. CHANGING SADDLES

be Sada and Inaba Masatake, her intermediary in finding work as a geisha, had started a sexual relationship by the end of her first month in his house. For Abe, their affair was romantic; she placed a great deal of trust in him. Inaba, on the other hand, recognized in Abe a source of not just pleasure but also income: he saw her as a plum to be picked and was not above being manipulative to grab it. As Abe herself described their relationship, he succeeded in wrapping her around his little finger.[1]

Although Inaba was not a full-time professional in the sex industry, he knew it well enough to be active as a semiprofessional intermediary. Members of the Abe family would have heard stories about him from his wife's sister, who had been married to Abe's eldest brother. Inaba provided the introductions for his own wife's other sisters so that they could become geisha. Consequently, when Abe's father decided to put Sada into a geisha house, Inaba would have been a sensible choice as an intermediary. He knew how to achieve results in the netherworld of legal brothels and their various clients and suppliers.

It was a network of personal connections among various communities of geisha, public prostitutes, procurers, pimps, brothel owners, and men looking for anything from short-term sex to long-term mistresses. On the outside, members often faced scorn. But when the public needed entry into this world—and they did so frequently—they were at the mercy of its initiates and connoisseurs. Without a personal connection, it was impossible to get through the door. A woman could not simply sign herself up as a licensed prostitute. Legally, a state-registered intermediary was necessary for an introduction to a geisha house or brothel. Nor could a woman switch houses—a process called "changing saddles" (*kuragae*)—without an intermediary. After Abe's entry into the sex industry, Inaba continued to play this role in her life for years.

The way Abe started her career lends credence to the story that she became a geisha of her own volition but without clearly understanding what employers and clients would expect of her. Had her father wished simply to be disciplinary yet maximize his profit, he would have placed her in a brothel from the beginning. But she started her professional career as an apprentice geisha at an establishment called Kanaya, in Yokohama. It is not clear whether her father or Inaba took a cash loan at the time she entered Kanaya. Within a month Abe found the demands intolerable. As the house's newest apprentice geisha, she was at the very bottom of a formidable hierarchy. No mistake in conduct would go unnoticed and almost every motion and every word were governed by strict rules of etiquette. Almost immediately she moved to another location, a geisha house called Shunshin Mino. She received a sum of two hundred yen for the move. Although she soon fulfilled her dream and attained full geisha status there, she still found the discipline onerous:

Once I had become a trainee I soon learned that "older" geisha like myself [who started relatively late in life] couldn't compare with the ones who had been in training since they were children. We just didn't have comparable skills and tended to get lost in the shuffle. The Shunshin Mino was a first-class establishment, and we had to be absolutely proper at all times. Since I had money to spend from what had been loaned me, I wasn't in financial trouble. Still, every time I had an engagement the men wanted me to sell them sexual favors, and I thought it was a horrible business. But because my parents had abandoned me, I threw myself to the fates and instead of thinking of it as work thought of it as play. I moved from place to place as I saw fit and had no hopes for the future as I worked as a geisha.[2]

A few short weeks of work opened Abe's eyes and ended her romance with the geisha ideal. Girls younger than she who had grown up in the geisha world were far ahead in their vocal and instrumental accomplishments, conversational elegance, dance repertoires, parlor games, make-up, kimono appearance, and other skills that constituted geisha culture. Customers tended to be more explicit in their expectations of sexual favors with a lower-ranking geisha than with one of higher standing, even in a sophisticated establishment like Shunshin Mino. Soon after her arrival, it would have become clear to Abe that she had no prospects whatsoever of becoming a leading geisha.

Ironically, the more a young geisha's skills were primarily sexual, the greater her monetary value, and consequentially the larger her startup loan. When Abe could no longer stand life in Shunshin Mino and went to Inaba asking that he introduce her to a different establishment, he was happy to do so because at a more explicitly sexual house she could receive a larger startup loan, six hundred yen from a Yokohama geisha parlor named Kamochû. Although Abe took some of this payment, she let Inaba keep most of it. In the meantime Abe visited him and considered him her lover.

On September 1, 1923, while Abe was visiting Inaba at his house, the largest earthquake in decades shattered the Kanto region. The fires that followed destroyed much of Tokyo and Yokohama; the old brothel quarters of Tokyo were especially hard hit, and many of the women who worked there died. It was not clear whether Abe's employer in Yokohama, Kamochû, also burned, but she did tell her police interrogators that Inaba's house burned before they could save anything inside. Abe also testified that her debt to Kamochû prevented her from helping her parents, whose home also had burned completely. Because they had previously moved to Saitama, it is unclear what remained of their business and property in Tokyo at the time of the earthquake. Fire possibly did keep Abe from returning to her previous employer, but it seems that Inaba already had a plan to improve his circumstances by taking both Abe and his family and moving to Toyama prefecture, on the Japan Sea side of the country. There, Abe entered a geisha parlor called Heianrô.

The farther they were from Tokyo and Kyoto, the more geisha parlors tended to be like simple brothels than places of sophisticated entertainment. This was evident from the thousand-yen loan that Abe took at the time of her initial employment at Heianrô. With this money she paid off her debts to Kamochû; she gave what was left to Inaba. He then rented a house close to her place of business and they continued their sexual relationship. Yet this time in Abe's life seems to have been one of growing frustration and resentment. She remembered disliking taking customers simply to have sex with them.

While she was working at Heianrô, several incidents involving theft got Abe into trouble. As on other occasions, her recollections were somewhat contradictory. Abe recalled having taken objects that belonged to other geisha and pawning them. But where on one occasion she said that she was motivated by Inaba's failure to give her adequate spending money, in other testimony she said that she had committed the thefts so that she could give the money to Inaba. Because she admitted to more than once having pawned objects that belonged to her co-workers, perhaps both versions of her story were true. Apparently the owner had all but overlooked several incidents, asking the police to investigate but not pressing charges. However, when she finally stole a plectrum for the shamisen and a tobacco pipe and pawned them for fifty yen—which suggests that both were extremely valu-able—the police arrested Abe. They did not charge her with a crime, but it was no longer possible for her to continue working at Heianrô.

In October 1924, Abe moved back to Tokyo along with the Inaba house-hold. She lived with Inaba and his family without working until the follow-ing May. During that time Abe seems to have had an awakening of sorts. She watched Inaba help his wife's sisters who had become geisha make arrange-ments to move between houses. Inaba started a sexual liaison with one of the sisters, and Abe was shocked when she realized that his wife knew all about the affair but did not complain. The women her husband helped pro-fessionally were simply sources of income; she apparently did not care if he had sex with them. Whether this realization or simple jealousy pushed Abe away, she decided to distance herself from Inaba by asking that he introduce her to a geisha house in the faraway country city of Iida, in mountainous Nagano prefecture. From an establishment called Mikawaya she then received a loan of 1,500 yen, enough to pay off her debts to Inaba.

At Mikawaya, living and working conditions seem to have frustrated Abe. The owner, Sakata Kintarô, remembered her as a hysterical woman. In 1936, he testified to the police:

> I called her into the drawing room. As soon as she said that she would be in trouble if I didn't telephone a doctor she then apologized, turned around, and went back to her room. About thirty minutes later there came word that Shizuko [Abe's working name at Mikawaya] was act-ing strange. I went to see, and found her sitting on the floor of her room with her legs sprawled out in front of her and pulling on her hair, her eyes rolled back. She was striking the floor with her legs and show-ing herself all the way up her thighs. This struck me as strange, so I called Dr. Furushima, who then gave her an injection. The doctor said he thought it was hysteria but added that she should quiet down within a couple of hours. He then went home. Soon after this she became uncontrollable, but just as the doctor said, she quieted down in a couple of hours.

The following day, when a steady client brought her a watch and thirty yen in cash, Shizuko struck the watch on the front of the client's head. He was so surprised that he came and told me about it. The day after that everybody in our house was saying how she had smashed the watch. Shizuko said that he had made a fool of her by saying that he would bring her any number of watches.[3]

Abe herself testified at her trial that she remembered little about this time other than that she had hated the client on whose head she had smashed the watch; she added that she had also broken combs, hairpins, and other objects. Her behavior was sufficiently extreme that both the geisha house owner and the physician started to wonder if she might have been abusing injected drugs. Because Abe had no needle marks in her skin, they quickly ruled that out. They agreed that she simply had a fit of psychologically induced temporary excitement, something that later sounded medical enough for both the police and the court to allow it to pass as a diagnosis.

This behavior also seems to have convinced Inaba that Abe was potentially a greater liability than asset. In his testimony on August 14, 1936, he said:

Around the time Sada was at Mikawaya in Nagano, I received a letter from the owner asking that I hold on to her should she appear, since she seemed to have run away. I knew where Sada was but couldn't keep her at my house since a doctor had diagnosed her as having fits of temporary derangement. I couldn't have her breaking watches and the like, so I wrote her a letter and asked that she find someplace else to live.[4]

Another major problem had appeared in Abe's life: syphilis. Because formally she had worked as a geisha, she did not undergo regular syphilis examinations. At Mikawaya, however, she was required to be examined along with the other women, and it was discovered that she had an open syphilitic lesion. There was no way of knowing whether she had been infected at Mikawaya or at a previous establishment, but for her it was a genuine shock.

Until then Abe had held on to the distinction of being a geisha and seems to have prided herself in not having become a prostitute. However, she soon realized that she already fulfilled two of the main qualifications: sex was the main service she sold, and she faced regular syphilis examinations in the future. If Abe had succeeded in pretending that she still was in any way a geisha until this point, venereal disease completed her disillusionment. For over five years she had worked as a geisha, but she would never do so again. Instead she chose the higher pay of the legally registered prostitute.

# 9. LEGAL PROSTITUTION AND ESCAPE

s Abe told the story, her switching saddles from geisha to licensed prostitute was the point at which she became reconciled with her parents:

I felt that if I had gone so far as to become a geisha who was required to have syphilis examinations I would be better off becoming a licensed prostitute. At age 22, on New Year's, I moved to a place in Tobita in Osaka called Misonorô. I took the professional name of Sonomaru and went to work. That was when I ended my relationship with Inaba. Just as I was moving to Misonorô my mother found out about my relationship with Inaba. This time, because I wanted to cut my ties with him, for the first time ever my mother became my go-between as a geisha. She asked an intermediary named Kaita in Yokohama. He went to the trouble of taking my mother with him to Mikawaya in Shinshû [Nagano]. I explained to her everything that had happened with Inaba and asked that she be my guarantor. From Misonorô I received an advance of 2,800 yen and from that I returned the money that I owed Mikawaya. Thereafter my father would be my sole guarantor, and I gave my mother 200 or 300 yen as spending money.

This was the first time I ever gave spending money to my parents. Until this time I had hated my parents, but I had a change of heart and I had given my mother some of my advance. Since I had fallen this far, I asked them to let me do as I please.[1]

It is unclear why Abe chose to enter licensed prostitution in Osaka rather than in Tokyo. Possibly she wanted to be farther from Inaba than living in Tokyo would allow. On the other hand, it is possible that the prospect of working in Osaka's famed Tobita brothel district at one of the most distinguished houses was genuinely an attraction for Abe. Prostitution in Osaka had a history that reached back more than a thousand years; many took pride in this. In any event, if the cash loan that she received at the beginning of her service at Misonorô is an indicator of her estimated earning potential, Abe had probably reached her peak. The average Osaka prostitute at this time would have brought in at the most five or six yen per day.

At first, Abe does not seem to have disappointed her employer. She threw herself into her work with an enthusiasm she had not shown before. According to her later testimony, she quit disliking her clients and learned to enjoy her work. Misonorô was, in her description, a "first-rate" establishment with a sophisticated clientele. One client inquired into buying Abe out of the business but then discovered that a business inferior also had relations with her and so cut off negotiations. In her interrogation Abe described this time in her life as rather uneventful, but the police investigation depicts her as unhappy with her circumstances and wanting to leave the profession.[2]

After approximately a year, she became discouraged at her inability to drop out of the business as she had told people she would, and moved to another Osaka brothel called Asahiseki. There, Abe soon made a name for herself as a troublemaker. Within six months she was accused of trying to elope with a customer. She denied this, saying that she had simply gone out to entertain him for an extended period of time as part of her employment. The circumstances were not clearly resolved, but soon it became evident that she was once again engaging in petty theft on the brothel premises. Cash went missing from clients' wallets, and the proprietor seems to have gone to considerable effort to get a change of saddles for Abe yet again. He succeeded in placing her in another Osaka brothel, Tokueirô, where she remained for nearly two years.

While at Tokueirô, Abe avoided bringing undue attention to herself. She was not accused of theft or attempted escape. Perhaps the prospect of changing saddles again to a less desirable establishment kept her from causing trouble. In her interrogation, she recounted this period in her life:

> At that time I liked to wear greenish brown things and the owner would always call me "parakeet" to bad-mouth me. The others all quietly did just what he said, but I refused to restrain myself and would speak up. Once, a friend approached me saying that she wanted to escape. I told her that I would help and sent her out through the window in my room. But she dropped a big make-up box, which crashed to the ground. They caught her.
>
> For the most part the owner didn't get very angry with us. But when he was drunk he would call me "parakeet" and yell at me about something. But I wasn't about to let him get the better of me and usually I got the better of him. Most of that was in jest. His wife was a nice person, too. And Tokueirô was a first-rate establishment with good customers. Around then I had a very strong desire to see my mother, and she came to see me.

I was able to take ten days off and gave her a warm reception. When she went home I gave her eighty yen in spending money. And for her and everybody else I bought local food specialties as gifts to take home.[3]

The owner's failure to become very angry with women who tried to escape suggests that it was expected behavior. Far more surprising was Abe's inclination to invite her mother to Osaka, take an extended vacation from work, and entertain her during that time. It is possible that brothel owners allowed this kind of break so that parents would continue to permit their daughters to work. Clearly, this was good for public relations, as it helped give the brothels the image of humane employers.

At this time Inaba, who had established a full-fledged geisha introduction service, attempted once again to contact Abe, but at first she refused to have any dealings with him. In response he sent his daughter to visit Abe, who this time responded warmly. The two spent several days together, but Abe did not become in any way intimate or friendly with Inaba again until nearly four years later.

Despite her relatively quiet time at Tokueirô, working there over the course of almost two years dampened Abe's enthusiasm both for that brothel and for life as a prostitute. She continued to experience health problems. Once again she contracted syphilis and underwent a series of injections as treatment, although she was not required to enter a hospital for syphilitic prostitutes. She also became ill with typhus, which meant that lice infested the brothel. Remarkably, during her time at Tokueirô, there were no reports of her having committed any thefts. Perhaps the police and the owner had made it clear that they would prosecute her should she once again steal. However, prosecution was also counterproductive to a brothel, which would lose an important source of income if one of its workers were convicted.

Following nearly two years at Tokueirô, Abe repeated her established pattern and attempted to flee. Rather than turn to Inaba, she went to the procurer who had previously helped her get a job in Osaka. The police had already notified him that she was attempting to escape, however, and he turned her over to Tokueirô's manager. He informed her that he was sad that she had been caught, since if she had not, he could have taken possession of her parents' rental properties in Tokyo. This scared her into submission, and she was sent to yet another brothel called Miyakorô in Osaka's Matsushima district, which was rougher than anyplace she had worked before. Abe's submission was short-lived; within two weeks she ran off to Tokyo, where she sought the help of yet another procurer. Of course, he simply informed Miyakorô of her whereabouts, and she was soon sent back to Osaka. Once again, Abe faced even worse treatment at a brothel called Taishôrô in Osaka's Tanba Sasayama. She recalled being forced to go out on the streets to pull in customers, much like a streetwalker.

Trying as she did, it was only a matter of time before Abe succeeded in escaping from legal prostitution. She later explained how:

> Around this time I stole about one hundred yen from a client so that I could escape. But we were closely watched and so I didn't have any opportunity to get out. Soon I realized that although the main lock on the door looked as though it was fastened, it really wasn't, and so when I saw a client out one time I made it sound as though the door was being locked when in fact it wasn't. The people in the establishment then relaxed their guard and I was able to get out. I waited for the first train and finally fled to Kobe. With that, I washed my hands of being a licensed prostitute.[4]

This time Abe did leave licensed prostitution behind, but she never said what happened to her parents' rental properties.

# 10. FROM PROSTITUTE ON THE LAM TO MISTRESS

Outside the legal brothel system, Abe faced the considerable challenge of making a living. As a prostitute, she had lived in the company of other women and servants who took care of daily needs such as shopping, cooking, and cleaning. On her own, Abe faced the responsibilities of everyday life for the first time. The prospect of earning money outside the sex industry surely seemed daunting. She tried, but succeeded for only a short time. Soon she was working as a prostitute again, if not legally. In her police interrogation, Abe described this period in her life as a time of some surprising turns:

When I ran away to Kobe from Tanba Sasayama I took the name of Yoshii Masako and for two weeks I worked as a waitress. But there was the problem of the advances that I still owed to the brothels and I was short of spending money, and in any event I wanted more money, so I asked customers if they didn't know of any work that would earn me about one hundred yen a month. One customer said that he had some good business and asked me to his place. I felt like having a good time and went and told him that we should start a business.

This man worked as a pimp for a brothel in Kobe. For the most part I could tell what he was up to, but I felt that if at this time I were to try to go straight I couldn't keep it up. So I went to his house and took it easy there for a couple of months before I started work as a high-class prostitute. But he took my pay to cover all my expenses until then. I was in over my ears, and in the end it was so terrible that after three months I quit the business. In 1932, when I was twenty-eight, I went to Osaka and started doing the same business, but I soon quit and became a mistress.

After that three men took care of me. Most months I received from 100 to 150 or 160 yen in spending money. From around this time I started to get strong pleasure from sex and I couldn't stand to sleep alone. When I was a mistress, my man would come to me only five or six times every month, so I had relations with two or three men who had been favorite clients when I was working as a prostitute. I had plenty of money and free time and so I became pretty hedonistic. In my free time I played mahjongg, went to the Takarazuka theater, and went to Dôtonbori [similar to Tokyo's Asakusa] to have a good time.[1]

By using the pseudonym Yoshii Masako and working as a café hostess, Abe succeeded in avoiding the net of the law and brothel owners looking for her. Abe said that she was worried about the money she owed the brothels but did not say if she ever repaid it, which was unlikely, or if perhaps the brothel owners took possession of her parents' rental properties, which also seems unlikely since they were looking for Abe well after this point in time, right up until her parents died. Clearly, Abe was not ready to live on a waitress's wages and could not resist becoming a prostitute once again. She worked only a short time in Kobe—the report of the police investigation says that she got tired of being exploited by her pimp—and the following year, 1932, she fled to Osaka's unlicensed brothel district. There she found greater possibilities for both profit and betrayal. Because they were outside police jurisdiction, the unlicensed brothels did not have extensive resources with which to hunt down a woman who escaped. Abe fled easily, but probably to connections that she had established while working from private brothels. It would have been more economical for both a prostitute and her customers to continue their relationship without a pimp involved.

The turn from private prostitute to mistress was important in Abe's life. It freed her from the institutional constraints of the brothels while delivering the luxuries to which she was accustomed. Perhaps even more important, the way she experienced sex changed dramatically. Once it ceased to be part of a blatantly economic transaction, Abe found sex not only enjoyable but a definite need. Sex suddenly became fun and not just a means to obtain things.

Once she had set herself up with a small number of customers who were happy to pay her what she asked, for a brief period Abe surrounded herself with indulgences. She had all the time, money, and men that she wanted. There were maids to do the menial work but nobody to control her daily activities. The Takarazuka theater's all-female revue was the cutting edge of popular culture at that time; Dôtonbori was a popular Osaka entertainment district. Mahjongg had become a popular form of gambling; the adept found it profitable and the rest found it fun. Abe seems to have become involved in the gambling world at this time: the police investigated her on gambling charges but did not indict or incarcerate her. Had they discovered her past and made an issue of it, Abe probably would have faced the consequences of having escaped her debts in the world of legal prostitution, not to mention having worked illegally as a prostitute. Abe's own description of what happened after the police had investigated her is revealing both of her life at that time and of how she tried to convince the police that she was, in fact, a good daughter:

That [brush with the law] made want to reform myself, and since I had about four hundred yen saved up I quit being a mistress and rented an apartment in Osaka where I did things like read books and lived a quiet life. But the longer I stayed away from men, I became increasingly irritated, so I went to a physician for an examination. The doctor told me that there was nothing in particular wrong with me and that was a natural way to feel for anybody. He told me that it would be better for me to become a serious wife and recommended that I read a difficult book on mental hygiene to make me change my feelings.

Eventually I started to play mahjongg and the like and I got a boyfriend. But in the autumn of my twenty-eighth year, a friend from Yokohama who was visiting Osaka told me that my parents were worried about me, which made me want to go home. I then stayed for three months with my parents, until winter. It was the first time in my life that I did anything that resembled filial piety toward my parents. So that they wouldn't worry, I lied to my parents and told them that a nice person in Osaka was taking care of me. Morning and night I would massage their shoulders and read the newspaper to them. I cooked the meals and did all that I could to show my devotion to them. They were so happy that they told me they could then die in peace.

But then three men from Sasayama came looking for me, so I couldn't stay any longer with my parents. I went back to my apartment in Osaka but in January 1933, when I was twenty-nine, I received a telegram telling me that my mother had died. I sent my father money and then gathered together my belongings and left Osaka. I got back to my parents' house one week after my mother had died and visited her grave. I stayed for about two weeks, but the people from Sasayama were looking for me and rumors about me had begun to spread around the countryside. I felt that I couldn't show my face to people. This made me feel confined, so I went to Tokyo. There, I found a place in Minowa and started to work as a prostitute once again under the name Yoshii Masako.[2]

Abe seems to have been genuinely surprised that she had a naturally occurring sexual desire. From the time she first became a geisha, ten years earlier, she probably had found sexual intercourse disagreeable or had not gone without it long enough to realize that a natural desire could exist. It certainly seems surprising today that anybody should go to a doctor to ask whether desire is normal. The physician's response is testimony to the male-centeredness of contemporary medical thought. There seems little doubt that Abe would have laughed at the thought of becoming a serious wife and have found the recommended book on mental hygiene a powerful soporific. Her own remedy was to find a boyfriend.

Abe's fortune changed at this point, in mixed ways. It gave her a chance to distance herself from Osaka while taking care of her parents, something that always scored big points with contemporary moralizers. Word of her mother's death brought her back to Tokyo, yet she had little chance to rest: the Sasayama men were on her trail even as she visited her mother's grave. Somehow they seemed to have more confidence in Abe's possible earnings than in the value of her parents' rental properties, should those still have been in their possession. In Tokyo Abe again worked as an unlicensed prostitute, using the professional name of Yoshii Masako. For sixty yen per month she established herself in October 1933 as the mistress of a man named Nakagawa Chôjirô, whom she described with affection. The following January, Abe received word that her father was seriously ill and rushed to nurse him. He died ten days later. She received an inheritance of three hundred yen and returned to Tokyo and her patron.

In Abe's interrogation, she seems to have done her best to play the filial piety card. Because that would have been a strategy aimed at survival, it suggests that by the time she was interrogated she had lost any desire to commit suicide or accept capital punishment as its surrogate. Perhaps her having taken care of her parents in their last days did influence the judges' views. But her actions themselves were by no means cynical. No ulterior motive was apparent when Abe did her best to help her parents. Their deaths ended an era for her. From then on, her family played a much smaller role in her life than did her patrons and lovers.

Following the deaths of her parents, Abe returned to Nakagawa. Unfortunately, his failing health prevented them from staying together past September 1934. Soon after their separation, she established herself as the mistress to a man named Kasahara Kinnosuke, a lobbyist for one of the most powerful political parties, the Seiyûkai. While Abe had spoken fondly of her previous patron, she could say hardly anything positive about Kasahara. Once again finding her situation highly disagreeable, she resorted to her usual remedy: flight. Kasahara followed, pressing Abe with breach of contract. Probably as a way to avoid him she moved to Nagoya, where she had never lived before. Nagoya was a growing industrial city between Tokyo and Kyoto. Although it was an old city and called itself the "Central Capital" (*Chûkyô*), it lacked the cultural stature of Kyoto, the merchant traditions of Osaka, and the political and financial clout of Tokyo. With a pseudonym and an assumed identity, Abe found it an excellent place to hide from Osaka brothel owners.

# 11. A SEARCH FOR STABILITY

I n Nagoya, Abe greeted the new year, 1935, with a new name, Tanaka Kayo, and a different approach to her situation. Rather than turn immediately to the brothels, pimps, or some other corner of the sex industry, she went to work as a maid in an established restaurant called Kotobuki. It is unclear how she arranged this situation, which would have required an introduction. That kind of business would have been scandalized were one of its maids found sleeping with clients, so it seems safe to assume that Abe went there with the intention of leaving the sex industry completely. Again, she found her intentions difficult to fulfill.

In April, Abe met a man who came to Kotobuki as a guest, accompanied by a maid from another establishment. His gentlemanly demeanor impressed her. Several days later he came to the restaurant and had sweets with Abe, who told him that her husband had died in Tokyo, where she had left her infant daughter so that she could work in Nagoya. Whether he actually believed her—and judging from his later testimony, he did—he gave Abe ten yen. She later asserted that the kindness of this man, who still remained anonymous to her, made her fall in love with him. In saying so, she at least superficially contradicted her statement that Ishida Kichizô, the man she murdered, was the only man with whom she had fallen in love. Abe's own description of what transpired at their next meeting revealed her attraction to this man:

> Once again, four or five days after that, he came alone, dressed in traditional men's kimono. This made me think that he must have feelings for me. He listened to me talk about my child and other things, and all the while I snuggled up to his lap and made it seem that I was very sad and tearful. He said, "You shouldn't put your hand there. Since I'm a man it makes me feel strange, so go sit over there. It would be a problem if somebody came." I thought that that was the right time and I made myself even sexier and pressed myself even closer against his lap. He embraced me and so I pushed him over and we had sex right where we were.[1]

Abe still did not know his name. Yet both their lives were about to change in ways neither could have imagined. He returned to Kotobuki some days later, and the two arranged to meet elsewhere. She then left the restaurant, saying simply that she would be going out for a while. They met at an inn near Nagoya's Maizuru Park. Presumably because she knew that the management at Kotobuki would not accept her sleeping with a customer, Abe ended her employment there simply by not returning. Instead she found work at a small restaurant in the same area and continued her relationship with this kindly if anonymous customer whom she called a "gentleman" (*shinshi*). Abe's first attempt to separate work and sex had failed.

In June she tired of Nagoya, which, compared to Osaka or Tokyo, was lacking in glitter and shine, and decided to return to Tokyo. Her emotional attachment to this man was not enough to anchor her to the rather dull Central Capital. Again Abe lied and told her gentleman lover that her daughter had died, making it necessary to go back to Tokyo. He gave her fifty yen and she promised to write him at the inn where they had had their liaisons. Abe's assertion that she had fallen in love with him seems rhetorical, since her feelings were not strong enough to make her want to stay close or to keep her from wanting to see other men.

Back in Tokyo Abe stayed again with Inaba; they reestablished their old connection. Soon, Kasahara discovered that she had returned. He immediately sued her for marriage fraud and sent the police looking for her at the Inaba residence. She succeeded in staying one step ahead of the police and, under the name Tanaka Kayo, ran off to an unlicensed brothel run by a man named Kimura Hiroshi, with whom she had been previously acquainted. Before long she wrote to her gentleman lover in Nagoya and asked him to visit her in Tokyo. He visited her once and they spent several hours together at an inn called Yumenosato. However, he soon returned to Nagoya. Abe continued to work in the brothel, but after getting involved with the owner, she again vowed to get out of the business.

A month later Abe's lover from Nagoya came looking for her at the house of the brothel owner for whom she had worked the previous month. She had told him that it was the house of her sister, but now he discovered that Abe was indeed a prostitute. Nevertheless he took her to Atami, the hot springs resort just south of Tokyo. Clearly, he had a genuine affection for Abe. While there, he told her that he did not mind that she had been a prostitute and that he thought he could help her start to lead a serious life. Yet he still would not tell her his real name or profession. His complete propriety was not particularly attractive to Abe, and she later testified that she had found him boring in bed. On the other hand, he showed genuine concern for her well-being in a way few, if any, other men had done previously. She seems to have found this truly touching. He was also very liberal with gifts of cash. In her testimony Abe described his sincerity and desire for her happiness in life as having been enough to make her decide to quit the sex industry and take up another profession. Upon returning to Tokyo from Atami she again went to live with Inaba. As part of her newfound seriousness she also quit smoking, if temporarily. However, she still felt sexually unsatisfied and continued to have encounters with her former patron, Nakagawa Chôjirô.

Her lover's anonymity bothered Abe, and she determined at this point to discover his identity. He had worn a lapel pin showing Nagoya's city logo, so she guessed that he was an official of some kind there. In August, she traveled to Nagoya to see what she might discover:

> After arriving I stopped by an inn called Kiyokoma that was next to the station. There, I saw a newspaper headline that read, CITY COUNCIL MEMBERS GO TO AMERICA. It showed a photograph of [the man I then came to know as] Professor Ômiya. For the first time I knew his position and occupation, and it made me happy. I quickly called him on the telephone and we met at an inn by the harbor called Nan'yôkan. He seemed to be extremely troubled and dispirited. He asked how I learned his name, and I told him by looking at the newspaper. "Oh," he said, and nodded. He then said, "Because I am a school president, if people found out about my relationship with you I wouldn't be able to go on living. You are a pistol pointed at me. It is up to you whether I live or die. In the future I hope to become a Diet [Parliament] member, so until then please keep things quiet. When I become a Diet member you can come visit me in broad daylight."[2]

The danger Abe posed to his career was not enough to persuade Ômiya Gorô—her lover's full name—to end their relationship. Obviously he trusted her, because as an established banker, president of a school of commerce, and aspiring politician, he was vulnerable to her. Although Abe could have blackmailed him, it remains a testament to her own character that instead she listened to his exhortations to pursue a life outside the sex industry. On this occasion he refused to have sex with her and sent her back to Tokyo with 130 yen in cash as spending money. They met again in Tokyo when he was on his way to the United States two weeks later, in mid-August.

Ômiya remained out of the country until October. During that time Abe stayed again with Inaba, where she said she "went to the movies and otherwise had a good time," spending over two hundred yen in the process. Whether she also earned money from prostitution during those nearly three months apart from Ômiya, she did not say. It was not until mid-November that they could meet again.

At their second meeting after Ômiya had returned from the United States, Abe told him that she had developed a sore on a knuckle of her finger. Immediately he concluded that it was caused by secondary syphilis and gave her 250 yen to visit a hot springs resort at Kusatsu, a therapy that people believed would cure syphilis. Abe stayed there from November until after the beginning of January 1936. Ômiya visited her only once, but that visit had considerable impact. Instead of having sex the first night they were together, he lectured her on the sexual morality of women. Abe recalled what he had told her:

> "For a husband and wife," he said, "the everyday affairs of life come first and sexual matters are secondary. For that matter, sex must be secondary to any relationship between men and women. Rather, they must be satisfied that they can truly feel for each other. When I look at you, I feel at peace. But your erotic drive is far too strong. Simply by holding my hand you get excited. You have to discipline yourself so that even when you sleep with a man you will be in control of yourself. When I tell you that I won't have sex, I mean it." I found it all a bore.[3]

Ômiya's sexual reticence at this time could easily have been pragmatic, based on a desire to avoid contracting syphilis. It would have been several weeks before Abe's secondary syphilitic lesions would have disappeared of their own accord, although clearly she was not cured of the disease and always would have been subject to tertiary symptoms, which could include brain lesions and aortal aneurysm. His lecture indicated that Ômiya saw his relationship with Abe as more than sexual. Although she found it boring at the time, she also said that when she had worked at becoming more placid she felt good in a way that made a deep impression on her. After she returned to Tokyo in January, they met again, this time in Kyoto. Ômiya recommended that Abe try to start a business and suggested a small restaurant. She had seen any number of women running restaurants and knew that they led economically independent lives. What she lacked was knowledge of the business that she could gain only by working in it, possibly as an apprentice. So in January 1936 Abe set out to find an appropriate position. She was newly determined to extricate herself from the sex industry.

# 12. DISCOVERING LOVE

be's resolve to quit prostitution carried her further this time than it had the previous year. While staying at her sister's house, she contacted a professional go-between for people seeking jobs in the restaurant trade and said that she did not mind if the pay was low; she wanted to work in a serious business. The go-between put her in touch with a local restaurant and on February 1, 1936 she started working as an apprentice maid at Yoshidaya, a reputable establishment in Tokyo's Nakano Ward. Its owner was a man named Ishida Kichizô. At Abe's interview, when Ishida and his wife asked why she wanted to work there, she prevaricated, saying that her husband's business had failed and she needed the job. It is safe to assume that had she been straightforward about her past, she would not have been hired.

Ishida had worked his way up through the business. He had apprenticed in his youth at an eel restaurant but eventually managed to establish his own place. This would have required both the support of others as well as a considerable financial commitment of his own. However, by the time Abe started to work at Yoshidaya, he was known as a philanderer who did little around the restaurant except make purchases at the wholesale fish market early each morning. His wife Otoku was the restaurant's talented and dedicated manager. The business had established a good reputation mostly through her devotion and discipline. She had put together a hardworking and serious staff that maintained an elegant and quiet demeanor. For Abe, the pay itself was a considerable benefit. When she started there she received a monthly salary of thirty yen to which she added about forty yen in tips; this came to more than she had previously earned as a mistress. There were four other maids, all of whom, like Abe, lived on the premises. Abe described Otoku as a decent person who was always in a good humor while she worked. Ishida and his wife had two children, a son aged fifteen and daughter aged thirteen.

Abe later asserted that she found Ishida attractive from her first interview with him, but added that at the time Ômiya had been on her mind. He had told Abe that he would be in touch with her through her sister. On March 3, the traditional celebration of girls' day, he contacted her. Abe took the night off to be with Ômiya. As much as she liked his elegance and his respectful attitude toward her, he never satisfied her completely, and especially not sexually. He told her that he planned to stay in Tokyo for three months and live like a student, spending most of his days reading. To her displeasure, he didn't want to sleep with her until he had completed this period of study. She told him that she could not stand "such a cold man." His response was to speculate that she had taken a lover, which she denied. Nevertheless, he informed her that he did not mind if she had a lover until he set her up in business. After that, were she to take a lover, he would act as an intermediary so that she could get married. He would then play the role of older brother until he died. Clearly Ômiya saw their relationship in the long term and wanted to do all he could to help Abe get out of the sex industry. Although he did not satisfy her sexual desire, he did satisfy her need for a stable relationship. And Abe seems to have appreciated his support of her efforts to become economically independent. These elements of their relationship seem to have created a genuine affection between them. When he invited her to a resort after his period of study, Abe first reprimanded him for his lack of passion, then bought a sewing kit and travel cosmetics in preparation for the trip.[1]

Shortly after Abe started work at Yoshidaya, Ishida challenged her with erotic banter. On various occasions he blocked her in the hallway, stopped her by putting a finger in her face, and made insinuating remarks. After she had been out late two nights, Ishida pressed against her, bit her earlobe, and pressed his knee into her buttocks. Rather than attempt to repulse him, Abe felt happy that Ishida found her attractive. She allowed him to hug and kiss her and to play with her breasts.

At the beginning of April, Ômiya and Abe spent two nights together; when she returned to Yoshidaya, Ishida pinched her arm and made remarks that suggested he was jealous. He continued to kiss and fondle her whenever they met, and their play started to become more intense. The way in which they first had sexual intercourse made it clear that Ishida had set up the situation. Abe recounted the incident:

It was sometime around the middle of April that Mrs. Ishida said, "Okayo, there is a customer in the annex." I went there with some bottles of sake and was surprised to find that the customer was Ishida himself, sitting there drinking. When I asked what the reason was for his actions, he said that he was not drinking outside anymore and so was going to have an evening drinking at his own place. He showed me an amulet from Narita Shrine that had "Total Abstinence" written on it. When I went to serve his sake he grabbed my hand and then hugged me. He started to play with my privates. It felt good and so I let him do as he pleased. In a few moments a geisha named Yaeji arrived and sang a long ballad for Ishida. Her voice was beautiful and I really fell for her. While the geisha was at the front desk we had sex for the first time.[2]

Ishida not only had seduced Abe but also seemed to have done so with his wife's complicity, although subsequent events suggest that Otoku did not expect Ishida and Abe to initiate a physical relationship. Ishida also divined Abe's love of a well-trained geisha's talents, especially in music. From the way she described this scene, it was the geisha's ability to create a romantic moment through music that completely entranced her. From that time she and Ishida continued to have sex whenever they could while on the restaurant's premises, which was not always easy since they were surrounded by numerous people. Abe later said that they became reckless. One night, while there was a boisterous party in another part of the restaurant, Abe and Ishida went to a parlor, turned off the light, and started to have sex on a sofa. Suddenly, a maid came in the room to get a cushion and switched on the light. Almost immediately everybody who worked at Yoshidaya knew about Abe and Ishida. His wife gave him a tongue-lashing for this but did nothing more.[3]

It might seem surprising that Otoku, Ishida's wife, put up with such behavior. However, she apparently had previously run off with a lover for a year and then come back to Ishida, who permitted her return for the sake of their children. Rather than a marriage in the conventional sense, they seemed to have a relationship based on professional and family convenience. Abe had once nursed Otoku while she was ill, and at that time she confided in Abe that Ishida was coldhearted and had a taste for women. Proving the point, even if unknowingly, he had called in a geisha to entertain him while his wife was recovering. Otoku had remained married to Ishida although he had kept a mistress for six years. Other stories of Ishida's philandering reached Abe's ears, but they did nothing to cool her passion for him.

After having been caught in the act, Abe and Ishida conspired to meet outside Yoshidaya on April 23 so that they could enjoy a more leisurely time together in bed. Abe had already asked for time off in June and tried to make it seem as though she was taking that time early. When Ishida also made it clear that he would be away for a shortwhile, starting the same day, he must have raised suspicions. In any event, it is clear that when Abe left on the morning of the twenty-third she planned to be back after two or three nights. A large party was planned at Yoshidaya on the twenty-fifth, and Abe knew that she was needed both that night and the next. She did not plan to terminate her position at Yoshidaya or her attempt to establish a life for herself outside the sex industry. They were just going out for a fling.

Abe called her relationship with Ishida at this point an "infatuation" and "just an impromptu affair," not unlike many others she had experienced in the past. It was something to be enjoyed briefly but not thought about deeply. She still had strong feelings for Ômiya because of his genuine concern for her well-being.

However, as soon as they met outside the restaurant the situation started to change. Ishida informed Abe that she could not stay much longer at Yoshidaya. He told her that debts were so bad that the telephone was in hock, something not even his wife knew. This suggested to Abe that Ishida trusted her in ways he did not trust his wife. She remembered, "I thought that since he had let me in on this secret, he really felt deeply toward me. Gradually, I fell more and more under his spell."[4] It also meant that the restaurant's financial situation was less than sound, or at least that he wanted Abe to believe that was the case. Ishida added that he wanted Abe to go into some kind of business, perhaps running a small hotel, so that they could continue to meet.

Abe might have seen Ishida's statement that she could not stay much longer at the restaurant as a warning flag regarding her future. Unlike Ômiya, Ishida did not have the means to set her up in business, so although he said that he wanted her to run a small hotel, he could not easily have provided the financial backing. Despite this, Abe allowed the romance of the moment to enchant her. She and Ishida went straight to a teahouse called Mitsuwa in the Shibuya Ward of Tokyo on the morning of April 23. He insisted that she refrain from addressing him with formal language, something she had done out of habit. This was yet another way in which he—with the power custom gave him as a man—could increase their intimacy. Although it was morning, they ordered sake. Ishida told Abe, "Today is our wedding day, so let's drink to it." They then immersed themselves completely in their mutual infatuation. For the next four days and nights they remained in bed together and completely neglected their obligations to the restaurant. On the evening of the twenty-seventh they switched to another teahouse called Tagawa in the neighborhood of Futago Tamagawa, well west of Tokyo proper, to make it more difficult for Ishida's wife to track them. They continued to drink and on at least two occasions had geisha come to their room to perform for them.

The ways Ishida paid attention to Abe, from his initial aggressive advances to bringing in a geisha to sing while she served him to his physical and linguistic intimacy, all fired a powerful passion in her. In her interrogation she asserted: "He was the first man I had ever met who made a woman feel important and who would do things to make her happy, and I fell completely in love with him."[5] For the first time in her life Abe experienced the combined erotic and emotional power of romantic love. This was about to change her life as well as those of Ishida, Ômiya, their families, and other people connected to them, all in ways nobody could have imagined. In Ômiya, Abe had found a man who expressed truly benevolent feelings toward her, and she found that extremely attractive, to the point that she thought she had fallen in love with him. But although Abe spoke warmly of her relationship with Ômiya, it was when she mentioned Ishida that she spoke of love's ecstasy.

# 13. LOVE'S INTOXICATION

In the English language, the word "love" means many different things. It includes religious ideals, long-term devotion, the habitual liking of something, a desire to be in another person's company, and physical attraction. In the Japanese language, different words have usually signified some of these different categories, especially before modern times. The term *ai*, which usually is translated as "love," signified the devotion of a parent to a child or of a ruler to the ruled, but it also had romantic and even carnal connotations. An early Buddhist text translated into Chinese during the fifth century included a range of seven distinct meanings.[1] During the mid-nineteenth century, a *daimyō*, or feudal lord, took advantage of this ambiguity and while he lay dying, spoke of his "loving relationship" (*ai en*) with a young male retainer. He ordered his leading advisors, who had surrounded his deathbed, to give the young man a lifetime stipend without any attached responsibilities. Those intimate with the *daimyō* knew that his beneficence stemmed from a powerful physical infatuation between the two men and was not simply a sign of lordly benevolence.[2] The term *koi*, on the other hand, clearly signified an attachment that was both psychological and physical. Generally, the same could be said for the term *ren'ai*, although it tended to have a more poetic nuance. By the beginning of the twentieth century, however, western ideals of romantic love had permeated Japanese culture, and *ai* tended to assume a range of meanings similar to those of the English word "love." The difference between "falling in love" and simply "loving" somebody was distinct.[3]

Abe loved Ōmiya, but she was in love with Ishida. The former she respected and revered; the latter was an object of total absorption and identification. It was definitely an erotic absorption, but it was much more as well. In the many films and works of fiction that have been based on the story of Abe Sada, the continued emphasis on her sexuality—rather than on how she expressed her emotions through it—at the time she murdered Ishida tells more about male attitudes than about Abe herself. Following her arrest, she continued for the rest of her life to fight assertions that she murdered Ishida Kichizō because she was "sex crazed." Nevertheless, from physicians and scholars to writers of prurient fiction, people have focused on her as a sexual being rather than as a woman capable of genuine love. Their descriptions are usually judgmental. Almost a century after her birth, one writer still described her as a "sex-crazy harlot."[4] That is the language of sensationalism, not of human understanding.

The reason for this misunderstanding is a confusion of erotic love with sex. "Erotic" denotes sexual love, not just the physical sex act. An erotic relationship requires desire, something few prostitutes feel for their clients. For most, as for Abe herself during much of her life, sex with clients was nothing but a means toward an unrelated end: money. She had plenty of sex in her

life, but little love. Time and again Abe emphasized the love in her relationship with Ishida, as when she unhesitatingly replied, "because I loved him"
when asked why she had killed him. In Ishida, she believed that she had
found true love, expressed at least in part through his sexual devotion to her.
In Abe's eyes he was the only man who ever desired her as the woman she
was rather than just as an interchangeable object of sexual play. Ironically, it
was because she had experienced sex with an enormous number of men
that Ishida's exceptional behavior in bed became a measure of his emotional
commitment to her. While his sexual skills were important, she did not love
him simply because he had good technique. When the police asked her what
had made her fall in love with Ishida, she answered at length:

> It is hard to say exactly what was so good about Ishida. But it was
> impossible to say anything bad about his looks, his attitude, his skill as
> a lover, the way he expressed his feelings. I had never met such a sexy
> man. He didn't seem to be forty-two years old. He had the skin and
> looks of someone in his twenties, twenty-seven or eight at the most.
> Emotionally he was a very simple man. Even little things would make
> him happy. He tended to show his emotions and was as innocent as a
> little baby. He was happy about anything that I did, and he adored me.
> Once, I had him put on my red under-kimono, and he wore it to sleep.
> While we were staying together he never once talked about his family.
> Ishida was very skilled in bed. When it came to sex, he understood
> a woman's feelings. He was very patient and did a lot to give pleasure.
> Even just after having sex he could get an erection again.
> Once, I tested Ishida to see if he was just using me to have a good
> time or if he made love to me because he was in love with me. Talking
> about it makes it sound rude or hateful, but on the twenty-third of
> April, when we ran away from Yoshidaya, I was a little dirty because of
> my period. But even that didn't bother Ishida, and he touched me and
> licked me. Around the twenty-eighth of April, while we were staying at
> Tagawa, I had ordered a broth with shiitake mushrooms in it. I said to
> him that if he really loved me he would put shiitake and sashimi on my

front and eat them from there. He said that of course he would do that, and took a shiitake out of the broth with a pair of chopsticks and put it inside of me. After putting it back in the broth and putting it on the tea table and teasing me with it, he ate half of it and I ate the other half.[5]

By the end of their first week in bed together, Abe was a changed woman. As she put it, "I fell completely in love with him."[6] They extended their tryst until they ran short of money. Abe then made a trip to Nagoya on April 29, where she met Ômiya and told him a lie about a former lover so that she could obtain a sizable amount of money from him. Ômiya gave her one hundred yen and promised more later. Abe had mixed feelings at this time. She recounted in her interrogation that although she definitely felt an affection for Ômiya, she was, in her words, "very much in love" with Ishida, and in the short time they were apart she longed to be with him.

Upon Abe's return to Tokyo, she and Ishida immediately went to another teahouse, Masaki, in a part of the city called Ogu. This was on the other side of the city from where they had been, in a red-light district close to the Sumida River and Asakusa, Abe's old home turf. The next few days they spent either in bed together or revisiting places they had previously stayed in order to pay their trail of debts at least partially, lest they be tracked down. While making love for days on end they frequently did without food or bathing. On May 3, they called a geisha to perform for them again, an extravagance considering their large, outstanding bills at several establishments. The fog of love had beclouded the judgment of both. It would soon become so thick that neither would emerge unscathed.

On May 5, Abe met Ômiya during the day in Shinjuku. They had originally planned to meet at noon, but Abe was late. Once again, she told him a lie about being involved with a man she wished to get rid of, and he gave her 120 yen. They had dinner together but didn't even shake hands when they parted. Abe said that she felt sorry for him, but once she had returned to Ishida she completely forgot Ômiya. Although their short-term financial worries were over, it was clear to both that they could not continue as they were without more money. Ishida also seems to have had qualms about

Abe's supporting their affair financially to that point. In any event, they decided on the sixth that Ishida needed to return to his restaurant, if for just a short time.

Parting was difficult for both. They went from Ogu to Asakusa, where they strolled in the rain through a park. Later, they went to a crab restaurant and continued to drink until midnight, when it closed and the manager asked them to leave. Still they could not bear separation. Instead, they continued to drink until they were asked to leave yet another restaurant when it closed. As the hour approached three in the morning, they went all the way across Tokyo together to Nakano, where Yoshidaya was located. On the way, a police officer scolded them for being out so late. Abe was afraid that were she out alone, she might be scolded by the police again, so Ishida took her to a neighborhood inn. Still unable to part, they spent the rest of the night together there. Finally, on the morning of May 8, Ishida returned to his restaurant and Abe went to stay with Inaba Masatake, who had moved back to Tokyo. Abe was overwhelmed for the first time in her life by feelings that reflected the dark side of her love and erotic desire for Ishida. Never before had she experienced jealousy.

# 14. MURDER

R omantic love, except in most movies, advertising, television dramas, and other fairy tales, tends to be more disturbing than blissful. This is as true for society as it is for individual lovers. It was certainly true of the effects that Abe's love for Ishida had on him, on herself, and eventually on people throughout the country. Inaba Masatake described Abe as "agitated" during her stay with him that May. In the past he had thought of her as reserved, but this time she surprised him with a request for something to drink. She then consumed three bottles of beer in front of him—an unthinkable amount for any woman at the time, including geisha and prostitutes. Abe remembered drinking excessively because she kept imagining that Ishida was making love to his wife. From the moment she arrived at the Inaba residence until she met Ishida some four days later, Abe was obsessed with the thought that he was with Otoku. In her interrogation she told the police: "I felt for the first time what it means to suffer from jealousy."[1]

This assertion supported her claim that with Ishida, she felt true love for the first time in her life. No matter how much she appreciated Ômiya's solicitude, he fulfilled only a paternal role for her. Abe repeatedly asserted that she felt deeply for Ômiya, if not that she was ever in love with him; but never did she say that she was jealous of him. She never seemed concerned about Ômiya being with another woman. Until she became Ishida's lover, Abe either subordinated herself to the wishes of her male partners, kept an emotional distance, or both. Some men gave her sexual pleasure, but that did not make them lovers. Consequently, with Ishida, her feelings of love and jealousy stood out, as if in relief, above anything she had felt before. Never in her life had she so desired to control a man.

Abe's thoughts of possession and control ultimately had no outlet other than the absolute extreme: murder. Already, between a week and ten days before she committed the act, she seriously contemplated it. The day after Abe and Ishida went separate ways, she tried to do something constructive and focused on making some new clothes and repairing old garments. She recounted her thoughts at that time:

> While I was sewing, all I could do was think about Ishida. Becoming his mistress and sharing him with somebody else didn't interest me, and so all that there was left to do was to get married. The only way we would be able to get married would be to run off together. But then I thought that Ishida wasn't the type to run off, and I even thought about killing him. Jealousy can make a person think like that, and so I thought there was nothing I could do to stop it.[2]

The official report of the police investigation quotes Abe at this point revealing her thoughts in words that do not appear in the interrogation record:

It wouldn't do for me to become his mistress or something like that; the only thing for me was to become his wife. But I thought that he wasn't the kind of man who would run away from his wife, and so I came to think all the more that I would kill him, to the point that there was no stopping me.[3]

For Abe to have asserted that "there was no stopping me" suggests that when she did kill Ishida, it was premeditated and no crime of passion. While she was at the Inaba residence during the second week of May, Abe seemingly had decided with some degree of conviction to commit murder. Yet even though she asserted that she could not have been stopped from killing Ishida, the situation was not completely clear. The police structured the investigation record to make it appear a case of premeditated murder; at a later point in time Abe could easily have had second thoughts. However, the narrative of the police investigation continues from this thought of murder directly to the act:

On the ninth, Abe went to a play at the Meijiza called "*Shinsaku tsuya monogatari*" [New tales of the erotic]. In it, there was a geisha named Koganei who hid a large knife in her kimono, went to the house where her lover lived with his parents, and attacked him with it. While looking at this play, all she could think about was Ishida, and upon seeing this she decided that she would buy a large knife and threaten Ishida with it. On May 12 [sic], she could no longer wait to see Ishida and bought a knife at a hardware store while on the way to the inn called Meijiya in Shinjuku. She found herself unable to ask for a large knife in front of the other customers, and so bought a smaller carving knife instead, and called Ishida from the inn in Shinjuku. They met again at about 8:30 that evening.[4]

This is one point where the interrogation and the investigation accounts contradict each other. In her interrogation, Abe draws a far more roundabout route to her reunion with Ishida, although she does say that the play mentioned in the police report was influential:

I went to a play at Meijiza, but the whole time I was thinking about Ishida. In that play there was a scene in which there appeared a large vegetable knife, and it made me want to go buy a large knife like that and to tease Ishida with it. I went back to the Inaba residence at about eleven that evening.[5]

Before separating, Abe and Ishida had agreed to contact each other through a sushi shop called Tama Sushi, whose owner agreed to act as an intermediary. The following day, May 10, Abe telephoned Tama Sushi to see if Ishida had left a message for her. He had simply left a request for Abe's telephone number, but that was enough to make her "swoon"—as she put it—and make plans to meet him. Abe then left the Inaba residence and went to Shinjuku, where she spent the night at an inn called Meijiya, which she had previously frequented with Ômiya. She later described how, the following day, after pawning some clothes, she used some of the money to buy the knife that the police described in their report:

> After that I bought some sushi at Sachi Sushi, and called Tama Sushi to leave the telephone number of Meijiya Inn. About three doors down from Sachi Sushi was a hardware store called Kikuhide. There, I bought a kitchen knife for ninety *sen*. I thought I would borrow some money from my older sister Teruko in Ôtsuka, but I got busy and didn't have time to go, and so returned to Meijiya.[6]

Although the police made much of it, Abe mentioned the knife purchase almost as an afterthought.

Later that night, Abe and Ishida met again in Nakano. Abe said that she was so happy to see him that she almost fell from the taxi. She described their meeting:

> We went to a place where it was dark, where Ishida said, "I'm so in love I'll always call back if we get disconnected." I pulled the kitchen knife out of my bag and threatened him as had been done in the play I had seen, saying, "Kichi, you wore that kimono just to please one of your

favorite customers. You bastard, I'll kill you for that." Ishida was startled and drew away a little, but he seemed delighted with it all, and
said that I had better put that thing away or somebody might see it,
which would get us in real trouble.[7]

She put it away and their conversation turned to money. In her elation
Abe consumed so much alcohol that she lost all memory of what happened
later in the evening. It is certain that they went from Nakano back to
Masaki in Ogu, where they remained until his murder except for short
intervals, during which Abe met Ômiya on May 15 and Ishida got a haircut
on May 16.

At Masaki, Abe had conflicting emotions: "I felt incredibly confused. I was
happy and hurt at the same time. I loved Ishida and hated him."[8] Ishida had
told her that he did not even go home their first night apart and that he had
not slept with his wife the whole time he was there. Yet she did not believe
this and expressed her displeasure by violently pinching and biting him. Abe
also threatened him with the knife. Ishida's response was to say that she
couldn't kill him with that knife, and to laugh and get excited:

> When I put the edge against the base of his penis and said that I would
> make sure he wouldn't fool around with other women, he just laughed
> and said that I was being stupid. On the next day, the twelfth, I
> thought that it would be a bad idea if the maid were to see the knife,
> so I hid it behind a picture.[9]

Clearly, she was teasing him. But Abe later followed through on it. At this
point her actions were playful, yet they also suggested a struggle for control.
One or two nights after they had reunited, their play took them in a direction
the danger of which was obvious in hindsight, if not at the time. When Abe
squeezed Ishida's throat in jest, he told her that he had heard that squeezing
the neck during sex increased the pleasure of intercourse and orgasm. In
response, she asked him to squeeze her neck with his hands while having
intercourse, which he did, but he could not continue doing it through the sex
act. Abe then tried it on him, but he did not like it and so they quit. Never-

theless, this was enough to get them started toward unexpected—if possibly not unintended—results a few days later.

As she had promised Ômiya the previous time she had seen him, Abe left Ishida to meet him on the fifteenth. They had dinner together and then went to a teahouse, where Abe felt obligated to have sex with him. She returned as quickly as possible to Ishida, who teased her about what she had done to obtain the fifty yen Ômiya had given her. He told her that the next time she went out with another man he would buy a big knife. Abe was pleased at Ishida's jealousy—it implied that her feelings were requited.

After Abe visited Ômiya, she and Ishida again tried to increase their sexual pleasure through play with strangulation. This led to an incident that, in retrospect, sealed Ishida's fate. On the sixteenth, Abe thought of wrapping her sash cord around his neck and squeezing it so that it cut off his breath for a few moments while they were having sex. Both enjoyed this. Ishida raised his hips, his penis engorged; Abe liked the sensation. He told her that he did not mind suffering a little if it gave her pleasure, so they repeated it for nearly two hours. Once, Abe pulled the cord too hard. Ishida's penis suddenly went limp and he clearly was in pain, his eyes bloodshot and swollen. A red line around his neck marked where the cord had been. She took him to the bath, washed his face, and tried to cool him down. Ishida's face remained distorted, which both of them found upsetting.

The following afternoon Ishida's face remained swollen and distorted, but they decided not to call a physician for fear he might notify the police. Instead, Abe went to a pharmacist, who told her that it would take a month or two before Ishida's face would return to normal. She then purchased some eye wash and a sedative called Calmotin, produced by Takeda Pharmaceuticals; nearby, she also bought some soup and watermelon for Ishida.

When Abe told Ishida what the pharmacist had said, he was upset that it would take so long for him to recover. They did not have much money and could not stay much longer at Masaki. Abe had a maid heat the soup and bring her a knife with which to cut the melon, having completely forgotten about the knife she had brought with her. They ate and Abe gave Ishida the prescribed dose of the sedative, which had little effect. He then took more, and finally took the entire package of thirty tablets.

Ishida was worried about paying their bill and wanted to leave as soon as possible. He wished to return home and for Abe to go to the Inaba residence in Shitaya. When she objected, he suggested another plan: they would go to a friend's house and have his wife come meet him there. Because that plan had no provision for her, Abe expressed her dissatisfaction. Ishida could think of no alternative but to part. When she recalled the pain of their previous separation, Abe felt that there was no way she could leave him for an even longer period:

> When I suggested that we commit a double suicide or run off together, Ishida said that he wanted to go on meeting me at teahouses. When we met, Ishida had already made a success of himself and his business. There was no reason for him to think of committing suicide or of running off. I knew all too well that he would refuse my suggestions and didn't even think of double suicide or of running off as serious options. So in the end, I decided that there was nothing I could do but kill him and make him mine forever.[10]

These were words of love—more accurately, of desire—not of anger and hatred. Abe's desire to make Ishida hers forever had the ring of a marriage proposal or pledge of commitment. Her decision to murder her lover came from her positive feelings about their relationship, combined with her recognition of the impossibility that it could continue on terms she could accept. Most lovers, drunk with mutual desire, wish that their moments of passion could endure eternally. Abe was no different. Yet the desire that Abe and Ishida had for each other was by this point toxic. In this private space their mutual desire mostly, if not completely, fogged and distorted their ordinary sense of morality. Even as she murdered Ishida, who was groggy from an overdose of the sedative, Abe asked his forgiveness:

> While Ishida was dozing, I lay down next to him. His pillow was to the south, and I put his right hand under my hips and stretched out toward my back as though he was holding me. I placed his left hand next to his

left shoulder and looked at his sleeping face. Now and then Ishida would open his eyes and see that I was next to him and then relax, knowing that I was there. Once, he said, "Okayo, you'll put the cord around my neck and squeeze it again while I'm sleeping, won't you." I said that I would and smiled. Then he said, "If you start to strangle me, don't stop, because it is so painful afterward." At that time I wondered if he wanted me to kill him, but after thinking it over I knew all too well that wasn't possible and that he must have been joking. After a while Ishida was sound asleep, and with my right hand I took my peach-colored sash cord that was next to his pillow and with my left hand pulled the end of it under his neck, wrapped it twice around his neck, adjusted the ends, and pulled on them. He opened his eyes and said, "Okayo." His body raised up a little and moved as though he was going to give me a hug. I put my face against his chest and cried, "Forgive me," and pulled on the ends of my sash cord with all my might. Ishida moaned once and his hands shook violently. When he went limp I released the ends of the cord. My whole body was trembling and I went over to the tea table where there was a bottle of sake. I gulped down everything that was in it and then, so that he wouldn't come back to life, I tightly tied my sash cord in a knot across his throat and wrapped the rest of it around his neck and placed the ends under his pillow. After that I went downstairs to see if there was anybody around. The clock at the desk said that it was about two in the morning.[11]

Abe's state of mind at this time was terrifyingly placid. She said to the police, "After I had killed Ishida I felt totally at ease, as though a heavy burden had been lifted from my shoulders, and I felt a sense of clarity."[12] For several hours she continued to lie next to Ishida's body, thinking both of her feelings for him and of a wish to apologize to Ômiya, whom she knew the police would investigate because of their relationship. When she realized that she would have to leave the scene, Abe calmly cut off Ishida's penis and scrotum with the knife she had hidden in their room. She then wrapped them in paper and constantly kept them close to herself until her arrest four days later.

When asked why she had done this, her answer was simple and straightforward: "Because I couldn't take his head or body with me, I wanted to take the part of him that brought back to me the most vivid memories."[13] On another occasion she said she had done it because she wanted to be close to that part of Ishida and for his wife not to be able to touch it again. This and the other acts of mutilation that she committed—carving her name into his body and writing on it in his blood—came as afterthoughts to the act of murder and were in no way premeditated. Finally, she put on his undergarments instead of her own, dressed, cleaned the room, and left Masaki at about eight in the morning with instructions not to bother Ishida.

Abe got her wish: she fulfilled her desire to control Ishida forever. But for the rest of her life, she paid dearly for the illusion of peace that she had created in the hours between her murder of Ishida and the discovery of his body. Once the maid at Masaki called the police, the "Abe Sada Incident" became a focus of national attention. Thereafter, it pursued her relentlessly for decades. According to what she wrote and said after her release from prison, she despaired that few if any people understood that she killed Ishida out of love. She despaired even more at correcting depictions of her as sexually motivated.

Those who focused on Abe's sexuality as a motive, especially Japanese psychoanalysts at the time, forgot that romantic love and desire to control the object of love are impossible to separate. Purely altruistic and compassionate love certainly exists, but romantic love implies a need to be united with the object of desire. In *Tales of Love*, the psychoanalyst Julia Kristeva aptly calls love "An unleashing that, in the absolute, can go as far as crime against the loved one."[14] This can just as easily be a crime against one's self as against another. Moreover, love is a threat not just to the individuals involved but even to the social order. Kristeva also emphasizes this point: "passionate love can be equated less with the calm slumber of reconciled civilizations than with their delirium, disengagement, and breach. A fragile crest where death and regeneration vie for dominance."[15] Contemporary fiction was awash with stories of love and death. Among the most popular were tales of young women in love who wasted away, usually from tuberculosis, because they could not be with their lover.[16] Previous generations were familiar with stories of women who joined their men in love suicides, beginning with the puppet and kabuki performances of plays by the eighteenth-century playwright Chikamatsu Monzaemon. Both scenarios resulted in the death of the woman, if not always the man, but nevertheless were politically suspect when they presented willful women. Abe was all the more dangerous because she actively murdered her lover, unlike other stereotypically willful women who passively wasted away in a sanitarium or died in a suicide pact. She had killed and survived without submitting to the phallocentric hegemony, and as a consequence could not be considered completely rational.

For Abe, as long as the object of her desire was close at hand, when unity with Ishida or at least its illusion was possible, hope of regenerating their relationship predominated. But when she was threatened with displacement, then separation through death became a plausible alternative. Abe was so in love with Ishida that she could not imagine her life without him, which also made her own death immanent. Suicide was just a matter of time—or so her state of mind made it seem.

For any lover, a threat of separation can arouse jealousy, which can, in turn, incite violent rage. In Abe's murder of Ishida, jealousy was central but did not lead directly to vengeful anger. At no point did the lovers quarrel, at least not according to Abe's testimony and to people at the teahouses where they stayed. In short, Abe did not murder Ishida in a crime of passion, a simple, jealousy-driven rage that blinded her to the gravity of her actions. Rather, she was aware she would pay a high cost, which for her meant her life. But she did not foresee the true price of her actions: unrelenting fame for an incident of murder and mutilation that remained frequently misunderstood and misrepresented. Paparazzi and tabloid reporters hounded her for decades. For Abe, the most painful consequence was the way people described her as motivated by sex rather than by love. Yet it was this imaginary view of her rather than the reality that contributed to her fame, since few have killed for sex but many have killed for love.

However, in the days after she committed murder Abe was hardly aware of the immense repercussions of that act. The fog that enshrouded her did not clear until after her arrest.

# 15. NO LONGER PRIVATE

It is hard to imagine a person committing murder and then mutilating the victim's body without subsequently being in some state of shock. In her interrogation Abe described herself immediately after killing Ishida as having gone about her affairs in a rather ordinary fashion, as people often do following traumatic experiences. She had little direction or urgency about her actions. Abe left Ishida's body at the teahouse, Masaki, at close to eight in the morning on May 18. She bought a change of clothes and then called Masaki to see if anything was amiss. The maid said that nothing was unusual, making it clear that nobody had discovered Ishida's body. Abe told her, "I'll be back at noon, so please be sure to let [Ishida] sleep until I get back." The maid assured her that she understood.[1] The naïveté and ordinariness of Abe's actions from then on both defy imagination and attest to her humanity.

Well before she committed the crime, Abe understood that Ishida's murder would have public implications. This was most obvious in the concern she showed for the devastating effect she knew it would have on the life of her Nagoya patron, Ômiya Gorô. In her interrogation Abe testified that after killing Ishida she had thought of Ômiya and the problems that her actions would cause him. This was no mere rhetoric. On the eighteenth, after changing clothes and ascertaining that Ishida's body had not yet been discovered, one of the first things that Abe did was to contact Ômiya at his inn. They arranged a meeting later that day. While with him, Abe did not confess to murder, but she repeatedly apologized for her behavior. Ômiya believed that she was apologizing for having a lover. He told her that she had given him more pleasure than anything else in life and that he wanted to go on seeing her. They had a meal together and then had sex at an inn near Ôtsuka Station in Tokyo. Abe later said that she did it out of a sense of obligation. Obviously Ômiya had no idea that not only his affair with Abe but also his career was at an end. And despite her concern for him, Abe did not have the courage to tell him what she had done.

Abe's worries about Ômiya did not give her insight into how this incident would change her own life. She had remained so focused on herself and Ishida that she did not imagine their affair as anything but private. Because she believed suicide was the only path open to her, she did not see herself and her actions as objects of public attention. But from the moment the maid at Masaki found Ishida's body and called the police, Abe had no privacy.

**FIGURE 2.** (Opposite: top) Article from the *Tokyo Nichinichi shinbun*, May 19, 1936, with photos of Abe Sada and Ishida Kichizô. The horizontal headline reads: GROTESQUE CRIME IN TEAHOUSE. The vertical headlines read: WOMAN OF THE NIGHT, A MATURE BEAUTY, KILLS SEX-CRAZED MASTER and "SADA, KICHI TOGETHER" INSCRIBED IN BLOOD, ESCAPES BY TAXI. Photo: The Mainichi Newspapers

**FIGURE 3.** (Opposite: bottom) Exterior of the teahouse Masaki, where the murder took place, May 1936. The man at bottom center speaking with the boys was said to be an investigating police officer. Photo: The Mainichi Newspapers

夜會巷の年増美人

# 情痴の主人殺し

滴る血潮で記す「定、吉二人」

圓タクで行方を晦す

情痴殺人の二人

男の所持金

持去つ

For over three decades, newspapers, magazines, the radio, and newsreels shown in movie theaters all made her the subject of intense scrutiny.

The detail with which newspapers described this incident and its protagonists reflects a close working relationship between the police and the press. The newspaper reports on May 19, 1936 included individual photographs of Abe and Ishida, of the teahouse Masaki with an arrow pointing to the room where Ishida's body had been discovered, and a map showing the floor plan, including that room. A headline announced that the president of the Chûkyô School of Commerce, Ômiya Gorô, age 49, was under police investigation in the case. The accompanying article described his career as a banker, educator, and politician in detail. The way the newspapers put Ômiya alongside headlines that described Abe as having A LICENTIOUS EROTIC LIFE and being AN EASY-SPENDING WOMAN must have pained him and probably shattered his family.[2] Without access to police evidence—including Abe's confession on the day of her arrest—the newspapers would have found it difficult to report this story so specifically.

In contrast, the press depicted the police as highly organized and efficient, doing their best to safeguard the public. On the nineteenth, newspapers described a police dragnet so tight it could hold water. They quoted a Metropolitan Police official as saying that the motive was unimaginable, so horrific was the crime. Most coverage that day spelled out Abe's movements in Tokyo immediately after the murder, as much as they could be pieced together from the accounts of witnesses. The tacit assumption was that the police, famous for their efficacy, could be counted on to catch the culprit. Yet by avoiding the places she usually frequented, changing kimono, and adding a pair of glasses, Abe avoided both the police and reporters.

The next day, May 20, brought no resolution. The incident had aroused enough public attention that it appeared in the *Tokyo Asahi* on page 2 instead of the next-to-last page, the place usually reserved for crime stories. The story ran with multiple headlines that dwarfed an article, which also included a photograph, about Adolph Hitler receiving an antique Japanese sword. News coverage of this murder overwhelmed that of other events as well, including visits to Japan by Jean Cocteau and Charlie Chaplin.

**FIGURE 4.** Police car stopped in front of an inn while officers search for Abe Sada, May 18 or 19, 1936. Photo: The Mainichi Newspapers

Police had tracked Abe to a used clothing shop where she had left the kimono she had worn from Masaki. As they were still unable to find her, all personnel in all Tokyo precincts, as well as some in Yokohama and other locations, had been mobilized. Further information was discovered about Abe, Ishida, and Ômiya. The papers reported details about Abe's life as a prostitute, how she had used multiple pseudonyms at various times, and how she had met with Ômiya on the eighteenth. He told the police that Abe never mentioned the crime to him. They didn't buy it. The police knew that Abe had met with

Ômiya during her affair with Ishida, and they continued to interrogate him. The *Asahi* wrote that Ômiya probably held the key to understanding the crime.

Another leading newspaper, the *Yomiuri*, tended toward the sensational in its tone. One headline called Abe an ENCHANTINGLY BEAUTIFUL FLOWER OF EVIL (*Yôbi na aku no hana*) and the protagonist in A TALE OF HORROR FROM THE HELL OF LUSTFUL DESIRE (*Aiyoku jigoku no kyôgeki*).[3] It described Abe's background as the daughter of a Kanda tatami maker, and said that she had known men from age fourteen or fifteen—but without noting that her first sexual experience was the result of rape. The report portrayed a juvenile delinquent who became a prostitute and then went on to commit murder. The *Yomiuri* also speculated that this crime was a historical first in modern Japan. It noted previous incidents in which women had cut off men's genitalia but wrote that there had been none in which a woman then walked off with the goods. The only known parallel was when a man had killed a woman in 1915 and carried away her severed pudenda.

Perhaps the most remarkable aspect of the *Yomiuri*'s coverage was its detail. Two days after the murder, it printed what Abe had eaten after she had met Ômiya and how they had spent an hour in private at an inn called Midoriya in the Nishi Sugamo part of Tokyo. From there, it described her trip to a used clothing store and quoted her conversation with a clerk there. She described Abe as carrying a package, which the clerk offered to wrap together with the clothing that Abe had worn into the shop. Abe told her, "Don't touch that package!" The same day's edition also included her conversations with a clerk in yet another used-kimono shop, a taxi driver, and a man whom she had met on the street who recognized her as "Sada from the tatami shop" in Kanda.[4] The newspaper did not reveal its sources for these stories.

A forensic psychologist for the Metropolitan Police Department, Kaneko Junji, quoted in the *Yomiuri*, asserted that this crime must have been motivated by sexual deviancy, for which he imagined four possible scenarios. In one, the criminal was a fetishist who wanted to possess a real penis as fetish and so had committed murder and mutilation. In the second, the woman was simply getting revenge for something the man had done. Another possibility was that the murder resulted from a love triangle in which Abe wished to demonstrate her affection for another man (Ômiya) by murdering and mutilating his rival. Finally, the killing could have been simply the result of jealousy, Abe's desire to control—literally to monopolize—the object of love, but based on a sense of anger and hatred so strong that she then mutilated him; in doing this, she had symbolically castrated all men. The *Yomiuri* wrote that most people seemed to support the jealousy theory. Kaneko believed that the fate of Ishida's missing parts would explain the case.[5]

Despite the ability of the police and the newspapers to follow her tracks, Abe managed to stay ahead of them. One of the first places she went following her meeting with Ômiya on the afternoon of the eighteenth was the public park at Hamachô, which offered a place for quiet reflection. Evening papers on that day carried no stories about Ishida's death, so, somewhat at ease, Abe then found a place to stay in Asakusa. She contemplated suicide and how to carry it out at Mount Ikoma on the one-week anniversary of Ishida's death. After her arrest, Abe reflected on her plans:

> At first, when I met Professor Ômiya, I had thought that I would go ahead and die. But after seeing him, although I was vaguely thinking that I would have to die, I felt safe since I had Ishida's important "thing" close to me. I felt attached to Ishida's penis and thought that only after taking leave from it quietly could I then die. I unwrapped the paper holding them and gazed at his penis and scrotum. I put his penis in my mouth and even tried to insert it inside me. All the while I was thinking about things and crying a little as well. I didn't sleep well that night. I felt that all that I wanted was to have another day to touch Ishida's penis. Then, I decided that I would flee to Osaka, staying with Ishida's penis all the while. In the end, I would jump from a cliff on Mt. Ikoma while holding on to his penis.[6]

This was not to happen. As events unfolded the following day, it soon became impossible for her to carry out her plans. The dense police presence at all of Tokyo's railway stations on May 19 prevented her from boarding a train, so she stayed in Tokyo. Abe told the police about events from that morning until she was arrested the following afternoon:

The next morning, on the nineteenth, I borrowed the paper at the registration desk and saw a photo of me from my youth along with an article written about what had happened in Ogu. It would cause trouble should one of the people in the inn see the newspaper, so I hid it under my futon. At about ten I left the inn, but since it was raining I hesitated to go to Osaka. I went to the movie theater Shôchikukan in Asakusa and around two started toward Ginza to get something to eat. But I realized that I might be recognized and so went to Shinagawa instead and bought a ticket for Osaka. Since I had two hours before the train departed, I bought five newspapers and went to a coffee shop in front of the station, where I bought a bottle of sake and got sleepy. At about five that afternoon I went to the inn Shinagawakan and took a bath, drank a beer, and called a masseuse. After dinner, I looked at the evening paper. I hadn't thought about things that way, but it compared me to Takahashi Oden [a woman who had become famous for a murder in the late nineteenth century] and said other big things, and reported that police were posted at every train station. It had become a big deal. I couldn't stay alive, but since it didn't seem possible to go to Osaka, I made up my mind to die at that inn. I asked the manager to get the money back for my ticket, which he did. If I were to stay at that inn the police would come looking and arrest me that night, and I wanted to die before they caught me. But the ledge over the doors was so low that if I were to hang myself by the neck my feet would still touch the floor, making it impossible to die that way. Resigned that I would be caught, I stayed up until about one that morning. Still, nothing happened that night, so on the morning of the twentieth I changed to a room that had higher doors. Once there, I wrote last testaments to Ômiya Gorô, Kurokawa Hana [sister-in-law of Inaba Masatake], and the victim, Ishida Kichizô. With the intention of dying that night, I drank three bottles of beer and fell asleep. At around four the next afternoon a police officer came into my room. I told him that I was Abe Sada and he arrested me.[7]

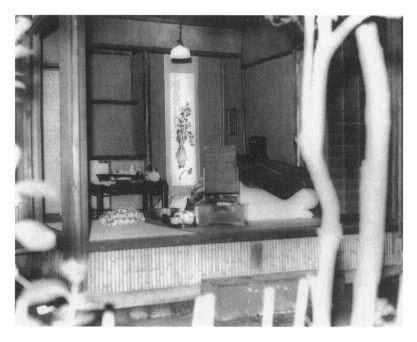

**FIGURE 5.** The room in which Abe Sada was arrested, May 20, 1936. Photo: The Mainichi Newspapers

Abe's memory of details was not completely accurate; she was arrested not at four but at approximately five-thirty in the afternoon. Just over an hour later, newspaper extras appeared announcing her arrest. They reflected the impact of this incident: extras were rare, and the most recent had appeared announcing the February 26 Incident; the next appeared only the following November, announcing a cooperative pact between Germany and Japan.

Some of the stories—obviously written before her arrest the previous afternoon—in the morning papers on May 21 still pondered Abe's where-abouts. On page 2 of the *Tokyo Asahi,* a story and accompanying photograph depicted a whirlwind of Abe Sada excitement continuing to sweep the country. The headlines and a photo of crowds stopped at the rumor of a "Sada

**FIGURE 6.** Extra, *Tokyo Nichinichi shinbun*, May 20, 1936. Headlines read: ABE SADA, CRIMINAL IN GROTESQUE MURDER AT OGU TEAHOUSE, FINALLY ARRESTED WHILE HIDING AT SHINAGAWAKAN IN TAKANAWA. Photo: The Mainichi Newspapers

sighting" overwhelmed a headline and photo of Prince Mikasa, the emperor's younger brother, participating in military exercises. One headline read: A FLOOD OF SADA SHADOWS, NONSENSE IN PURSUIT OF A PHANTOM; it referred to the third element of the triad of *ero-guro-nansensu* (erotic, grotesque, nonsense) that was a current fad. To contemporaries, the first two elements were obvious in the news of this incident. Excitement over nothing added the third element. A

**FIGURE 7.** A crowd gathered outside the Ogu police station at the word of Abe Sada's arrest, May 20, 1936. Photo: The Mainichi Newspapers

reported sighting of Abe in Tokyo's Ginza district froze traffic. Other sightings were reported in the Kanda, Tokyo Station, Shiba, and Nihonbashi neighborhoods of the city. Outside Tokyo, there had been at least two reported sightings in Osaka, and the Yokohama police had been mobilized in the search. The pursuit of a dangerous criminal on the loose could not have generated more excitement. People debated whether she had fled to a distant location or simply gone underground.

The main headlines concerning Abe on the twenty-first, however, reported her arrest. Police had previously visited the inn where she was stay-

**FIGURE 8.** *Tokyo Nichinichi shinbun*, May 21, 1936 with story of Abe Sada's arrest. Top headlines read: BIZARRELY DRAWN PICTURE OF LOVE AND DESIRE. SADA, FEMME FATALE IN TEAHOUSE MURDER, ARRESTED. The vertical headlines on the right read: MONOPOLIZES THE MAN SHE LOVES. A DEVIL INCARNATE LAUGHS AT BLOOD. SADISM BEYOND IMAGINATION. A WEIRD INCIDENT RARELY SEEN IN THE HISTORY OF CRIME. The vertical headlines on the left read: ARRESTED AT SHINAGAWAKAN JUST BEFORE ATTEMPTING SUICIDE. Photo: The Mainichi Newspapers

ing, but another officer returned late the same afternoon. The newspapers dedicated at least one full page to this story. The *Asahi* ran a photograph of Andô Matsukichi, the police detective who arrested Abe, along with an interview in which he described how he had taken her into custody:

> I assumed that the culprit was laying low in Tokyo, so from the morning of the twentieth we kept a watch on Shinagawa Station. But from

**FIGURE 9.**  Abe Sada surrounded by police officers, leaving Takanawa Police Station, May 20 or 21, 1936. Photo: The Mainichi Newspapers

the evening we started investigating the inns. First we went to the Keihin Hotel, and from there to the Shinagawakan. The registration book there showed a guest named Ôwada Nao (age 37), a name that didn't reveal whether the person was a man or woman. I had the maid show me to the room. There, a woman was wearing a nightgown and an eye mask. I thought it couldn't be her, but then I said, "That's a fake name, isn't it?" I added, "Sleeping this time of day, you're no ordinary person."

Without looking in the least bit surprised, she said, "In fact, I'm the Abe Sada you are looking for." And so I took her away immediately.[8]

According to newspaper reports based on the maid's testimony, Abe smiled at the detective, got dressed and did her make-up, and went out with the police, carrying only a small package in a brown oiled-paper wrapper. A photograph in the *Asahi* showed a smiling, almost radiant Abe holding this package, surrounded by police officers. The fact that a petite, beautiful woman could have committed such an atrocious crime did all the more to capture the public's attention. Headlines next to the photograph read: "WE DIDN'T HAVE A MARRIAGE RELATIONSHIP"; KILLS WHILE WATCHING HIS SLEEPING FACE; and CONFESSES, "BECAUSE I LOVED HIM."[9] One account included a conversation Abe had with the police at a police station. It described her as carrying a package wrapped in oiled paper that she had kept between her breasts for three days, and which as a result reeked of decay. The police asked, "Doesn't it make you sick to be carrying around something like that?" She replied with a smile, "What? Why should it make me feel sick? It belonged to that beautiful man."[10] After this, the police preserved Ishida's body parts, which later became the subject of questions about ownership.

Another report included a partial confession that began with Abe's near-strangulation of Ishida during the early morning hours of the seventeenth. Abe then clearly asserted that she had started preparing for Ishida's murder several days earlier:

> I looked at this man's sleeping face and thought that since I was in no position to become his wife, no matter how much I loved him, in the end he would belong to another woman, which would be a pity. I thought it would be better to kill him and die myself, and so on the fifteenth I started making preparations for killing him when I bought a butcher's knife while I was at Ueno.[11]

None of the police speculation about her motives had been completely correct. Indeed, compared to the truth, they lacked imagination. Abe could not have incriminated herself more. In the confession that the newspapers printed, she told how she had gone to work at Yoshidaya and had started an affair with Ishida. Their brief period of separation in the beginning of May had been extremely painful for her. She continued:

> When I thought about my future with Ishida, I realized that he had a fine wife. No matter how much I loved him, I could expect to be together with him like this no more than about two weeks in any month. Because I had already bet my life on Ishida and had come to adore him so completely, I would not be able to stand the pain [of this separation]. So I decided that it would be best to throw away everything for the love I had for Ishida at present and to kill him and die myself. That's how I decided to kill him. It was a pity that although I was the person who loved him the most, I couldn't attend his funeral. That's why I cut off the part of the man I loved the most.[12]

Abe's focus was on Ishida and her love for him, not on the jealousy she felt toward his wife or other women; this was what both defied and captured the imaginations of her contemporaries. She had killed not out of jealousy but out of love.

The newspapers also printed the short testaments that Abe had written immediately before her arrest. Briefest was her message to Kuroda Hana, which read, "You have done much to help me for a very long time. I am very grateful for all you have done for me. Please give my best wishes to all." Abe's message to Ômiya Gorô was the longest. She wrote: "There is no excuse for the inconveniences that I have caused you. You have treated me as a serious person and done many kind things for me, but my selfishness has made me less than happy. Because of circumstances I cannot control I'm about to die. Thank you for all you have done." Finally, her message to Ishida was in an envelope addressed, "To You, Who Are Mine." It read simply: "You, whom I love the most, even when dead you are mine. I'll be with you soon." These messages left no doubt as to her intentions.[13]

The following day the *Tokyo Asahi* ran a story with a headline that quoted Abe as saying, "HA, HA: THE DEATH PENALTY IS FINE." Other dailies carried similar headlines. The piece described Abe as talking to the police as though she were still with Ishida. When they asked if she regretted having killed him, she replied: "He (Ishida) is underground, happy that I killed him. I feel good, as though something has been completed. Execution or anything is just fine. Please execute me quickly. If I were to get the death penalty, do you think I'm silly enough to appeal?"[14]

After this, newspapers reported little more on Abe until the following month. On June 10, the *Tokyo Asahi* carried a headline that read: SADA SCORNS THE WORLD. Police investigators had finished her interrogation the day before and were ready to indict her for murder and mutilation. Still she showed no regret. The story quoted Abe as saying, "I'm sorry to have caused such a commotion, but I don't think I did anything bad by killing Yo [as she called Ishida]. I think that Yo is underground, delighted with things as they are." The article concluded by saying that it was Abe's dream to die for Ishida, and quoted her: "I want to climb the gallows' steps with my souvenir of Yo in my hands and to die with a smile on my lips."[15] Her two weeks of police custody and interrogations had not changed her state of mind. In one respect, at least, it never would change: long after her release from prison, she still did not believe that her murder of Ishida was wrong.

What had changed, however, was Abe's place in public life. From then on, nearly everything she did attracted attention, from her trial and imprisonment to her release from prison to her later attempts to make a living. The media found that Abe's story, retold every few years, made for solid sales. Abe Sada had ceased to be a private individual and had become a public figure.

Of course, she was not the only person thrust into the spotlight because of her crime. Ômiya Gorô was probably put in the most difficult position. The police, finally convinced that he had nothing to do with the murder, released him from custody on May 21. He then made a public announcement in which he stated that he had met with Abe only eight times and apologized to his students. She had led him to believe that she was in a difficult situation, which made him want to help her; in all, he had given her about one thousand yen. In the end, despite the trouble she had caused him, he called her simply "a pitiful woman."[16] Ômiya had already resigned from his formal positions before the incident became public, and following his statement to the press, he disappeared from view.

Others fared better. Initially Ishida's wife was overwhelmed by her husband's death and did not even make an appearance at his funeral. However, she and the general manager kept the business running and before long, due to the publicity that the incident had brought, Yoshidaya profited as it never had before.[17] The various teahouses where Ishida and Abe had stayed also benefited from the publicity. Masaki in particular made a profit, with couples wanting to stay in the room where Ishida and Abe had spent their last days. Shinagawakan, the inn where Abe had been arrested, also did well; it kept the room supposedly in the condition it was at the moment Detective Andô discovered her there. In short, the two men central to Abe's life, Ishida and Ômiya, suffered great misfortunes because of this incident, and it certainly caused pain to many others, such as members of Abe's family. Yet it also brought unforeseen profit to some of those it touched.

# 16. INTERROGATION AND INVESTIGATION

A more amiable felon than Abe Sada would be hard to imagine. With the mere appearance of a policeman in her room, she cheerfully prepared herself for arrest. She accompanied officers to Metropolitan Police Headquarters not only without resistance but quite literally with a smile. Her attitude reflected relief more than anxiety. Later, she remembered having no fear of the police but doing her best to tell them what a good person Kichizô had been.[1]

Abe slept for much of her first three days in jail, during which she also received medical treatment for chronic stomach pains. She also complained about the conditions of her incarceration. She wanted a better futon, a higher pillow, and other amenities. Her jailers told her to get used to what she had. In reality, conditions were good: she was allowed to purchase various items, including tissue paper, sweets, women's magazines, and flowers to decorate her cell. Soon after she arrived she had flowers brought in, which she then dedicated to the memory of Kichizô.

The woman in the cell next door in the detention center where Abe was first held remembered her clearly. Talk between the cells was forbidden, but one night, Abe's neighbor could hear her voice:

> "I'll be executed. It'll be good if they execute me soon," she repeated in a sad voice, talking to herself.
>
> "They won't execute you, so go to sleep and don't worry about it," [the guard replied].
>
> "That's wrong. It will be better if they execute me. And I want them to do it soon."[2]

Once she had been apprehended, decisions about how to commit suicide, the subject that had preoccupied Abe since killing Ishida, were no longer of concern. The courts would seal her fate. She testified to the police:

> If I hadn't thought I would receive the death penalty, I wouldn't have told everything in such detail at police headquarters. Because I have told everything, people will think I am a pervert. But if I hadn't told everything, people couldn't be expected to understand what Ishida and I did together. When I asked for a lawyer it wasn't so that I might get off lightly. It was so that he could tell people that I wasn't a pervert.[3]

Abe's greatest fear following her arrest was being misunderstood. To avoid this, she did her best to reveal everything possible about her life and her relationship with Ishida. Abe wanted not only the courts but the general public to remember that she had killed Ishida because of her deep love for him and not because of sexual deviancy. After her imprisonment she re-created her life story with a slightly different twist, but at the time of her arrest she believed that the only way to be understood was to tell the whole truth simply and directly.

The later comments of her interrogating officer, Adachi Umezô, support Abe's assertion that she had held back nothing. He described her behavior in her interrogation:

> That woman named Sada had a very straightforward manner. She answered questions without hesitation and she didn't wring her hands. The interrogation was easy. She said, "I'm very sorry for all the trouble I've caused" with great fervor, but it was possible to see that deep inside she was very satisfied that she had managed to take complete control of the man she loved. I could tell that when I was sitting across from her. So when she said, "I'm sorry," I could tell that the words had no real content. Nevertheless, there was nothing about her that made her seem criminal.
>
> She was a woman in the prime of life, a woman in the smart, old Edo style who was sexy in a way one doesn't usually think of a geisha or restaurant woman. What really left an impression was when I asked her, "Why did you cut him?" Immediately she became excited and her eyes sparkled in a strange way.
>
> At the time, people were saying that she had cut off Ishida's thing because it was larger than average. But in reality, Ishida's was just average. She told me, "Size doesn't make a man in bed. Technique and his desire to please me were what I liked about Ishida."[4]

This policeman's description is revealing not only of Abe but of himself as well. How he knew that Ishida's penis was of average size, he did not say. As one who had considerable contact with various criminals, he was in all likelihood an experienced observer of them. Clearly, Abe had fascinated him. And there is no doubt that they became well acquainted over the month during which he interrogated her.

Abe's interrogation determined her fate, not only in court but for the rest of her life—and beyond. In the Japanese legal system, based on the French and Prussian systems, police gathered evidence to establish the truth rather than to answer the question whether it could be demonstrated beyond doubt that a defendant had broken the law. The accused was expected to reveal all details and had no right to avoid self-incrimination. There was no legal requirement that counsel be present during interrogations. Furthermore, the police determined the final shape that the interrogation and investigation records took. These records were admissible as evidence in court. Trial by jury was not an option; rather, a three-judge panel presented the court's decision based on the evidence. This gave the police tremendous powers open to abuse, especially in cases that involved "thought crimes" against the state and similar "offenses" that were becoming increasingly common at the time. In the case of Abe Sada, however, the interrogation and gathering of evidence was far more cooperative in character than oppositional. Still, the police largely determined the structure of the evidence presented to the court.

Because the interrogations lasted for a full month, it is hard to believe that the records as presented to the court include everything that Abe said to the police. The existing document of her interrogation is entitled "Notes from the Interrogation of Abe Sada" (*Abe Sada jinmon jikô*), suggesting that it does not contain the complete record.[5] It consists of forty-six questions reportedly asked during six meetings with her interrogator. Oddly, it also contains testimony from one other person besides Abe herself. This was Kasahara Kinnosuke, for whom Abe briefly had been a mistress and who remembered her angrily.

Of the two official records from the police investigation that have been made public, the other being the "Police Investigation of Abe Sada" (*Abe Sada no chôsho*; more about it follows), this is the more compelling because it faithfully preserves Abe's voice—or at least appears to have done so. The first set of six questions asked why she committed murder, whether she had considered a double suicide, and if Ishida expected to die. The second interrogation included the most questions, fourteen. They concerned her family background, household, and childhood up to the time she became a public prostitute. Based on the amount of material covered, these first two periods of questioning must have extended over several days. The next two periods included only four questions each. The first set focused on the time from when Abe quit licensed prostitution until she began her relationship with Ômiya Gorô. In the next four questions, the police asked about the time from when Abe started work at Yoshidaya until she and Ishida ran away together. The fifth set of questions focused on the reasons Abe loved Ishida with such passion and the events of the murder and mutilation. The final interrogation focused on more details of the murder, her flight afterward, and descriptions of confiscated articles. Throughout this document, the police voice is minimal. Abe's own voice is intelligent and insightful. Although she lacked formal education beyond primary school, she was very perceptive. Her desire to reveal all that she could about her feelings and the details of her relationship with Ishida gives this document a candor unusual for a first-person account of a Japanese woman's life during the first half of the twentieth century. Therefore, it became the basis for the short stories, novels, theatrical performances, and films made about Abe. Without this document, the story of Abe Sada would be remembered in a radically different way. Even the first-hand account that Abe wrote in 1947 lacks the immediacy and straightforwardness of her interrogation record.[6]

The rough editorial state of the record is most obvious in its inclusion of the statement by Kasahara Kinnosuke, whose testimony would better fit the "Police Investigation of Abe Sada." He was a political operative who had been head of the Yokohama branch of the lobbying office for the Seiyûkai, one of the mainstream political parties at the time. His was the only testimony by anybody other than Abe included, although the official record of the court investigation contains testimony by many others who knew her.

A friend of her older brother in Kanda, Kasahara had sprung Abe from the Yokohama police station after she had been apprehended in a raid on an unlicensed brothel in 1934. He had found Abe attractive, taken her as a mistress, and set her up in a house. Abe then asked him to give up his wife and to marry her, but he refused. Things quickly went sour between them. He was unable to satisfy her sexually, and when she told him she wanted to take a lover he said he would kick her out if she did. It was at this point that she fled to Nagoya. Kasahara tried to follow her, threatening her with legal action for breach of contract because of the money he had spent on her. Their entire relationship lasted only two weeks. In his testimony, he described Abe in mixed terms. On the one hand, he said, "Even though I am pretty jaded, she was enough to astound me." Obviously he found her sexual intensity attractive. Yet on the other hand, his anger brought sharp words: "She is a slut and a whore. And as what she has done makes clear, she is a woman whom men should fear."[7] Without being aware of it, Kasahara explained the combination of sexual magnetism and threat that Abe embodied not only for him but also for many other men both at the time and since.

For her part, Abe described him in less than positive terms: "Kasahara was a real reprobate and wouldn't give me much spending money. He didn't love me and treated me like an animal. He was scum, but he then pleaded with me when I said that we should break up."[8] Following this experience as a mistress, Abe's attraction to a man as kind and considerate as Ômiya is understandable. In her own testimony, Abe also left out the incident in which she first met Kasahara following a police raid; this suggests that she was attempting in any way possible to create a favorable picture of herself in the interrogation record.

The judges who tried the case probably perused this account, but the official court record was entitled "Record of the Abe Sada Investigation" (*Abe Sada no chôsho*). Of the two court records available now, this has remained the more obscure, generally ignored by the many writers who have created works about Abe Sada. It has not been included in recent collections of documents printed in Japanese. Possibly, it remained unavailable when the transcript of her interrogation became public. It contains numerous statements by Abe not in the interrogation record, as well as testimony from many others, including relatives, former employers, lovers, clients, and friends. Most important, the investigation record was structured to create a clear narrative of her life, followed by an attempt by investigators to explain her behavior. It ends with a statement by an expert witness, a physician from Tokyo University, concerning her physical and mental condition.

Nearly half of the investigation record focuses on Abe's family background and life story, taken from her own testimony and that of others. This is followed by detailed comments on her menstrual period, medical history, tobacco use, alcohol use, and sexual appetite. According to contemporary belief, a woman's menstrual period could cause irrational behavior; hence it was a focus of attention in this investigation. However, nothing abnormal was apparent: "She experiences no abdominal pain, and says that she does not quarrel with people or act impulsively during her period. In addition, she said that at the time she committed the crime, she was between periods. She said that she has not been pregnant."[9] Abe's medical record did show that she had suffered from gonorrhea and syphilis, the latter having progressed to its tertiary stages but without physical or psychological abnormalities. The use of tobacco and alcohol, common among women of the sex industry and restaurant and bar businesses, was considered a sign of moral degeneracy and frowned upon among middle-class women living with their families. Abe had started to drink after becoming a geisha, and to smoke cigarettes after becoming a prostitute. Except for a short time when she had tried to quit smoking just after beginning work at Yoshidaya, she continued to smoke approximately a pack a day up to the time of her arrest. Although Abe liked to drink alcohol, she had never become alcoholic. The investigation did not conclude that alcohol had been a determinant in her murder of Ishida, despite the fact that each had consumed approximately a liter of sake every day from the time they had run off together.

While the investigation presented only a short paragraph concerning menstruation, medical history, and tobacco and alcohol use, it devoted nineteen paragraphs to Abe's sexual behavior. The intensity with which she enjoyed sex was a point of considerable attention. She told the police that she had started to enjoy sex only in her twenties, and that only in her late twenties had she become extraordinarily sensitive to it. As might be expected, she did not receive much sexual pleasure as a prostitute with a customer, but she became highly excited with men in whom she had a personal interest. The investigation report presents testimony concerning her sexual behavior from four different men with firsthand experience. All asserted that she had an extremely strong sexual appetite, was extraordinarily sensitive, enjoyed giving oral sex, desired intercourse for hours on end, and experienced orgasms so powerful that she would sometimes stop breathing and turn blue in the face. Ômiya Gorô said that she had him pull her hair and spank her. The investigation stated, "Clearly, these behaviors reflect a type of pathology."[10] At the time, the Japanese medical community, like those of Europe and North America, considered hysteria and nymphomania genuine pathological categories, although neither had a clearly established or universal definition.[11] For the most part, any woman with a strong and pronounced sexual desire could fall into the category of nymphomaniac, and in several places in the investigation record there are assertions that Abe herself did.[12] Similarly, almost any behavior outside the norm for a woman could garner a diagnosis of hysteria.

Yet this document also seems to contradict itself. The authorities wanted to depict Abe as normal and abnormal at the same time. They most clearly expressed this in their conclusions regarding the relationship between Abe's sexual appetite and her murder and mutilation of Ishida:

Nevertheless, if it is correct that her various sexual activities did not exceed what she described above, she remained in the realm of normal sexual behavior for the achievement of pleasure through foreplay and other forms of sexual play. The issue is only one of the strength of her sexual response and her abnormally strong desire for great quantities of sex. When considering her employment history and her penchant for becoming mildly intoxicated, it is difficult to say that she is qualitatively abnormal. Because her activities in foreplay, in sexual intercourse, and even in acts of cruelty were ultimately aimed at achieving sexual pleasure in a normal sense, it is impossible to say that she is sexually perverted.

Even so, the act of murder itself clearly was rooted in the defendant's sexual appetite. Based on her ardent sexual desire, she wished to have sole control over the victim's physical body for all eternity so that she could wantonly engage in an eternal sexual debauch. She realized that would be impossible and she could not stand the idea of

being sidelined while he was with another woman. Rather than allowing that to happen, she decided to fulfill her desire to control him completely through murder. Although it is difficult to assert that her desire
to control the victim sexually was pathological, the strength of that
desire easily emerged from the strength of her sexual appetite. This
also was clearly shown by her peace of mind following the murder.
Furthermore, several facts make it hard to think that she was driven by
a pathological lust to kill: she had an impulsive character and committed the murder impulsively; she was in a state of light intoxication and
a heightened state of sexual excitement on the night of the crime; and
she did not commit the murder for the purpose of stimulating sexual
pleasure or any other such perversion. With regard to her treatment of
the body and her actions after the murder, it is impossible to understand them based solely on her enormous desire for sex.[13]

This passage spells out what became the official state position regarding
Abe's motive in her murder of Ishida. It depicts Abe's physical sexual desire—
and not a psychological desire based on love—as the basis for her wish to
"monopolize" Ishida. Yet it cannot reconcile the very real physical demands
of sex with what it contends was her desire for an eternal sexual debauch,
which could only be metaphysical. In short, the investigators could not
accept Abe's own description of her motive as based on love no matter how
many times she repeated it. This was exactly what Abe herself wished to
avoid and what had motivated her to describe herself as deeply in love with
Ishida.

In the last sections of the investigation record are the report of the physician, Matsumura Tsuneo, who had examined Abe both physically and psychologically. Matsumura's qualifications as a Lecturer at Tokyo University
suggest that his perspective represented the forefront of contemporary
medical thought. Following a thorough physical examination that included
measurements of her head, chest, hands, and arms, he found no marked
physical abnormalities, although he did think her rather short index fingers
and thumbs somewhat unusual. In his psychological profile of Abe, Mat-

sumura described her as of average intelligence but without education, and emphasized her vanity, willfulness, and powerful sexual desire. His final conclusions summarized his findings:

1. The defendant's mental state at present reflects an inborn degenerative character that was strongly encouraged from childhood and has indications of both physical and mental hysteria. In addition, she has indications of an extreme nymphomania. However, her abnormalities of character are not extreme. Hence it is impossible to recognize them as temporary insanity or a condition of mental weakness.

2. The defendant's state of mind at the time of the crime, as indicated in the previous testimony, upon the basis of her abnormalities of character and her nymphomania, alcohol use, and other minor causes, helped facilitate the crime. Yet in a narrow sense, this murder was not the result of a deluded sexual desire. Nor was it simply the result of a pathological impulse. It is not possible to diagnose any mental abnormality at the time the defendant committed the murder. Likewise, with regard to the mutilation of the corpse, while this suggests a tendency toward a delusional sexuality, it was impossible to diagnose any specific abnormality. Thus, at the time of the crime, it is impossible to diagnose temporary insanity or a condition of mental weakness.[14]

Here, the dilemma that the judges faced becomes apparent. Matsumura could not attribute the crime simply to sexual desire, he could not diagnose Abe as psychologically pathological either. Most important, even as an expert medical witness he did not note in Abe any sign of temporary insanity or condition of "mental weakness" (*shinshin kôjaku* in Japanese), a contemporary diagnostic category.

Once the initial interrogation was complete, the state was prepared to press charges. The *Asahi* reported on May 10 that Abe was to be tried for murder and mutilation of a corpse. On the fourteenth it announced that she was to be indicted that day. The following day she was moved from a holding cell in the Metropolitan Police Headquarters to Tokyo's Ichigaya Prison. She remained there until the time of her trial.

For several weeks there appeared no news concerning Abe, but in October, newspapers carried several stories about her. On October 1, the *Asahi* ran a story, with a photograph, reporting that the pretrial investigation had been completed. The article included a synopsis of the report, which presented a brief biography of Abe and a recapitulation of the crimes with which she was charged. It described her motive as a desire to gain complete control of Ishida, again using the Japanese term for "monopolize." Two days later, the *Asahi* reported that with the pretrial examination over, Abe had been allowed visits from her older sister and her lawyer, Ôta Kinjirô. Reporters also asked for interviews, but she declined, instead agreeing to give a written statement. In it, she apologized profusely to Ômiya Gorô, saying that although she did not regret having murdered Ishida, she greatly regretted the trouble she had caused Ômiya.

Another story on October 9 reported that Abe had fired both of her lawyers, Ôta Kinjirô and Takeuchi Kintarô, who until then had represented her. Her stated reason was that she did not care whether she was punished lightly or severely and she admitted to everything with which the state had charged her.[15] Ôta disappeared from her case after that, but because Takeuchi did represent Abe at her trial, either the court did not allow her to be tried without counsel or she changed her mind. In a memoir written later, however, Abe does say that she asked for counsel so that her perspective would be represented fully in court.[16]

Perhaps surprisingly, once the trial was under way, Abe herself was in agreement more with the prosecution's case than with the defense's attempt to claim she was out of her mind at the time of the murder. She did not want to be remembered as mentally deranged, and especially not sexually deranged. The judges who tried her agreed less with the prosecution than with the defense, although they could not go so far as to find Abe innocent because of insanity.

# 17. JUDGMENT

ollowing her arrest, Abe Sada's fate lay in the hands of the court system and the three judges who tried her case. The outcome was surprising not only for Abe but also for many others: instead of the capital punishment that she had expected, she received a sentence of six years in prison. Questions about why this was so were answered when the lead judge in the trial, Hosoya Keijirô, published his memoirs twenty years later. There, he presented the perspective of one who was both an observer and participant in the action.[1]

Hosoya wrote about this case with apparent candor. He admitted that at the time Abe murdered Ishida, he was frequenting what were then called *kafe* in Japanese, which was to say "cafés." These were places where attractive young women served men drinks and light foods in an erotically charged atmosphere.[2] Not infrequently the women and men involved then arranged assignations outside. Abe herself had worked as a "café hostess" immediately after her escape from legal prostitution and before becoming a call girl and mistress. In short, Hosoya admitted to having consorted with women of backgrounds similar to Abe's before he was assigned to her case.

This assignment was not Hosoya's choice. That decision was made by officials in the Ministry of Justice based on an assessment of the content and difficulties the case presented, and of Hosoya as the legal mind best suited to it. At the time, he had mixed feelings about it. The assignment was something of an insult: the incident was nationally famous but had become an object of laughter and derision in many circles. Still, he felt curious about the case and set out to do his best.

Hosoya had considerable control over the proceedings. He was apprehensive that others might find fault with his handling of the case, so he did his best to be careful in all respects. Worried about how best to run the trial, he consulted three prominent judges. One, the head of the Tokyo Court of Appeals, instructed him to follow a French case he knew about: ask the defendant whether she was guilty; if she said yes, then all that was left was to sentence her, which could be done quickly. The Minister of Justice told him to handle it as though it were a simple robbery and give it no more attention. Finally, his mentor during his probationary period as a judge replied that the general public wanted to know the facts of the case, so Hosoya should do his best to bring them forth with as much detail as possible. Hosoya decided to follow this course.[3] It was the most difficult of the three: it required that he be somewhat explicit but without offending public morals.

One of the most difficult issues was how to deal with the documents from the investigations by the police and prosecutors. He remembered three bound volumes. These included the formal "Record of the Abe Sada Investigation" and the "Notes from the Interrogation of Abe Sada." It is unclear what the third volume might have been, or if these two documents had been bound in three separate volumes. Hosoya himself was astonished by their explicitness. At the time, simple public displays of affection were taboo. Films did not show couples kissing until the 1950s, and any kind of discussion of sex in print was subject to censorship. Despite strict orders that only the trial judges were to see them, when Hosoya received his own copies of the documents they already were smeared with the fingerprints of unauthorized readers in the office. People were curious. Another problem was keeping them under wraps while reading them at home. Preparing for cases at home seems to have been the custom of Hosoya and the other judges. He put off his children's questions by saying that they had to wait until they were adults; then they could understand. Hosoya was also worried that his wife might see the documents and made sure not to mention them in front of her. Of all the cases he tried, he remembered this one as having been the most difficult with regard to keeping evidence confidential.

The trial presented other difficulties to Hosoya and his fellow judges. It was necessary under constitutional law to discuss the specifics of the case in a setting open to the press and observers. This meant that it was necessary to address openly the erotic and grotesque, but these topics were subject to restriction under the fifty-ninth article of the Meiji Constitution, which governed public discussion of anything that could possibly harm the stability and order of the state or public morality. Hosoya got around this dilemma by mandating a careful use of language. For example, when it became necessary to discuss Abe's removal of Ishida's penis, a word he could not allow in court, he required people to say "Ishida's extremity." In other instances, he required the use of pronouns.[4]

Another difficulty presented itself when Hosoya read the documents related to the case: he found himself sexually excited. Although the other two judges on the case were extremely serious individuals, he could not expect more of them than what he expected of himself. Contemporary sensibilities supported taboos on sexual intercourse during a woman's menstrual period; Hosoya did not want the case to arouse the other judges sexually if they might then discover that their wives were having their periods, since they would be without the proper means of relieving their excitement. Consequently, he determined when their wives were having their periods by asking them about who had bathed the children or if their wife had taken a bath, since bathing also was taboo during a woman's period. This way he established a time when all three wives would not be menstruating, and he set the trial for that time.[5]

The trial opened on November 25. Approximately 200 spectators, a large number of them young women, competed for seats and filled the courtroom to capacity. The audience included Abe's older sister, Toku, and the owner of Masaki, the teahouse where the murder had occurred. Ishida's wife did not, apparently, go to the trial. The *Yomiuri* called interest in the case "Sada mania" and referred to the young women in attendance as "Sada fans."[6] This implied that there existed considerable sympathy for Abe, quite possibly because many young women themselves wished they could "monopolize" a man they loved. Before opening the proceedings, Hosoya made it clear that any public display of laughter, applause, or other disturbance would result in the ejection of the individuals involved. Despite this, the appearance of some evidence in the courtroom—including Ishida's genitals, which the police had preserved in a jar, the wrapping paper in which Abe had carried them, the knife with which she had removed them, and other objects—elicited gasps. Abe herself appeared with her head entirely covered in a conical straw hat, keeping her face from public view until the trial began.[7]

Members of the press competed for scoops. When Abe appeared in the courtroom, camera flashes bathed the scene in light. One photographer managed to capture an image of Hosoya dressed in his robes, looking as though he were smiling. In reality, he was telling the photographer to get out, but the picture ended up in the papers nonetheless, and Hosoya was reprimanded by his peers for allowing this to happen. Thereafter the court took measures to escort Abe to and from her cell in ways that kept the press at bay. Photographers then attempted to shoot pictures through the courtroom's windows.

Had Abe pleaded innocent to the charges against her, a long and attention-getting trial would have resulted. However, she pleaded guilty, so the first part of the trial, at least the part that remained public, consisted of little more than questions that made her restate important facts she already had asserted in her interrogation. This made it clear that Abe did not kill

**FIGURE 10.** Abe Sada, head covered in conical hat, escorted by guards to courtroom, November 1936. Photo: The Mainichi Newspapers

Ishida out of a desire for revenge on his wife. Hosoya also asked Abe directly whether she thought a woman's chastity was important, to which she responded affirmatively, adding that she had lost her virginity by force.[8] When asked if she had been a habitual liar while working as a prostitute, she answered that it was expected as part of the profession, and added that all the men in her life, with the exception of Ômiya Gorô, also had been liars. When it came time to discuss the details of the murder itself, Hosoya cleared the courtroom of all spectators and proceeded in a closed session that ended the same afternoon. At the end of the day, Abe left the courtroom as she had entered, wearing a straw hat reaching down to her shoulders.

Abe's next appearance in court was for a hearing concerning her sentencing, held on December 8. Throngs of people stood in line for the 250 tickets available. All speculated on her punishment. Under contemporary criminal code, the maximum for murder was death, and next was life in prison; the minimum was three years of incarceration. Some journalists as well as a number of officials in the Ministry of Justice thought that Abe should be punished severely, with either death by hanging or a life sentence. Many others saw her crime as committed out of love, implying that it was a crime of passion, and called for leniency. In the hearing, the prosecution demanded a ten-year sentence. The lead prosecutor asserted that Abe had committed premeditated murder. He emphasized the findings of the expert medical witness who had examined her psychological disposition for the court and found that she had been in a clear and sane state of mind when she murdered Ishida. Indeed, this was how Abe saw herself. Much to her chagrin, Abe's defense lawyer, Takeuchi Kintarô, asserted that she had been either fully insane or at least mentally impaired at the time of the murder and so should be found innocent. He asserted that she had been only partly conscious of her actions.

The opinions of the three judges were split. Although their positions remained anonymous, it became clear that at least one thought she should be imprisoned for four years while another believed eight years more appropriate. The sentence was announced on December 21, a cold and snowy day in Tokyo almost exactly seven months after Abe's arrest. It appears to have been a compromise: she received six years, with her incarceration following her arrest to count toward the total time served. When told that she had the right to appeal, Abe answered immediately that she would not. Newspapers carried detailed reports, which were widely followed throughout the country.

The official reason for the sentence amounted to little more than a recapitulation of the events between April 23, when Ishida and Abe ran off together, and May 18, when she murdered him. The most revealing part was the last sentence, which read, "At the time of the crime, the defendant was suffering from a mental handicap, which was to say a condition of mental weakness."[9] This raises questions about the influence that the judges and the court had on its expert witnesses. There is no doubt about the conclusion that Matsumura Tsuneo reached in the investigation report, and about the court's blatant rejection of that conclusion. Yet to justify the decision, Hosoya quoted an extensive passage by Matsumura, one that differed considerably from the doctor's earlier assessment. In part, this later passage read:

> The defendant displays the characteristics of mental and physical hysteria and a marked sexual oversensitivity (nymphomania). Hence at the time of the crime the defendant had, as I have noted, an abnormality of character and oversensitivity to sex. On the basis of this, for a week before the crime she immersed herself in a life of extreme sexuality that paralyzed her moral sensibility.[10]

Matsumura went on to say that Abe's behavior at the time of Ishida's murder and immediately following reflected the symptoms of sadism and fetishism. He did not go so far as to use the diagnostic term for mental weakness, which he had not found present in his previous assessment, but Hosoya and the other judges seem to have found the combination of hysteria, nymphomania, sadism, and fetishism, along with her alcohol use, sufficient to declare Abe in a state of mental weakness at the time of her crime. Hosoya used this statement by Matsumura to counter charges that Abe's penalty was too light.

Although he might have contradicted the expert witness, Hosoya's reasoning was not spurious. The research on forensic medicine had long emphasized a link between sexuality and crime. Women received considerable attention in this literature, which explicitly linked nymphomania and criminality, hysteria and "mental weakness."[11] The implication was that the experts, though perhaps divided, knew more about Abe than she knew herself.

Another document, an official admonition of Abe, was more telling of Hosoya's thinking in this case than the official reasons for the sentence. Under the contemporary penal code, this was a legally sanctioned document that allowed the judge in a case to state what he expected of the defendant's future life. Later, many people mistook this as the official explanation for the sentencing. It was important because it not only explained the court's attitude toward the defendant but its attitude toward the victim as well:

> This case, as the statement regarding the sentencing makes clear, is the result of the defendant having fallen into a life of sexual debauchery, making her into one habituated to sexual excess. Having reached an age of full maturity, she then happened to meet the victim, who became interested in her habits, and then without restraint did his best to fulfill her. As a result of their sexual play they then quickly developed an extremely powerful love for each other. This [the running off together of Abe and Ishida] by itself resulted in what could be called criminal behavior, the result of an impulse arising from a mild mental impairment.
>
> However, the crime at hand developed out of the defendant's habituation to sexual excess, which led to an extreme mental impairment causing impulsive behavior without respect either for human life or for the influence of her actions on social mores. Of course, this cannot be expected to be rectified easily. On the other hand, the victim in this crime was himself lascivious and old enough to understand the consequences of his actions. Without consideration for his family or household, he engaged in sexual excess for over ten days with the defendant, making himself the subject of sexual indulgences, a plaything for the defendant's whims. Without restraint he fulfilled her desires. In this way, it is impossible to overlook how [the victim] was central in causing this crime.[12]

At this point Hosoya interpreted Ishida's behavior as having led to his own demise. Abe was the perpetrator, but Ishida made himself a willing victim, first to her desires and then to her wish to control him completely. In Hosoya's view of the situation, he should have known better.

Also important to Hosoya was the penalty for the crime of mutilation, which had done more than the murder itself to make the incident a national sensation. He believed that Abe's intention to commit suicide and the fact that she would have done so had the police been only a few hours later was enough to offset this crime.

Furthermore, Hosoya explicitly refused to accept Abe's own reasoning. Toward the end of this admonition, he wrote:

> However, if one interprets this incident as one of love taken to an extreme, or of a double love suicide, or even as the actions of a person close to insanity, and thus believes that the decidedly light penalty is appropriate, then this is to fail to understand the true nature of this case. This perspective neglects the need to correct the defendant's habitual lasciviousness and the impact it has on respect for human life and social mores.[13]

Hosoya thus justified a longer sentence than what the defense demanded, but he also ended this admonitory statement optimistically. During her incarceration, he asserted, Abe already had begun to reflect deeply upon her lasciviousness and correct her misguided ways. However, he did warn her not to repeat her actions and commit another crime following her release from prison.[14]

Abe was not pleased with the court's reasoning with regard to either the verdict or her sentence. When Hosoya had asked her about her motive, she had responded repeatedly that had Ishida lived, he would not have belonged to her, but in death he belonged to her completely. Rather than accept this at face value, Hosoya interpreted the evidence in a way that disagreed with the prosecution, the expert medical witness, and Abe herself. Furthermore, Abe claimed that she had committed murder in order to establish the same right over a man that men had over women, and thus emphasized the gender-based disempowerment of women in contemporary Japanese society; had Hosoya judged her completely sane, it could have indicated that her reasoning had a valid basis. Hosoya wrote in his memoirs that his greatest fear in this case was that Abe might commit another, similar crime, placing his judgment with regard to her sentence in question. Twenty years later, he wrote that he was relieved she had never again broken the law. By saying this, he showed that he never did understand or accept Abe's feelings toward Ishida or her reason for killing him. Perhaps most tellingly, Hosoya's admission that he became sexually excited while reading the court documents reveals that he found Abe an object of sexual and erotic attraction while never grasping completely the social and cultural implications that her case presented.

In his memoirs, Hosoya also recalled another exchange that he had had with Abe, one that revealed a gap common between middle- and upper-class men and their wives. He asked Abe if she thought that sex was central to a marriage relationship. Without hesitation she replied that it was, and that any woman would admit as much. Hosoya later asked his wife what she thought. At first she told him, "Of course not," but he did not find her tone very convincing. In a few moments she then said, "Well, perhaps there is some truth to that."[15] The idea that good wives were not subject to sexual desire was so deeply ingrained in the minds of numerous men, many of whom took it for granted that they should find their own sexual pleasure outside of marriage, that they failed to recognize the needs of the women closest to them.

As the main judge in this case, Hosoya was haunted by one last issue. That was the disposition of Ishida's "extremities." Under the current legal code, they were the property of Ishida's legal heir. Soon after the crime, that person, whom Hosoya did not identify, declined any claim to them, so they remained in police possession. Some time later, a friend of the Ishida family went to Hosoya and said that he felt it was wrong for Ishida's penis and testicles to be an object of public scrutiny. Hosoya considered this and agreed that he would feel the same were it a matter concerning his own family. Yet without a formal claim from Ishida's family for their repossession, there was nothing he could do.

At a later point in time, Ishida's penis and testicles were moved to the Tokyo University Medical School pathology museum. At the time of this writing, they are missing.

# 18. IMPRISONMENT AND RELEASE

be herself was relieved at her sentence. Her life regained direction and she acquired clear priorities. By the end of the trial, she seemed to have put aside thoughts of suicide and instead to see herself as a living memorial to Ishida. When she returned to the jail in Ichigaya, the guards told her that she had gotten off lightly and that she should do her best during the remaining five-and-a-half years of imprisonment that lay before her. They encouraged her to pray for Ishida in his afterlife. The day before she was to begin serving her sentence, Abe's sister Toku told her that no matter how far away she might be sent, she would come to visit. Abe was not isolated.

On December 26, Abe, dressed in a red prison uniform, was moved from Tokyo to the Tochigi Women's Prison, which held approximately 200 inmates. Unlike most convicts, who enter prison with sadness and anger, Abe remembered feeling refreshed and full of happiness.[1] The guards were troubled by her carefree attitude; like the Ichigaya guards, they thought she should take her situation seriously. For her, the most shocking aspect of prison life was her material surroundings. Abe had a three-mat room (approximately six feet by nine feet) with a single, high window; a pillar on which hung a small mirror; and a toilet. Until this time she had lived in relative luxury, even while working in the seediest brothels. But compared to her prison cell, her holding cell in Ichigaya had been well appointed. Now, Abe had only the bare essentials. Until her release, her name was simply "Cell Block 1, Number 11," or "Number 11" for short. Nevertheless, she described the guards and other prison workers as loving and caring people who acted politely to the inmates. With time, Abe said that she grew accustomed to doing without things she had taken for granted on the outside. She accepted the stark surroundings and the strict rules of behavior as the price she had to pay for her actions.[2]

Her most embarrassing moment in prison, Abe wrote, was when she was told to do the "radio calisthenics" and realized that she did not know how. "Radio calisthenics" were a set series of exercises accompanied by an announcer and piano, aired by the national broadcasting company, NHK (for Nihon Hôsô Kyôkai) at the same times every day. People throughout the country, in rural and urban areas, in apartments and factories, schools and prisons, all participated. This was a significant event about which Abe wrote, "The moment I was taught how to do the radio exercises I felt that I had become human."[3] Although she did not explain any more clearly what she meant by this, it is easy to imagine that for the first time she felt as though she had become part of the national community, doing the same thing that other people throughout the country were doing at the same time. She was going through a socialization process in prison that she had never experienced on the outside.

While in prison, Abe was required to do hand work, and was taught to make small cellophane bags for packaging camphor. She threw herself into the work and became adept at it, taking pleasure in completing a large number of bags. Not long after she arrived, the cold became much more extreme. Despite the lack of heating, prisoners were expected to continue their work, and Abe's fingers became stiff and almost purple in the frigid air. Still, she continued making the small bags through the cold of winter and felt happy with the warmth of early spring.

The new year's festival in prison also was a source of comfort. For three days the prisoners were given relative leniency, allowed to bathe and have some special holiday foods. Later they listened to the radio and phonograph records. Normally they were allowed to write to people outside prison only once a month, but at new year's they received permission to write letters for the first three days of the year; they could also read newspapers and magazines at times not usually permitted. Abe remembered that first new year's as the first time since she had killed Ishida that she again felt like a woman, a whole human being. She was not entirely happy—she burst into tears when she thought of Ishida and what the two of them would be doing together were he still alive. Nevertheless, it was a time in which she remembered all the prisoners becoming childlike and enjoying themselves.[4]

In the warm days of spring, Abe found herself thinking about the coming first anniversary of Ishida's death. On that day a nun from the True Pure Land sect of Buddhism was allowed to read sutras in Ishida's memory in the prison chapel, which Abe was permitted to visit. Abe asked her to chant the longest sutra possible. The nun who performed the service for Abe seemed to inspire her to consider Buddhism and religious faith more seriously. The young nun had spent her life immersed in Buddhism. She had been raised in a temple family and inspired to practice the faith rather than to pursue a life as a wife and mother, although she did eventually marry.

Yet once the service was finished, Abe found herself more dispirited than ever. She could not eat or do her work and remained in her cell, weeping, all day long. Once again, thoughts of suicide preoccupied her. She fantasized about hanging herself, biting off her tongue, or stabbing herself with scissors. It became impossible for her to respond to the guards. Previously friendly, they ceased being gentle. They carried her to the office of the head guard, who slapped her cheek so hard that it remained swollen for two days. On the way there and back some of the other prisoners taunted and teased her, although some gave her encouragement. Back in her cell, she continued to weep and think of Ishida, contemplating death.

Abe did not improve over the summer. In the fall she suffered a fit of rage and cut off most of her hair. When the guard came for a normal inspection, Abe dumped a bucket of dirty water on her. She held no grudge against this guard; she simply wanted to do something bad. The head guard told her that she had never heard of such a thing in all her time working in the prison system, not even in the men's prisons. Soon thereafter, Abe was put in a small detention cell, restrained with her hands tied behind her back and a rope reaching from her neck down her torso to her wrists. Her hands went numb and breathing was difficult. She thought she might die, and even hoped she would.

At around noon on the next day, after more than twenty-four hours of being bound tightly, Abe received a visit from the nun who had performed the service for Ishida. She told Abe, "Number 11, how would you tell Ishida about what you have done? If you act like this, not even Buddha will come to you. What an evil woman you have become." She added, "Number 11, unless you get serious, I'll have to quit being a nun."[5] Abe was ashamed and encouraged at the same time, and for the sake of this nun, for whom she felt great respect, did her best to reform her ways.

Abe also tried to become more religious, but chanting "Praise be to Amitabha" (*Namu Amida Butsu* in Japanese), the formula for salvation in the Pure Land tradition, never inspired her. However, she did find the descriptions of the Nichiren sect in books in the prison library to her liking. She read more than fifty books on Nichiren, the medieval Buddhist priest who founded the sect known by his name, and felt an affinity for the sect's teachings. Nichiren was similar to the Pure Land sect in that it was one of the most popular types of Buddhism in Japan and dated back to medieval times. Both sects also emphasized chanting; Nichiren adherents used the formula "Praise be to the wondrous law of the Lotus Sutra" (*Namu myôhô Renge Kyô* in Japanese). Although Abe does not describe her last three years in prison, this encounter with Buddhism seems to have given her the strength to continue, and once released, she did maintain her faith in Nichiren Buddhism. She did not, apparently, cause any more trouble in prison.[6]

On May 17, 1941, the warden summoned Abe to her office. After her early resistance to prison life, she had apparently become a model prisoner and received consideration for early release based on good behavior. Further helping Abe's cause, on November 10 of the previous year the nation had celebrated the 2,600th anniversary of Japan's mythical founding, and as part of that celebration the emperor had granted a large number of pardons. Abe received one, which allowed her release the following spring. On that day in May, the warden informed Abe that she was about to be released and encouraged her to get a job as soon as she got out. Abe took these words to heart. She had spent almost five years to the day in state custody. After that, her life changed:

> As the guard accompanied me down a long, stone-paved hallway, I thought that tomorrow at the same time I would no longer be here. The moment I realized this, without any warning whatsoever, my face felt as though it had been ripped apart at the seams. Suddenly, the chapel and the roof of the large factory that I could see from the hallway looked different.
>
> When I got to the door to my cell, the guard told me, "It's good that your sister is coming to meet you," and smiled at me. At that point I had to look down, overwhelmed with a desire to weep. Lunch and dinner went by uneventfully, and with the bell marking the end of the day, my last night in prison had begun. Ah, when I think of that night, I remember having fallen asleep when I heard the sound of the guard's sandals approaching my cell. Just when they had stopped in front of my door, I heard the sound of the key to which I was so accustomed. In a cautious, low voice, the guard said, "Number 11. Get up." I started to smile. "You're getting released," she said. I was so happy. By the time I had put away my futon I could feel my heart pounding. I felt the same way until I got to the room where my sister was waiting. I wondered

why they would release me so late at night. At that moment, my sister put a kimono on me, and I ran my hand down the silk crepe lining. It had been five years since I had worn silk and felt how soft it was against my skin. With true feelings of affection, I said my good-byes to everybody, and then my sister took my hand and we went out a small gate. A car was waiting to take us to my sister's house in Ôi, in Tokyo.[7]

At the time of her release, Abe entered an identity protection program. Because her real name was universally known, the courts had obtained police cooperation in sponsoring a pseudonym so that Abe could gain employment and create a stable life for herself. The police also made it impossible for anybody to trace her through the usual legal means. The newspapers reported her release but also said that she had been taken in by a society for the protection of women. Abe's sister told her that for the next six years she was to be known officially as Yoshii Masako, the name she had given herself following her escape from legal prostitution. Abe soon felt guilty about staying at her sister's residence without any income to contribute to household expenses. Her brother-in-law reminded her that they were living under a rationing system, implying that Abe was consuming part of a fixed amount that the family was receiving. Before long, she received an offer to manage a *kafe* in Manchuria, which was governed by the Japanese puppet state, but she felt that taking on such work would let down the people who had supported her during her prison stay, especially the nun who had helped her out. Some time later she received an offer to become a maid. Under the pseudonym of Yoshii Masako, she accepted the position. Through no fault of her own, however, the family for which she was working discovered her true identity and immediately terminated her employment.[8]

By this time Japan was consumed by a total war, and it was more difficult than ever for a single woman to support herself, especially one who had no higher education and no skills beyond making cellophane bags. So when Abe received an offer from a "serious man" named "Y" (as she referred to him) to become his mistress, she accepted. According to her memoir published in 1948, she felt that this placed her in a difficult position because it both betrayed Ishida and made life stressful. She did her best to stay out of sight. Daily, she read the sutras before Ishida's memorial tablet and became increasingly devoted to Nichiren Buddhism.[9]

She tried to live a quiet life, but Abe and Y, as part of a policy of evacuation, were moved from Tokyo. They lived out the duration of the war in the Ibaragi countryside north of the city. Abe found the simplicity of country life appealing, and she worked in the fields dressed the same as the farm women. She got along well with the farmers in the village and always thought warmly of them, even when she later heard people say that they sold everything on the black market to maximize their profits. Abe later wrote that she could easily have stayed there. But the man who was supporting her had continued to commute from Ibaragi to his job in Tokyo throughout the war and was determined to move back to the city. According to Abe, his work was his life, so they returned to Tokyo. While on the train back, Abe thought that she really did not want to leave.[10]

It was at this time that Abe clearly saw the fate that would be hers for the rest of her life. Her real name had become, as she wrote, "poisonous." Back in Tokyo, she had to wait some time before she could return to life with Y. She wrote:

> I looked for a place to live in Tokyo with the Inaba family. It had been a long time since I had called them "mother" and "father," and before long I was getting used to living with them, talking with them as if we had returned to the time when I was a young girl. But this was not a place where I could rest at ease. One after the other, people who knew that I had made the mistake that I did ten years before came to visit.
>
> People who knew me long ago came and said, "Sada, I'm so glad you are doing well." When I heard this, it hurt as though a needle had pierced my chest. It filled me with embarrassment and horrible thoughts, making me depressed. As quickly as possible I wanted to go someplace where nobody knew me, and I walked the streets of Tokyo every day, looking for a place to live.[11]

Ironically, once she had moved back to Tokyo, Y's family circumstances required that they relocate to another rural village, this time in Saitama prefecture. After they had lived there for some time, her identity caught up with her again and neighbors pressured her to move away. Despite her devotion to Y, their relationship did not last much longer. Once Abe's identity became known among his friends and relatives, they urged him to end it. He did. Again Abe had to fend for herself, but within economic, social, and cultural boundaries that permitted only certain kinds of work. Abe had been released from prison, but the social and economic walls that surrounded her on the outside were nearly as restrictive. She fought back in the ways available to her.

It is of note that Abe wrote little about the influence of the war on her life during these years. Her separation from Y came just when Japanese cities were devastated by incendiary bombings and life became increasingly difficult. Possibly, the tumult in Abe's life made the hardships of war seem relatively minor.

# 19. CELEBRITY, HARDSHIP, AND ESCAPE

B y no means did Abe Sada pursue fame. Yet from the moment the mass media discovered her, she suffered all the disadvantages that other celebrities face, but without the wealth and other advantages that many celebrities enjoy. She had no source of royalties or other financial benefit from her fame. From the day after she murdered Ishida in 1936, she became the subject of innumerable discussions, but none paid their subject. The semifictionalized figure that such discussions created, moreover, took on a life of her own. From the time of Abe's arrest to the present day, commentators have interpreted her personality and her actions in ways that have had far more to do with their own ideas, fears, and desires than with the real Abe Sada and the crime that she committed.

Consequently, Abe's life after her release from prison illustrates the advantages and disadvantages of being a public figure, a person with celebrity status. Her first reaction to the newspaper coverage of her role in Ishida's murder was naïve surprise. Photographers and reporters massed to her arrest and trial. Had the state not protected Abe's identity, they certainly would have climbed over each other to cover her release from prison. As it was, they were forced to cover it from a distance. Abe Sada sold print because her name conjured up lurid images that mixed the erotic and the violent. It signified an imagined figure, that of the sexually dangerous woman in a man's world. This imaginary Abe Sada became a prison without walls for the living woman with that name.

After prison, Abe first tried to avoid the celebrity role by serving as a maid and then as a mistress. Later, in order to fight what she believed was slander, she actively assumed her public identity and initiated a libel suit against a novelist who had used her case as the basis for a best-selling novel, which is discussed further in the following chapter. For some time after that she used her notoriety as a way to make a living, having quickly learned the business advantages of name recognition. But after several years, she once again attempted to withdraw entirely from public view; although it took decades, she eventually succeeded.

After Abe left Y, she returned to the Inaba household. Her one-time lover and intermediary once again saw her as a source of income. If writers and publishers could make money from Abe's reputation, so could those closest to her. Soon, Abe became part of a theatrical troupe under the direction of Nagata Mikihiko. She performed in a one-act play called *Showa Ichidai Onna* [A woman of the Showa period] that was staged in Tokyo and toured the country. Advertisements said that profits would be contributed to the rehabilitation of women prisoners, but it is unclear how much, if anything, was donated to this cause.[1] In 1947, an interview of Abe Sada by the writer Sakaguchi Ango appeared in the first edition of a serious literary magazine called *Zadan*. Sakaguchi raised eyebrows with the comment that he had never met

**FIGURE 11.**    Abe Sada, photographed July 26, 1951. Photo: The Mainichi Newspapers

a more ordinary woman. He sympathized with her situation and agreed with the logic that she used to rationalize her murder of Ishida.[2] This interview and the media attention surrounding Abe's libel suit helped publicize her case and bring larger audiences to the play in which she was appearing. As late as 1949, Abe was still performing at least part time in that play. That year, she also started to work in restaurants and inns around Kyoto and Osaka.

Abe remained outside Tokyo until 1952, when she began work at an established restaurant and bar called Hoshikikusui. She was employed under her own name, which drew customers, and she stayed there for an extended period, probably until 1966. For approximately six months after she left Hoshikikusui, Abe ran a bar called Queen in Asakusa, which soon went out of business. An account by the film critic Donald Richie captured the Abe Sada of this period: "Like many a pub woman she became manly, just one of the boys. Unlike many, however, she had actually choked a man to death and then cut off his member. There was a consequent frisson when Sada Abé slapped your back."[3] Richie described her as descending a set of stairs into the midst of her working-class customers and cowing them into silence, only then to join them in laughter and drinks.[4]

Despite the media attention, few details of her later life were recorded. In 1956, Inaba Masatake died, removing yet one more piece of Abe's earlier life. Between the time she quit working at Queen and 1967, when she opened a small restaurant and bar of her own called Wakatake, it is unclear what she did. If she continued as in the past, she stayed with old friends and acquaintances. While operating Wakatake, which specialized in stuffed rice balls (*onigiri*), Abe saved a considerable sum of money but had it stolen, reputedly by a young, gay lover with whom she had a platonic relationship. She had trusted him to become a partner in starting another business. Her savings gone, Abe closed Wakatake in 1970 and lived with friends for several months, after which she took a job working as a maid at the Katsuyama Hotel in Chiba prefecture. She stayed there for only about six months. Then she disappeared, leaving only a note saying that she could no longer do the work required of her and that she wished to apologize for not being a better person. She took with her only a change of summer kimono and her savings of 500,000 yen (at the time, worth about $2,000). She wrote that she would be seeing one of the hotel's owners in Tokyo, and it is possible that he helped her start yet another new life.

What happened to Abe after that remains a mystery. Reporters and writers followed a number of theories and leads concerning her ultimate whereabouts. There was speculation that she died from illness; some conjectured that she had committed suicide. Others followed leads to residences for the elderly. A reporter found a woman by the name of Abe Sada at a home for the aged, but she clearly was a different person with the same name. Others tracked Abe to Buddhist temples, under the assumption that she might have become a nun. Yet none of these leads resulted in any firm information concerning where she had gone.[5]

On several occasions following her release from prison Abe Sada had tried to remove herself from public scrutiny. This time, she succeeded.

# A TRAIL OF RE-CREATIONS

From May 18, 1936, when the newspapers made her life the subject of scrutiny, Abe Sada became known to innumerable people in Japan and even outside the country. However, the woman about whom most people heard was usually fictitious, the product of an imagination only rarely her own. The crime that she committed was by itself enough to mesmerize millions and give her an enduring place in modern Japanese culture. People have understood her in many ways. For some, she has merely been the object of a prurient gaze, generic and interchangeable with other objects of pornographic release. Yet Abe Sada and her crimes told many others something they needed to learn about the boundaries that governed women, gender, and sexual power in their own society and culture. Her story lit up the sexual skeletons in many a Japanese family's closet. While the incident that made Abe famous marked an outer boundary of sexual violence, it also encompassed the norm and helped people understand how their gender roles informed their sexual identities.

During the days and months immediately following Abe's arrest there appeared numerous writings about her and what she had done. In July 1936, for example, a neighbor woman and her daughter were interviewed by the women's magazine *Fujin kôron*. Their images of the neighborhood and their memories of the young Abe Sada were illuminating. They described Abe herself as a strong-willed and sometimes astonishingly brave young child. As a firsthand description of life in a Kanda neighborhood during the 1920s, this account remains a valuable document in its own right. Also, in December of that year, one of the lawyers who had given Abe counsel until October published the record of his interviews with her. He thought all women were primarily emotional creatures, but he believed Abe was far more emotional than most. Although he was personally acquainted with her, he did not know her well; yet he did not keep this from presenting his interpretation of her personality as though it were based on an intimate knowledge.[1]

Before long, others who did not know her at all started to present their own interpretations of Abe's personality. For example, in July 1936 the widely read magazine *Tsûzoku igaku* [Popular medicine] published a lengthy piece by Kawaguchi Shûshi that compared the "Abe Sada Incident" to Oscar Wilde's *Salome*. The story of *Salome* had become well known in Japan when Wilde's play was performed in Tokyo in 1914. People knew it as a tale of erotic allure and explicit violence. Under the guise of foreign culture, *Salome* provided an exotic and novel context in which Kawaguchi voiced his opinions concerning sadism, masochism, fetishism, and phallicism. The article ended with a discussion of artificial insemination and the possibility that cloning would eventually create a society in which women had no need for men in order to reproduce. The Abe Sada Incident was best understood, Kawaguchi concluded, as both an event in history and a harbinger of what science would soon bring to the world of men. He speculated that if Eve had been born into the Garden of Eden without Adam but could still have reproduced, she might have been there forever.[2] Had Abe read this piece, she probably would have put down the magazine and scratched her head, wondering what this odd mix of literary criticism, anthropology, psychology, eugenics, reproductive biology, and religion had to do with her.

In January 1937, there appeared a collection of psychoanalytic essays on Abe.[3] The authors used the language of psychoanalysis to diagnose her, reaching conclusions similar to those of less scholarly writers. The lead author wrote that Abe was abnormal but not pathological, echoing the often-heard opinion that she was wrong to have murdered Ishida, but by no means evil. Not all the authors in this collection were of the same mind. Kaneko Junji, the police psychologist whom the newspapers had quoted immediately after the discovery of Ishida's body, wrote that she epitomized the four major sexual perversions: sadism, masochism, fetishism, and nymphomania. As she had chosen to be a prostitute of her own free will, he found her nymphomania particularly pronounced. A Freudian psychoanalyst, Nagasaki Bunji, once again raised the theme of Oscar Wilde's *Salome* and saw parallels between the removal of Ishida's penis and the severing of John the Baptist's head. Abe was not conscious of the forces that drove her to murder Ishida, he asserted, although he agreed with Abe herself that the main reason was her desire to control Ishida. Takahashi Tetsu, a pioneering sexologist, wrote that Abe had suffered from penis envy all her life, but that the feeling was normal among all women. He also noted that this was not the first case in Japan in which a woman had removed a man's penis and cited an earlier case of a prostitute having done so out of jealousy. Takahashi contrasted Abe with this earlier case, saying that she had become an object of adoration, with people attempting to buy the kimono she was wearing at the time of the crime and coming to visit the sites associated with it. Another writer in the same volume, Ôtsuki Kenji, asserted that Abe was no more guilty of a crime than an animal might be. He also compared her to Salome, but concluded that Abe was in fact a vampire who embodied love and hatred in the same stream of emotion.

Soon after the crime, many notables penned their opinions of Abe Sada. Hiratsuka Raichô, the feminist writer and activist, wrote that Abe's mother had spoiled her badly, and as a result, the daughter had become a delinquent. Her moral was that mothers needed to pay closer attention to their children. A well-known physicist, Ishihara Jun, wrote that Abe had manifested a kind of primitive but universal pathology. The murder was an expression of love taken to an extreme. A literary critic, Sugiyama Heisuke, compared the Abe Sada incident to the fiction of Tanizaki Jun'ichirô. Sugiyama observed that women in high society almost invariably scorned Abe and her behavior, but women of the working classes almost invariably sympathized with her. He emphasized that many people had reacted to this case with humor and laughter and asserted that although Abe was bad, she certainly was not evil.[4]

This is only a sample of the writing about Abe that appeared before the outbreak of war with the United States in 1941. The most important pieces were the printed records of her interrogation and police investigation. These were published in the *Sôtaikai kenkyû hôkoku*, the in-house record of an innovative research group on contemporary sexuality. The group was headed by a scholar named Ogura Seizaburô and included a number of serious researchers, writers, judges, police officials, physicians, historians, and others who brought documents together for publication in the journal. It was Ogura's wife, arrested for dealing with "obscene" materials, who had been in the cell next to Abe's at the time of her arrest. The limited circulation of the group's publication before World War II kept it from censorship, but it also prevented many from reading the interrogation and investigation records. Once reprinted, the journal became an important source for these documents.[5]

Both during and after the war, the record of Abe Sada's police interrogation was studied by numerous writers of fiction and films who then based their works on it. In the 1946 short story "Sesô" [Worldly conditions], the novelist Oda Sakunosuke described his jubilation when he discovered that an acquaintance owned a copy of the interrogation record. However, because it was wartime, when any reference to sexuality faced censorship and suppression, the author refrained from writing the novel based on it. He later wrote a novella, "Yôfu" [A dangerous woman], recounting Abe's early life, based on the interrogation record.[6]

After 1945, Abe commanded attention because of social and cultural changes that were occurring in the wake of World War II. The culture of *ero-guro*, the erotic and grotesque, offered a distraction from memories of wartime suffering and present-day difficulties, and the story of Abe Sada and her murder of Ishida became a favorite topic of conversation during the postwar years. In 1947, the record of her interrogation appeared in an unauthorized version under the classical-sounding title *Enkonroku* [A tale of passion and hatred]. This helped start a new Abe Sada publishing boom.

Pulp magazines, called *kasutori*, frequently featured her, as did a number of novelists and short-story writers; none of this attention, however, benefited Abe financially. One of these works, entitled *Abe Sada iro zange* [The erotic confessions of Abe Sada], by Kimura Ichirô, was published in 1947 and became a best-seller.[7] Kimura had used the transcript of Abe's interrogation to create a work that had the appearance of a confession made to a friend. Abe discovered it one day while looking in a store window. Incensed by the book's premise of being based on her confessions to the author and by his description of her primarily in sexual terms, Abe sued the writer for libel and defamation of character. The result of the court case did not appear in the press; possibly it was an out-of-court settlement. Had Abe won, the fact certainly would have appeared in the popular press. In any event, the publishing company used her case as a way of gathering more attention for the book. It became a national best-seller with sales in excess of 100,000 copies.

Kimura's book prompted Abe to write one of her own in response. The result was *Abe Sada shuki* [Memoirs of Abe Sada], which retold her life story up to that time and was published in 1948. In this work Abe had a clear goal, which was to counter the image of herself as a sexual pervert. She repeatedly attested to her love for Ishida and described the pain that being the center of this case had caused her. Her main point was that the account of her affection for Ishida should be a love story, not an erotic potboiler. Yet her descriptions of past events sometimes contradict the records of her interrogation and investigation. Not infrequently she presented incorrect dates, saying, for example, that she had lost her virginity at age seventeen rather than at age fifteen, and changed other facts to spin a more positive image of herself. As a result, her book lacks the power and immediacy of the interrogation record and is of questionable historical value. Moreover, it did not achieve its goal. Other writers continued to write more or less fictional depictions of Abe, usually using her real name, which they based on the interrogation record. They often used her own words, but they rewrote and edited them in ways that, in fact, created many Abe Sadas. Some writers, such as Sakaguchi Ango, saw Abe as an ordinary woman from the Low City. Others saw her as a subject more suitable for lurid imaginations.

Ever since she committed murder in 1936, Abe has remained a subject of interest to creative writers. This was not because her actual crimes were particularly unusual. In 1981, there appeared a book entitled *19 nin no Abe Sada* [19 Abe Sadas] that told of nineteen criminal incidents in which men had lost their penises.[8] All had occurred after 1936, but none gained the attention that Abe Sada had because almost all were the result of simple jealousy. And unlike Ishida, many of the men described in this book lived after their losses. The writer also found at least one case in which a homosexual man had murdered and dismembered his lover's corpse and cooked the penis.

Throughout the ensuing decades, re-creations of Abe Sada's story have continued to appear. They mirror changing attitudes toward women, sexuality, and murder. Most have been fictional, while some have been poetic.[9] A few have been more scholarly in tone, and others have used Abe Sada as a means of exploring issues concerning sexuality today.[10] Films also continue to use the Abe Sada story. A documentary by Ishii Teruo about women criminals appeared in 1969 that featured Abe herself, and three feature films about her story have appeared since: Tanaka Noboru's *Jitsuroku Abe Sada* in 1975, Ôshima Nagisa's *Realm of the Senses* in 1976, and Ôbayashi Yoshihiko's *SADA* in 1998.[11]

The vast corpus of works on Abe Sada is a subject that merits a book in itself. What is important here is simply that ever since she committed murder and mutilation, her story has kindled imaginations. While her actions were extraordinary, her life opened a window on all-too-ordinary human desires and passions, raising themes that have continued to resonate in the minds of people in Japan and elsewhere. If this book has convinced the reader that Abe Sada's passions and desires were understandable in the context of her life and times, it has been successful. In any event, Abe Sada's story seems perpetually meaningful, one that others will ponder and recount far beyond this attempt to tell it yet again.

# NOTES FROM THE POLICE INTERROGATION OF ABE SADA

Translated by William Johnston

## First Interrogation of Abe Sada

Permanent address: Nagoya, Higashi Ward, Chikusa dôri 7–79
Place of birth: Tokyo, Kanda Ward, Shingin-chô 99

**Question of Police Interrogator [hereafter "Q"]:** We are now to begin a preliminary investigation regarding the facts concerning an incident of murder and the mutilation of a dead body that the prosecutor has presented regarding the defendant. Do you have a statement to make regarding these facts?

At this time, the judge read aloud the facts concerning the charges made against the defendant from the indictment.

**Abe Sada [hereafter AS]:** The facts are as you say; there are no mistakes.

**Q:** Why did you want to kill Kichizô?

**AS:** I loved him so much I couldn't stand it, and I decided that I wanted him all to myself. We weren't married, so if he had continued living he would have had relations with other women. But dead, he would never again lay a finger on another woman. And so I killed him.

**Q:** Was Kichizô in love with the defendant?

**AS:** Sure, he liked me well enough, but as would be the luck of the draw, I liked him a lot more than he liked me. From start to finish he always thought of his home as home and of me just as me. He had two kids at home, and he felt that he was getting old. So he said that there was no way we were going to elope. He told me that I should go and get some shabby place to live in and open up a tearoom, and that we could then see each other for a long time. But with a half-baked idea like that it would have been impossible for me to get my way.

**Q:** If you loved Ishida so much, why didn't you bring up the idea of a double suicide?

**AS:** From start to finish Ishida spoke of me as someone he wanted to make his mistress. As a joke he would say things about dying, but in reality he had absolutely no desire to commit suicide. And since I knew about how things were for him at home, it never crossed my mind to consider talking about double suicide with him.

**Q:** On the night that you killed Ishida, did you say that you'd make him die?

**AS:** No, I never said anything like that.

**Q:** That evening, did Ishida show any signs of having any suspicions that he was about to die?

**AS:** He didn't show any suspicions at all. But at around one in the morning on the eighteenth he told me that if he went to sleep again I would be sure to strangle him again. Then he said that he wouldn't want me to let the cord go loose before finishing him off. He added that he didn't feel it while the cord was tight around his neck, but after I let go it was very painful. I thought he said that as a joke.

**Q:** Why was that?

**AS:** When I had had sex with him before this and choked him, he said that it had felt good. But on the evening of the sixteenth of May, when we had sex with me on top while I pressed down on his throat with my hands, he said that he didn't feel anything, so I wrapped my sash cord around his neck. I was tightening and loosening it while we had sex, and because I had been looking down the whole time I tightened it too strongly without realizing it. Ishida moaned and his organ suddenly got small. I was startled and loosened my sash cord, but Ishida's face had turned red and wouldn't go back to normal. That day and the next day I cooled his face with water.

Since we had done that, at around one in the morning on the eighteenth, while

Ishida was asleep I thought about how he had said that he wouldn't want me to let the cord go loose before finishing him off. At the moment he told me that, I thought that he wouldn't regret it if I killed him, and I laughed and agreed. Ishida had said that while laughing and looking at me in the face. He added that if he felt like dying he wanted to have me kill him. But I thought he was just joking. About thirty minutes after that, I sat down next to Ishida while he was sleeping, but I didn't say that I was going to kill him. Ishida had always thought I was pretty frail and believed that I had consumption. So when he said things like, "Okayo, if it were for you I would die anytime," I always thought he was saying it in jest, and I also thought that he was joking when he told me that night. When I quietly went up to Ishida and started to wrap my sash cord around his neck with the intention of killing him, he said, "Okayo," and went to embrace me, so he had no idea that I was going to kill him. I think he was startled, but I did not loosen my sash cord, and while thinking to myself that he should forgive me, I continued to pull it as tightly as I could.

### Deposition by Kasahara Kinosuke

**Kasahara:** I was born in Noge, Naka Ward in Yokohama, graduated from the upper level of Ishida Elementary School, and then went to work on the Yokohama stock exchange, where I worked for a brokerage company for a long time. From November 21, 1930 until the present I have been the head of the Yokohama branch of the Seiyûkai lobbying office. My office is in Noge, Yamashita, Miyakawa-chô. I have a salary of about eighty yen. My wife, who is fifty-five years old, and I have lived together since 1907. My son, Kikutarô, is twenty years of age and is in his fifth year at the Kantô Academy middle school. That is all.

**Q:** Do you know a woman named Abe Sada? If so, what is your relationship to her?

**Kasahara:** Yes, I know a woman named Abe Sada. I feel a bit awkward talking about my relationship with this Sada, but I will tell you everything in detail.

I became acquainted with Sada about a year ago, sometime around October 1934. I've completely forgotten what day it was, but I had an acquaintance who lived in Naka Ward, Fujimi, a man named Yamada, who ran a brothel. Around that time the place was raided and the women were all taken to the Isezaki-chô police station. Yamada asked if I could get the women released, and we went to the Isazaki-chô station. At the time I asked if they could be released they still hadn't been charged, so the police let them out. One of those women was Abe Sada.

Since she was good-looking and had a nice figure, I couldn't forget her, and so I went and had a talk with Yamada about her. Luckily she didn't have any debts, and I negotiated to make her my mistress. She agreed to it and so the matter was settled. On the twentieth of December the same year I spent about two hundred yen to set up a house for her in Miyakawa-chô, and for living expenses I would give her three or four yen every now and then, but I didn't regularly give her a set amount.

The rent was fifteen yen a month, and I paid that and the cost of rice for her. We never lived together, but at first I would stay with her every other day or once every two days. She was really strong, a real powerful one. Even though I am pretty jaded, she was enough to astound me.

She wasn't satisfied unless we did it two, three, or four times a night. To her, it was unacceptable unless I had my hand on her private parts all night long. It didn't bother her to lick my tool. It is hard to put it into words what it was like; we went without sleeping almost the whole night.

At first it was great, but after a couple of weeks I got a little exhausted. Of course, it was my own fault. But because I have a wife of thirty years who has helped me through difficult times, it was impossible for me to stay all the time with Sada, and little by little I started to see her only once every five days. Moreover, at my office there are always five or six helpers, and taking them out to eat all the time runs into quite a bit of money, so I thought that it would be cheaper if I were to provide the ingredients and have Sada cook meals for them. When I mentioned this to Sada, she would have none of it. Not only that, but she asked me to spend every night in bed with her until she was satisfied. But for the reason I stated before I told Sada that I could not fulfill all her desires. Sada then said that I should get rid of my wife and make her my legal spouse and satisfy her that way, but I refused. When I told her that I couldn't do something as stupid as that, she asked if she could take a lover. That was on the twenty-ninth of January last year. I was giving her an allowance for food and incidentals and I couldn't stand to have somebody I was supporting like that blithely take a lover, so I told her, "You have to be joking," and said I would kick her if she were to do that. That night she ran off by herself and wrote only one letter. It was mailed from inside a train on the Tôkaidô line, postmarked Hamamatsu. In it, she said that she had caused me a great deal of trouble but that it wasn't good to be involved in a triangle with me and my wife, and took her leave to go to Kansai to work there and asked that I forget her. I was pretty angry, but I still had some feelings for her and so looked all around for her. But that was the last time I saw her and after that I never heard from her again.

We have no relationship at present. Nevertheless, because of this incident, I have been subjected to police investigation. Also, while she was my mistress I knew her older brother, who lived in Kanda in Tokyo. Luckily, because I had the good fortune to break up with her then, I didn't end up losing one of my important parts. While I was together with Sada she never toyed around with knives or poison or talked about killing someone or dying or anything like that.

She is a slut and a whore. And as what she has done makes clear, she is a woman whom men should fear.

That is all that I know about her.

## Second Interrogation of Abe Sada

**Q:** Have you ever been convicted of a crime before?

**AS:** No.

**Q:** Have you ever been investigated by the police?

**AS:** Yes, on four different occasions. The first time was when I was sixteen and indentured as a maid. I put on a kimono and a ring of my employer's daughter and went out sightseeing. The next time was when I was twenty-one, when I took five or six shamisen plectrums and a pipe that belonged to a girl I was working with and pawned them. After that was when I was twenty-six and indentured as a prostitute and I took one hundred yen that belonged to a customer. And then, when was when I was twenty-eight or nine, the police investigated me for gambling with cards and mahjongg, but they released me [without filing charges].

**Q:** How far did you go in school?

**AS:** After graduating from primary school in Kanda in Tokyo, I had a private tutor in my home and learned calligraphy.

**Q:** What about your parents and brothers and sisters?

**AS:** My father was Abe Shigeyoshi and my mother was called Katsu. My mother died in January 1933 and my father died in January 1934. Both died at around age seventy-five from natural causes.

I had seven brothers and sisters. I was the fourth daughter and the youngest child. My second and third oldest brothers died when I was about ten, and my fourth oldest brother died soon after he was born. My remaining brothers and sisters include my eldest brother Shintarô, age fifty; a sister, Imao Toku, age forty-nine; and another sister, Tatsumi [Teruko], age thirty-eight. At present, Shintarô works as a tatami maker in Yokohama; Toku is the wife of Imao Seitarô, who worked as a trucker in Saitama prefecture but who quit that and since last year has been running a general store in Tokyo. My sister Teruko is the wife of Tatsumi Toshisaburô, a tatami maker in Ikebukuro.

**Q:** How is your health?

**AS:** I might look frail, but I am in perfect health. When I was twenty-three and working as a prostitute in Nagoya, I got syphilis and received about ten injections. After that I did not have any more symptoms of syphilis, but around October last year I started to get swellings on my hands. Because of that I went to Kusatsu hot springs, where the hot-water therapy cured me. This January, a doctor told me that I had tertiary syphilis but it looks as though it will not develop symptoms. At age twenty-four I contracted typhus, but since then I have been in good health except for once, when I developed hemorrhoids and spent two months in the hospital recovering.

**Q:** Is your period regular?

**AS:** I started to menstruate from late in my sixteenth year and ever since then it has been regular. It lasts for about four days. During my period I get a headache and become irritable, but it isn't so severe that I need to go to bed.

**Q:** In your direct family or among any of your relatives are there any who are mentally diseased?

**AS:** There are none. Both of my parents died of old age, one of my older brothers died of heart failure due to beriberi, and the other died of typhus. All of my other brothers and sisters are in good health, and among my relatives there are none who are mentally ill.

**Q:** What were the circumstances of your household while you were growing up?

**AS:** I was born in Kanda. My older brother Shintarô got himself a wife; my older sister Toku had gone off to marry; the next oldest, Teruko, was of age but was still staying around the house. While I was being brought up my family was prospering as it never had before. We always had six craftsmen in the house, and when they got busy they hired as many as ten or fifteen. We were wealthy and as the youngest child my parents spoiled me.

My mother liked garish things and was very vain. From around my second year in primary school she had me learn the shamisen and would dress me up and parade me around. That kept me from doing my studies, and I naturally started to hate school. My teacher told me that I had to quit taking those lessons, but I took lessons during the entire time I was in elementary school. About one year after my graduation I started to take sewing lessons, and my parents had a teacher called to our house to teach me calligraphy. But there were many craftsmen in our house and I heard them talking about many things. Because of that, by age ten I knew what men and women do with each other. Of course, I was a bit precocious.

My brother Shintarô was something of a hedonist. When he got rid of my older sister, who was rather difficult, for the first time he started to let his women friends who worked in bars and restaurants hang out around the house. It must have been around the same time that a craftsman in the house was adopted into the family as my sister Teruko's husband. Shintarô had been led to believe that Teruko would inherit the house and business, so he and his wife gave Teruko and her husband a hard time. My mother sided with Teruko. Every day our house was a mass of confusion. My parents didn't think it would be good for me to see everything so shook up, so every day they said, "Go play outside." I thought it was a good thing and I went and spent most of my time at friends' houses. As a result I got in the habit of staying out.

**Q:** Did the defendant start to keep the company of delinquents from around this time?

**AS:** No, not at all. Rather, if anything, I was far too serious in my thinking at that time. But when I was fifteen an older student took advantage of me at a friend's place, and that changed me in no time. After that, I spent a lot of time hanging out in Asakusa with a bunch of no-goods.

**Q:** What happened?

**AS:** At that time, I went out with Fukuda Minako almost every day. This was when I was fifteen. At her place I got to know a Keiô University student named Sakuragi Ken, who was a friend of Minako's older brother. I acted a little older than my age and we started to get intimate. While we were playing around on the second floor he forced himself into me. Because it hurt horribly and I bled for two days after that, I was frightened and felt that I had to tell my mother about it, so I did. Some time later I met that student again at Minako's house. We went out for a walk together and I told him that because I had told my mother what had happened between us I wanted him to tell his parents, too. After that he quit showing up around Minako's. My mother then went to his parents' house, but they wouldn't even talk with her. I just stayed in my bed and cried. At that time I didn't think that I wanted to marry that student, but I couldn't stand to think that he was making a fool out of me the whole time. When I realized that I was no longer a virgin [*shojo*], I hated [that I had] to hide the fact so that I could get married. It was worse to think of discussing the facts concerning my virginity [with a prospective marriage partner] before I could get married. Because [now] it was impossible for me to get married, I wondered what I would do with myself and got really angry about it.

My mother saw that I was very agitated and comforted me by telling me that if I kept quiet about it, things would be okay. Besides, a man had taken advantage of me by doing something to me that I didn't understand, so it was nothing to worry about. She bought me a new koto and other things and otherwise spoiled me more than before. But the more she spoiled me the angrier I became, and so one day I took fifteen yen from the house and went out to have a good time.

At that time, there were a lot of no-goods in the neighborhood. When I walked by they always teased me by calling out my name, but I would never turn around and look at them. But that time I called out to them and told them that because I was in a bad mood that day I wanted them to take me someplace where we could have a good time. Two or three of them came along and we went together to Asakusa, where we had fun until evening. I thought that if I took any money home with me I would get caught, so I divided it among them and let them have it.

I'm sure that was around the time when my older sister Teruko and her husband were in the process of leaving our house and everything was a mass of confusion. My parents increasingly ignored me. My mother said that I was very late and so I told her that I had been to the hills around Ueno. It was absolutely splendid when I could give money to the no-goods in my bunch and buy them meals and drinks. They would all boisterously call me "Saachan, Saachan" [an endearing and diminutive form of "Sada"]. It was fine with me that my parents didn't say anything about these things so I became increasingly contemptuous. Even if I was awakened in the morning I wouldn't get up. I got very lazy. Once I had awakened I would make somebody bring me my breakfast in bed. After eating I got up, dressed, and immediately went to Asakusa. There, I went to the Kinryûkan [a fashionable restaurant] and mainly three other establishments where I would stay all day long, refusing to go home until after nine at night.

Once, I grabbed a handful of money from my parents. When I went out and counted it I got scared because I had twenty yen. I went to return some of it but there were too many craftsmen around [who might notice what I was doing], so I just went out and spent it all. I hung around with this group of no-goods for about a year. That was the year my sister Teruko ran away from the house and left her husband. After she had returned home she took a craftsman as her lover and had illicit relations with him. I knew about this and my parents started to scold me for it but I yelled, "It's Teruko who did it, not me," and they shut up.

When I think about it now, my father didn't mind my going out. For instance, he spoiled me by ignoring me when I went out all dressed up. And my mother spoiled me by letting me back in quietly when I returned home late at night. This made me more and more contemptuous of them.

Even so, my father suddenly got angry and nailed shut the door to my room on the second story. After that I wrapped my best kimono in a bundle and threw it down to the storage shed. I would call the young mother next door and she would help me from my window onto the roof. Or else I would have one of the craftsmen take my kimono out for me and I would get out that way.

There were ten men and two women in my gang. Usually I gave them spending money at Asakusa and we all had a good time, but nobody had sexual relations. Only once, when I went to Kamakura, I had sex with two men who were about twenty years old.

**Q:** What happened between then and the time you became a geisha?

**AS:** In April of my sixteenth year arrangements were being made for my older sister Teruko to get married. Maybe it was because they had gotten their fill of my being a no-good, but I think it is more likely that they were afraid that I would tell people about my sister's misdeeds and become an obstacle to her getting married. My mother was afraid that I might cause the negotiations to miscarry and so she said, "So that we can get your sister out of the way you are going to have to stay quiet for a while. You have to go be a housemaid." She then put me into service in a mansion across from Seishin Academy in Shiba Ward. I was maid to the young daughter. But because I had been completely spoiled until that time, I felt horribly constrained. Not only that, but I had to eat in the kitchen, which was the worst. I felt so lonely that I wept at every meal. It was impossible for me to forget my good times playing around Asakusa. Just about a month after I had started there I put on the daughter's best kimono and ring, rather naïvely thinking it would be all right if I put them back after I returned, and I went to the Kinryûkan in Asakusa. My older sister came looking for me there and took me back. That was the first time I was taken to the police.

After that I stayed quiet. When I was seventeen, my older brother Shintarô and his wife ran off with all the family's money. My parents got worried about what they would do, so they quit the tatami business, sold their house in Kanda, and built a house close to my older sister Toku's, in the town of Sakaishi in Saitama prefecture. My parents and I moved there together.

My father didn't have a business in the countryside, and I didn't have any work either. So I started to take shamisen lessons again. Sure enough, it was impossible for me to stay quiet for very long, and I became infatuated with a local man and had sex with him once; people saw us together when we went out for walks. Now and then I would go alone to a local western-style restaurant. Since it was the countryside, rumors about me started to fly thick and fast. My father couldn't take it and got angry. He said, "If you like men all that much I'll sell you off to a brothel." My mother and Toku were worried about me and made my father hold off. That really scared me, too, and I cried for three days and asked my father to forgive me, but he wouldn't listen. In July of 1922, when I was eighteen, he took me to a distant relative in Makita-chô, Yokohama, named Inaba Masatake, and asked him to make me into a licensed prostitute. In the train on the way there I didn't say a single word to my father. Since I had a blemished body anyhow there was nothing I could do about it, and I promised myself that I would never again live with my parents. But I was still too young to become a licensed prostitute, so I went to stay with the Inaba family for about a month. After that, Inaba went through an intermediary who had me take an advance of three hundred yen from a geisha house called Shunshin Mino in Sumiyoshi, Naka Ward. They made me into a trainee with the professional name Miyako. I soon became a full-fledged geisha.

Around that time my family had five or six houses that they rented out, so it was easy to find a place to stay. Since I had plenty of money, I gave some of the money I had been lent to Inaba and used some of it for the goods that I needed and for spending. I hated my father then, but later I heard that he had told my mother and sister that if I were to experience taking on temporary male companions as a business, I was certain to tire of it quickly and want to return home, in which case he would have welcomed me back.

**Q:** What do you remember from the time you were a geisha?

**AS:** Once I had become a trainee, I soon learned that "older" geisha like myself [who started relatively late in life] couldn't compare with the ones who had been in training since they were children. We just didn't have comparable skills and tended to get lost in the shuffle. The Shunshin Mino was a first-class establishment, and we had to be absolutely proper at all times. Since I had money to spend from what had been loaned me, I wasn't in financial trouble. Still, every time I had an engagement the men wanted me to sell them sexual favors, and I thought it was a horrible business. But because my parents had abandoned me, I threw myself to the fates and instead of thinking of it as work thought of it as play. I moved from place to place as I saw fit and had no hopes for the future as I worked as a geisha.

**Q:** What were the circumstances that led the defendant to go from place to place working as a geisha?

**AS:** To tell you that I have to tell you about my relationship with Inaba Masatake. Inaba was the husband of Kurokawa Hana, who was the older sister of my brother's first wife Ume. He worked as a wood carver in Yokohama and my family had previous contact with him. Inaba knew from before that I had been running around with a bunch of no-goods, and after he had helped me out for about a month he forced me to have sex with him. He was a smooth talker and I was still wet behind the ears. In no time he had me wrapped around his little finger. So we could continue our relationship, even after I had become a geisha I would go see Inaba when I had time off. When I was nineteen I told him how horrible Shunshin Mino, was and he helped me move to a geisha house called Kamochû in Haruki-chô, Kagawa Ward.

There, I had to take a loan of six hundred yen. I didn't worry too much about it at the time, but later I realized that Inaba had swindled me. While I was working at Kamochû, visiting Inaba's house one day, the great earthquake hit. Inaba's house burned to the ground before we could take anything out. Because of the money on loan to me it was impossible for me to return to my parents, so I helped out at Inaba's house for a while. In October of that year I went with the entire Inaba family to Toyama so that I could pay back my debts. There, he got a loan of one thousand yen from a geisha house in Shimizu-chô named Heianrô. I paid back my debts to Kamochû and gave the remaining two or three hundred yen to Inaba. With that money he rented a house close to Heianrô. When I didn't have any customers I would go to Inaba's place and we continued to have sexual relations.

At that time I worked under the professional name of Haruko and assumed complete responsibility for Inaba. I gave him all my spending money, but by itself my income was not enough and things got difficult. From one of my colleagues I stole a plectrum for the shamisen and a tobacco pipe, put them into hock for fifty yen, and gave Inaba the money. That was in 1924, when I was twenty-one. The police arrested and investigated me but let me go.

I worked for a year in the Heianrô in Toyama, but after being arrested it became impossible to stay there. That October I moved back to Tokyo with Inaba and his family and rented a house in Shiba Ward, Kirizuki 31. I lived with Inaba and spent the next six months wandering around having a good time.

The sisters of Kurokawa Hana, Inaba's wife, were all geisha and he helped them out. He got intimate with one of them and sold her as an upper-class geisha. This started a real brouhaha, but during the whole time his wife just ignored it all. Suddenly I realized for the first time that Inaba and his wife were just using me to line their pockets. They were eating me alive. This all made me very angry, and I immediately decided to end my relationship with Inaba. But since he had cosigned my loan in Toyama it would be impossible to get rid of him straight off. To do that, in May of 1925 I had to cosign with Inaba on an advance of 1,500 yen from a geisha house called Mikawaya in Iida, Shinshû. I started work there under the professional name of Seikô.

Because all the geisha who went to Shinshû hadn't previously been examined for venereal diseases, the [geisha in the] teahouses and customers both were required to have syphilis examinations. It was clear that I had contracted a venereal disease some-place that didn't require examinations.

I felt that if I had gone so far as to become a geisha who was required to have syphilis examinations I would be better off becoming a licensed prostitute. At age 22, on New Year's, I moved to a place in Tobita in Osaka called Misonorô. I took the profes-sional name of Sonomaru and went to work. That was when I ended my relationship with Inaba. Just as I was moving to Misonorô, my mother found out about my rela-tionship with Inaba. This time, because I wanted to cut my ties with him, for the first time ever my mother became my go-between as a geisha. She asked an intermediary named Kaita in Yokohama. He went to the trouble of taking my mother with him to Mikawaya in Shinshû [Nagano]. I explained to her everything that had happened with Inaba and asked that she be my guarantor. From Misonorô I received an advance of 2,800 yen, and from that I returned the money that I owed Mikawaya. Thereafter my father would be my sole guarantor, and I gave my mother 200 or 300 yen as spending money.

This was the first time I ever gave spending money to my parents. Until this time I had hated my parents, but I had a change of heart and I had given my mother some of my advance. Since I had fallen this far, I asked them to let me do as I please.

**Q:** What happened while you worked as a licensed prostitute?

**AS:** Misonorô at that time was a first-rate establishment and I was no slouch. From that time I quit disliking taking on my customers, so I had a good time while I was work-ing. After about a year, a customer from a certain company said that he wanted to buy the rights to me. But when he learned that someone who worked under him also was a customer of mine, he broke off negotiations and asked me how much he owed me, so at that time I got some money.

Then, I was sweet-talked into moving to another establishment that was a little rotten, and soon after the beginning of the new year I moved for a sum of about 2,600 yen. But when I got there the owner was expecting a cute little girl, and if anything, I was a real shrew. Apparently the intermediary had pleaded with the owner to take me. At the time I didn't know about any of this. But when I heard that he was lamenting that there wasn't anything he could do but hire me and that I could call myself anything I wanted, I knew what had happened. I thought that if he didn't like me now, I would make him like me. I took Sadako as my professional name and worked as hard as I could.

I worked at Tokueirô only for a couple of years, but I have a lot of memories from that time. At that time I liked to wear greenish brown things and the owner would always call me "parakeet" to badmouth me. The others all quietly did just what he said, but I refused to restrain myself and would speak up. Once, a friend approached me saying that she wanted to escape. I told her that I would help and sent her out through the window in my room. But she dropped a big make-up box, which crashed to the ground. They caught her.

For the most part the owner didn't get very angry with us. But when he was drunk he would call me "parakeet" and yell at me about something. But I wasn't about to let him get the better of me and usually I got the better of him. Most of that was in jest. His wife was a nice person, too. And Tokueirô was a first-rate establishment with good customers. Around then I had a very strong desire to see my mother, and she came to see me.

I was able to take ten days off and gave her a warm reception. When she went home I gave her eighty yen in spending money. And for her and everybody else I bought local food specialties as gifts to take home.

A letter came from Inaba saying that this time he had started a procurement service for geisha, but I told him we were not having anything to do with each other. Then, Inaba's daughter went to the trouble of coming to see me. I put her up for about a week and sent her home with presents of local food specialties.

After that I got typhus, and little by little I started to get sick of business. With the intention of moving elsewhere, I went out of the house without permission and went to the procurer who originally helped me out in Osaka. But they already knew about me, and somebody came from Tokueirô and took me back. The owner said he would have been better off if I had escaped. Had I done that, he said, he would have taken possession of my parents' rental property, so he got me pretty scared. We had a quiet discussion, and he allowed me to move to the brothel called Miyakorô in Matsushima in Osaka, where I took the name Azuma. I'm certain that I received an advance of about two thousand yen. But unlike the places I'd worked before, it was a bit tacky and the clientele was fairly rough, so I got sick of it. I wanted to free myself and drop out of the business, so about two weeks after I started there I ran away from the place and went to Tokyo, where I stayed in the inn across from Tsukuda, a procurer who had helped me in the past. The man who came looking for me from Miyakorô found me and took me back to Osaka. They forced me to move to a place called Taishôrô in Tanba Sasayama. There, I assumed the professional name of Okaru. That was in the winter of my twenty-sixth year. Taishôrô was a worse place than before, worse than being a streetwalker. Even on cold, snowy nights we had to go out and pull in the clients. I got more and more sick of it all and after about half a year I used a client to escape. I tried to make it look as though we had eloped, but it didn't work and they caught me and brought me back.

After that I changed my professional name to Ikuyo. Around this time I stole about one hundred yen from a client so that I could escape. But we were closely watched and so I didn't have any opportunity to get out. Soon I realized that although the main lock on the door looked as though it was fastened, it really wasn't, and so when I saw a client out one time I made it sound as though the door was being locked when in fact it wasn't. The people in the establishment then relaxed their guard and I was able to get out. I waited for the first train and finally fled to Kobe. With that, I washed my hands of being a licensed prostitute.

## Third Interrogation of Abe Sada

**Q:** What did you do after you quit being a licensed prostitute?

**AS:** Since then I have worked as a waitress and as a prostitute, and have been a kept mistress. Until last July I spent most of my time as a prostitute, but after that I distanced myself from men for a while and worked as a maid and for a while went and took care of my parents.

**Q:** Explain in detail the events that took place while you were [an unlicensed] prostitute.

**AS:** When I ran away to Kobe from Tanba Sasayama I took the name of Yoshii Masako and for two weeks I worked as a waitress. But there was the problem of the advances that I still owed to the brothels and I was short of spending money, and in any event I wanted more money, so I asked customers if they didn't know of any work that would earn me about one hundred yen a month. One customer said that he had some good business and asked me to his place. I felt like having a good time and went and told him that we should start a business.

This man worked as a pimp for a brothel in Kobe. For the most part I could tell what he was up to, but I felt that if at this time I were to try to go straight I couldn't keep it up. So I went to his house and took it easy there for a couple of months before I started work as a high-class prostitute. But he took my pay to cover all my expenses until then. I was in over my ears, and in the end it was so terrible that after three months I quit the business. In 1932, when I was twenty-eight, I went to Osaka and started doing the same business, but I soon quit and became a mistress.

After that three men took care of me. Most months I received from 100 to 150 or 160 yen in spending money. From around this time I started to get strong pleasure from sex and I couldn't stand to sleep alone. When I was a mistress, my man would come to me only five or six times every month, so I had relations with two or three men who had been favorite clients when I was working as a prostitute. I had plenty of money and free time and so I became pretty hedonistic. In my free time I played mahjongg, went to the Takarazuka theater, and went to Dôtonbori [similar to Tokyo's Asakusa] to have a good time.

It was around this time that I was arrested for gambling.

That [brush with the law] made want to reform myself, and since I had about four hundred yen saved up I quit being a mistress and rented an apartment in Osaka where I did things like read books and lived a quiet life. But the longer I stayed away from men, I became increasingly irritated, so I went to a physician for an examination. The doctor told me that there was nothing in particular wrong with me and that was a natural way to feel for anybody. He told me that it would be better for me to become a serious wife and recommended that I read a difficult book on mental hygiene to make me change my feelings.

Eventually I started to play mahjongg and the like and I got a boyfriend. But in the autumn of my twenty-eighth year, a friend from Yokohama who was visiting Osaka told me that my parents were worried about me, which made me want to go home. I then stayed for three months with my parents, until winter. It was the first time in my life that I did anything that resembled filial piety toward my parents. So that they wouldn't worry, I lied to my parents and told them that a nice person in Osaka was taking care of me. Morning and night I would massage their shoulders and read the newspaper to them. I cooked the meals and did all that I could to show my devotion to them. They were so happy that they told me they could then die in peace.

But then three men from Sasayama came looking for me, so I couldn't stay any longer with my parents. I went back to my apartment in Osaka but in January 1933, when I was twenty-nine, I received a telegram telling me that my mother had died. I sent my father money and then gathered together my belongings and left Osaka. I got back to my parents' house one week after my mother had died and visited her grave. I stayed for about two weeks, but the people from Sasayama were looking for me and rumors about me had begun to spread around the countryside. I felt that I couldn't show my face to people. This made me feel confined, so I went to Tokyo. There, I found a place in Minowa and started to work as a prostitute once again under the name Yoshii Masako.

Eventually, in October of my twenty-ninth year, I became the mistress of a man of about thirty-seven or -eight who was in the sack business in Muromachi, Nihonbashi Ward. We liked each other, and he promised he would come see me every day. I then rented first a place on the second floor of a small *oden* [boiled food] restaurant in Shingin-chô, Kanda Ward, and then I moved to another room on the second floor of an *ikebana* teacher's place. I was getting about sixty yen a month at that time. Then, in January of my thirtieth year, I received word that my father had become ill, so I went to him and stayed for about ten days, during which I did everything I could to nurse him and take care of him. Even now, I think that that was the only time I really showed any filial piety.

Around the time my father died, he told me with tears in his eyes that he had never thought I would take care of him. He died on January twenty-sixth.

After receiving three hundred yen from my father's estate, I soon returned to Tokyo, where I continued to be Mr. Nakagawa's mistress.

It must have been around that time that I went to Yokohama on business and saw an old friend who told me that Inaba's daughter had died. She and I had been good friends, so I went to visit her grave in the countryside. Once again I saw Inaba, whom I had once sworn never to see again. I couldn't stand to see the circumstances they were living in and so I pawned one of my rings and gave him 150 yen.

In September of my thirtieth year, Mr. Nakagawa became ill and worried about what I would do. After we talked it over, we decided to separate and I went to stay with Inaba. For about two weeks I just wandered around having a good time. But since I was lonely and didn't have any real skills, once again I went to Yokohama, Naka Ward, Fujimi-chô, where I started to work as a prostitute for a place called Yamadaya. It was from my connections there that a year ago I met Kasahara Kinnosuke, a middle-aged man of about fifty who worked for the Seiyûkai lobbying office, and became his mistress. Kasahara was a real reprobate and wouldn't give me much spending money. He didn't love me and treated me like an animal. He was the kind of scum who would then plead with me when I said that we should break up. I soon started to hate him, and last January I called Mr. Nakagawa on the telephone and he came and stayed with me at an inn called Jôshûya in Asakusa. When I tried to run away from Kawahara he came looking for me as far as Sakaguchi, in the country. He told me that I was his mistress and threatened me. Finally, in January of the following year, I was able to flee to Nagoya, and after that I cut all ties with Kasahara.

In Nagoya, I started to work as a maid in a restaurant called Kotobuki on Chikusa-dôri, Higashi Ward, under the pseudonym of Tanaka Kayo. I was the only maid there, and it was a very strict and formal kind of place. One evening last April I met a man whose name and position I later learned, Ômiya Gorô, a Nagoya city councilman and head-master of Chûkyô College of Commerce. He was on his way back from another restau-rant and brought a maid from that place with him.

Professor Ômiya's attitude toward that maid showed that he was a real gentleman and nattily groomed. It was the first time we met, but I had a real crush on this beautiful man. Four or five days later he came by himself and had some sweets to eat. He seemed to want to hear all about me, and so that he would take pity on me I told him a sad cock-and-bull story about a daughter that I had to leave in Tokyo, and since my husband had died I had to do this kind of work to raise her. Hearing this, he gave me ten yen and told me to buy something for my daughter. His kindness made me fall even more in love with him.

Once again, four or five days after that, he came alone, dressed in traditional men's kimono. This made me think that he must have feelings for me. He listened to me talk about my child and other things, and all the while I snuggled up to his lap and made it seem that I was very sad and tearful. He said, "You shouldn't put your hand there. Since I'm a man it makes me feel strange, so go sit over there. It would be a problem if some-body came." I thought that that was the right time and I made myself even sexier and pressed myself even closer against his lap. He embraced me and so I pushed him over and we had sex right where we were.

Two or three days later Professor Ômiya came to Kotobuki once again, and I told him that I would like to meet with him someplace where we could take our time. He replied that we should go to Matsukawa Inn, close to Maizuru Park. I told the people at the restaurant that I was going out for a while and he and I went to the inn together.

I didn't return to Kotobuki after that and instead went to a small restaurant close by named Ijû, where I lived and worked. Around that time I had sex with Ômiya again at Mat-sukawa, but I was getting tired of Nagoya, so in June of last year I told him that my daugh-ter had died and that I had to return to Tokyo. I told him that I would write care of Mat-sukawa Inn, and he gave me fifty yen, after which I left for Tokyo. For about ten days I stayed with Inaba again in Shitaya, during which I went around having a good time. But it was not long before Kasahara, whose concubine I had been, sued me for marriage fraud and the police apparently came looking for me at Inaba's. It seemed time to clear out, so I went to a bordello in Hama-chô run by Kimura Hiroshi, whom I had become acquainted with while I was working as a prostitute in Tokyo before. There, I once again worked as a prostitute under the pseudonym Tanaka Kayo. With clients I used the name Tanaka Kimi. I wrote a letter to Professor Ômiya and told him to come see me at Kimura's place.

Then, sometime around the middle of June last year, Professor Ômiya came to visit me at Kimura's. I lied to him and said that Kimura's was my older sister's house. That day the two of us went to a place called Yumenosato in Shinagawa and enjoyed each other for about two hours. Then we saw a movie in Asakusa, and after dinner he went back to Nagoya. At that time he gave me thirty yen.

Even after that I remained at Kimura's, but then I got involved with him and his wife, Kanako Shizu, got jealous and made everything chaotic.

Kimura Hiroshi was a real rake. While he had been living with his previous wife, Ohashi Hide, he had fallen in love with Kanako. His wife Hide then said that she would give Kanako her husband and made the two of them live together while she lived separately but close by. This time, when things got messy because of the relationship between Kimura and myself, Hide let us stay together on the second floor of her place.

I quit being a prostitute from that time, but one evening in mid-July of last year Kanako came to get me, saying that Professor Ômiya had come to visit. When I went to Shizu's place I found him there in a hot living room. He said that he had been there for three hours.

I was delighted and hurried up to get ready. We went from Tokyo Station by train to Atami, where we stayed at Tamanoi Inn. Professor Ômiya said that he had heard what had been going on from Shizu, and said that he wasn't surprised that I was a prostitute and that I had taken another woman's husband. From the beginning he didn't think I was much for propriety, but he felt he could somehow help me and asked me to do what I could to start leading a serious life. He said that he wouldn't tell me his real name, but well into the night he explained how he would never fail to take care of me in the future. From the beginning I had felt that I was just having a short affair with him.

Under no circumstances would he tell me his name or profession, and told me a cock-and-bull story that his name was Tamura Masao. He told me that if only I would tell him where I lived he would always take care of me. He carefully put away his clothing himself so that I would not learn his name and he was so fastidious that he was boring even in bed. I thought that there was little hope in him. But then I thought that he had, after all, gone to the trouble of coming to see me and was showing me every kindness. When he met me he was completely sincere and wanted only to do me well. This time, I was truly grateful. He had moved me to decide that I would be serious in the future, and I went with him all the way to Numazu, where we had a tearful parting.

At this time I received thirty yen from Professor Ômiya. After that I completely washed my hands of prostitution and after returning to Tokyo didn't go back to Kimura's, and instead let Inaba take care of me. I thought I would even quit smoking and went to a Nichiren priest to ask for assistance. I met Professor Ômiya twice in August, in Nagoya and Tokyo, and after that we set up about ten meetings in Toyohashi, Osaka, Kusatsu, Kyoto, Tokyo, and other places. And immediately after I killed Ishida Kichizô, I met with him for the last time in Tokyo on May eighteenth.

**Q:** Did you not have relations with other men during this time?

**AS:** Since Professor Ômiya couldn't satisfy me, I stayed with Nakagawa Chôjirô, whose mistress I had been, five or six times in Asakusa, where we had sex.

**Q:** Continue explaining your relationship with Ômiya Gorô.

**AS:** Around the middle of July last year, after leaving Professor Ômiya and going back to Tokyo, I stayed with Inaba. But after a couple of weeks I wanted to see Professor Ômiya again.

He wore a lapel pin that had a circle with the Chinese character for the number eight inside it [*maruhachi*] and I knew that this lapel pin meant that he either was a member of the Nagoya City Council or an official in the Nagoya City Hall. I thought that if I tried to find out who he was I could, so in mid-August I went to Nagoya. After arriving I stopped by an inn called Kiyokoma that was next to the station. There, I saw a newspaper headline that read, CITY COUNCIL MEMBERS GO TO AMERICA. It showed a photograph of [the man I then came to know as] Professor Ômiya. For the first time I knew his position and occupation, and it made me happy. I quickly called him on the telephone and we met at an inn by the harbor called Nan'yôkan. He seemed to be extremely troubled and dispirited. He asked how I learned his name, and I told him by looking at the newspaper. "Oh," he said, and nodded. He then said, "Because I am a school president, if people found out about my relationship with you I wouldn't be able to go on living. You are a pistol pointed at me. It is up to you whether I live or die. In the future I hope to become a Diet [Parliament] member, so until then please keep things quiet. When I become a Diet member you can come visit me in broad daylight." I told him that I was the only one who knew who he was, that I hadn't told anyone else, and that I didn't want to bother him in any way. After that he told me that he was very busy that day and asked that I quickly return to Tokyo, since he couldn't even walk straight if he knew that I was in Nagoya. I wanted to have sex with him then, but he said that it was best that I leave straight away and that he would come visit me in Tokyo on the 13th. Since he wasn't in good spirits I took 130 yen that he gave me for spending money and returned to Tokyo.

On the thirteenth he came to Tokyo on his way to go to America and we met at Yumenosato. After that Inaba took care of me the whole time. In late October I found out that he would be returning and I went back to Nagoya to wait for him there. But he stayed in Tokyo on the way back, and I waited around for two weeks for him. During that time I went to movies and otherwise had a good time. In the process I spent over two hundred yen.

On November eleventh he finally met me, but he was busy and after only about an hour he had to leave. I received one hundred yen from him.

On that day we promised to meet in Toyohashi on the 16th of November. We spent the day together taking it easy, and he gave me 50 yen when I returned to Tokyo. Soon after that we met in Osaka. I told him that I had developed a sore. He told me that because I had previously led an evil life I had contracted syphilis and that I should go to Kusatsu for hot springs therapy. With 250 yen that he gave me, from November of last year until January 10th this year I stayed at Kusatsu. He visited me once while I was there. When he found out that I had quit smoking he was surprised. He spent one night at Kusatsu, but we had two futon spread and when I approached him he said that he was tired, and we didn't have sex. Instead, he talked about husbands and wives and the proper conduct of women. "For a husband and wife," he said, "the everyday affairs of life come first and sexual matters are secondary. For that matter, sex must be secondary to any relationship between men and women. Rather, they must be satisfied that they can truly feel for each other. When I look at you, I feel at peace. But your erotic drive is far too strong. Simply by holding my hand you get excited. You have to discipline yourself so that even when you sleep with a man you will be in control of yourself. When I tell you that I won't have sex, I mean it." I found it all a bore.

The next day we went together to Ikabo, where we spent the night. Professor Ômiya went home around noon the next day, and gave me one hundred yen in spending money. At Ikabo, I was happy when he had told me that I had become more placid and that my manner of speech had changed. Even now, I can't forget that feeling. After I left Kusatsu in mid-January of this year I met him once in Kyoto. As he had before, he told me again in Kusatsu and Kyoto that I should get serious and start some kind of business. So that I could open something like an *oden* shop or other small restaurant, he suggested that I start as an apprentice cook someplace. I thought it was a good idea and returned to Tokyo from Kusatsu. While there I stayed with Toku, my older sister in Fujiwara Ward, Kamishinmyô-chô, and with Inaba in Shitaya. In February this year I contacted a go-between called Hinode and told them that I didn't mind if the pay was low; I wanted to go to work in a serious business. Before long, I became the maid at a small restaurant called Yoshidaya, 538 Nii-chô, Nakano Ward, owned by Ishida Kichizô, who at the time was 42 years old.

Professor Ômiya had said that he would learn my whereabouts from my older sister, Imao Toku. On March third of this year he came to Tokyo and asked her where I was, and telephoned me, asking me to meet him at Tokyo Station. I became excited, and without thinking about how busy Yoshidaya was, I asked for time off and spent the night at Meijiya in Shinjuku with him.

This time he had his hair in a crew cut and said that he was going to spend March in Tokyo, planning to study the whole time as though he were a youth again. He added that he wouldn't sleep with me the whole time, but once his studies were over he would take me to Shiohara. I told him that I couldn't stand such a cold man, and he thought I had taken a lover and wouldn't believe me [that I hadn't]. Then he told me that he didn't have a monopoly on me and that I could do whatever I wanted, but that once I started business I would have to get serious with him. If I had a lover at that time, he told me to tell him about it. If my lover seemed good enough for me, Professor Ômiya said that he would act as a go-between for us to get married. After that, he said that he would think of me as his younger sister and would take care of me until he died.

At that time he gave me fifty yen and left. I didn't feel sexually satisfied with Professor Ômiya, but I was grateful to him for the way he was serious with me and I remember him even now for it. And when I went head over heels over Ishida, I'm sorry that I didn't think of Professor Ômiya. At any rate, I listened to what he had to say, and the idea of meeting him now and then and going with him to Shiohara sounded like it would be a good time. Once I got back to Yoshidaya I made preparations by buying a sewing box and cosmetics. It is quite a stroke of fate that I'll be using these things in prison. After going to work at Yoshidaya, little by little I got involved with the owner and we had a physical relationship. Even after we made a date for the twenty-third of April to meet and take a room to spend the night together, around that time I also met with Professor Ômiya on about four occasions.

Once, on the 29th of April, while I was staying with Ishida at a place called Tagawa in Futago Tamagawa I ran short of money, so I went and spent a night at an inn in Nagoya and the next day I met with Professor Ômiya at Nan'yôkan and he gave me 100 yen plus travel expenses. We promised to meet on the 5th of the next month. We next met on the fifth of May, while I was staying with Ishida in a place in Ogu called Masaki. I met with Professor Ômiya in Shinjuku, and we spent the night at the Meiji Inn and he gave me 120 yen. The next time was on the 15th of May, again while I was staying with Ishida at Masaki in Ogu. I went to Tokyo Station and met Professor Ômiya there. We had lunch in Ginza and took a room at a place called Yumenosato, where he gave me 50 yen. The last time was on the 18th of May, after I had killed Ishida. We met in front of a place called Mansô in Suda-chô. We had noodles at a shop in Nihonbashi and then spent a couple of hours together at an inn called Midoriya in Otsuka. After that we went our separate ways. We had sex twice that day, both at Yumenosato and at Midoriya. Whenever we met, Professor Ômiya always said he was worried about my future and encouraged me to start a serious business.

## Fourth Interrogation of Abe Sada

**Q:** Could you explain what took place between the time the defendant was hired at Yoshidaya and the time you became intimate with the owner?

**AS:** When I started to live at Yoshidaya I was guaranteed a salary of thirty yen. In actuality I received about forty yen in tips. There were five maids, all of whom lived in, and it was a serious restaurant. Ishida's wife was a good person who always worked in a good humor.

The first time I went there both Ishida and his wife asked me why I wanted to work there. I lied and told them that my husband's business had failed and that we both had to go to work.

The first time I saw the owner, Ishida Kichizô, I thought that he was a nice person in good circumstances. In a way he enraptured me, but I didn't show it openly. But after I had been there for about ten days, when we met going in opposite directions in the hallway he would put his finger into my face or would stand in the hallway and block my way on purpose, while he looked at me. Of course, this made me think that he was interested in me. While I was a geisha I had experienced a lot of banter with older men, and I saw this as just more banter. Then, sometime around the twenty-fifth of February, I took some time off and went to Inaba's house to take care of some business. I returned two nights later. On the night I got back I was in the telephone room calling a geisha and Ishida came into the room, although he didn't have any business there, and said to me, "You must be tired out from all the good things you were doing last night." I said, "You must be joking." Ishida replied, "Liar." Then he bit my earlobe and pressed his knee against my buttocks. I gave Ishida a sidelong glance and was happy that he was giving me desiring looks.

Ishida got up early in the morning to go to the fish market and the next morning, while I was going to the toilet, Ishida was walking in the hallway outside the maids' room. He grasped my hand, said, "Your hand is cold," and gave me a hug. After that, whenever I had a chance I would give him a hug or a kiss or let him play with my breasts, but we still hadn't had sex at this point.

On the evening of April third Professor Ômiya called me on the telephone. I spoke with Mrs. Ishida and got some time off and spent two nights out. I got back at about eleven in the evening. Ishida was in the hallway and pinched my arm so that it hurt very badly. During the middle of the following day Ishida and I nonchalantly went together to a room on the second floor. In the corner of the living room, he said, "That telephone call was from your husband, damn it." I didn't say anything and only laughed. But Ishida was hugging me and gave me a kiss, and we went down after that. It was sometime around the middle of April that Mrs. Ishida said, "Okayo, there is a customer in the annex." I went there with some bottles of sake and was surprised to find that the customer was Ishida himself, sitting there drinking. When I asked what the reason was for his actions, he said that he was not drinking outside anymore and so was going to have an evening drinking at his own place. He showed me an amulet from Narita Shrine that had "Total Abstinence" written on it. When I went to serve his sake he grabbed my hand and then hugged me. He started to play with my privates. It felt good and so I let him do as he pleased. In a few moments a geisha named Yaeji arrived and sang a long ballad for Ishida. Her voice was beautiful and I really fell for her. While the geisha was at the front desk we had sex for the first time. But that time, I just had him put it inside me, and we couldn't take our time.

**Q:** After a while, did you and Ishida go together to stay in hotels because everyone in the house was hearing about you?

**AS:** That's right. On the evening of April 19th this year Ishida and I shut off the light in the parlor and started to have sex when a maid found us and told on us. On the morning of the 22nd Ishida and I talked things over and decided that we would run off together to a place called Mitsuwa in Shibuya, at 80 Sonoyama-chô.

**Q:** What were the circumstances?

**AS:** Very early on the morning after we first had sex, I went to the toilet. Ishida was already there waiting for me. He suggested we do it again, so we quietly went to the annex and did it. After that, whenever we could get away from people's eyes we would quickly have sex in the annex or the second floor, and eventually we got pretty reckless. On the nineteenth we had a big party and there was a real ruckus. Ishida and I went to the parlor and turned off the light. We were playing around on the sofa and started to have intercourse when a maid said, "Oh, the light is off in the parlor," and came in to pick up a cushion. Both of us left the room in a hurry, but not before she had seen us.

The next morning, Ishida said that his wife had gotten angry with him the previous night and suggested that we go outside and have a leisurely chat. I was planning on coming back in soon after talking with Ishida. On the evening of April twenty-second I asked his wife permission to go home for just two or three nights. Then, as Ishida and I had planned, we met at eight on the morning of the twenty-third of April at Shinjuku Station and from there went to the teahouse in Shibuya called Mitsuwa.

My infatuation with Ishida was just an impromptu affair, and even after I had started working at Yoshidaya I had thought about Professor Ômiya and was looking forward to being with him. I had told Mrs. Ishida that I would want some time off from the first of June and had bought a soapbox and cosmetics to get ready for our trip to Shiohara. He was sincere but didn't understand a woman's feelings. He didn't write even once. When we met, if I asked him to write me a letter, he would say that I would be happy if I received a letter full of lies. No, he went on, even if we were separated for five years or ten years he still would not forget me, and asked that I believe him. After he said that I thought that I should be patient, but I found it easy to have an affair with someone else.

Even on the morning of April twenty-third, when I ran off with Ishida, I didn't plan to run away with him for good and thought that we could go back after talking things over. There was a party for eighty guests planned for the twenty-fifth, and on the twenty-sixth we had been asked to help at another restaurant, so his wife had asked that I return by the twenty-fifth at the latest. Ishida also knew that we were busy, and so knowing him, I think that he also planned to be back by then. It seemed certain that at Yoshidaya, after I had gathered my baggage and left, people would have thought I was running off with Ishida. But since I had asked for time off from the first of June, I thought that maybe they would think that although it would be something of a burden to everyone else, I was taking my time off early. I talked it over with Ishida and immediately returned, planning to take time off soon and send my baggage to Inaba's and my handbag to Tsutaya.

**Q:** What did the defendant do after running off with Ishida?

**AS:** At around eight o'clock on the morning of April twenty-third, we called for some food to be brought to our room at Mitsuwa in Shibuya. Ishida and I talked for a long time. He said that the previous night his wife had told him off, and that it was a maid who had told on us.

He said, "It will be difficult for you to stay much longer, so it would be best if you take your leave then. At my house, even the telephone is in hock. It won't be possible very soon, but I want for you to run a small hotel, at least, and we will be able to enjoy ourselves for a long time after that."

I then asked him, "If you have as nice a wife as you do, what do you want from a woman like me?"

"Otoku [Ishida's wife] herself had a lover once and ran away for a year. It was only because of the children that I took her back. No matter how much a man might be unfaithful, the thought of a wife cheating on a man makes me sick. I don't have any real feelings of love for her."

At this point, I would like to say something about the relationship between Ishida and his wife. Ishida's wife used to tell us all kinds of gossip about him, maybe as a warning, saying that he was a real bother when it came to women.

For example, in his pursuit of women, Ishida kept a mistress for six years. Once, when his wife went to his mistress's place, the moment she crossed the threshold she saw the two of them stark naked on top of each other. Or, when she went to a hotel to get him back, he debated whether to leave his mistress and in the process he dyed the pond at the hotel to look like blood. Pretending to be in a play, he opened a bamboo umbrella and grabbed a woman's hair while she was washing it and hit her. Maybe women loved Ishida, but he didn't have the guts to talk with other men. She said lots of other things about him, describing him as though he were a real beast.

Once when his wife was ill, I took care of her and stayed next to her bed for two or three days. She said that one shouldn't take a man like Ishida as a husband. She said that he was coldhearted and had a taste for women. Worst of all, while his wife was down sick, he had done things like call in geisha to drink with.

Even though I had heard all of this gossip about Ishida, I didn't think the worse of him. Rather, I thought that she was a fool to be saying such bad things about her husband.

When I had sex with Ishida he was cheating, but their relationship had become so difficult that he had pawned their telephone apparently without telling her. And I thought that since he had let me in on this secret, he really felt deeply toward me. Gradually, I fell more and more under his spell. He thought that I was married, and told me, "Your husband mustn't be much of a man, so let's do something about it," and I consented. When we were at Mitsuwa, he said, "Today is our wedding day, so let's drink to it." Since he still had the amulet from Narita Shrine with "Total Abstinence" hanging around his neck, I said, "But you have quit drinking." He told me, "Today I become one with you and so I'll drink, and I'm giving this to you." He gave me the amulet and said, "It'll be all right if we go to Narita Shrine sometime and apologize." I'm a bit confused as to exactly when it happened, but even when we had relaxed at Mitsuwa I was still calling him "sir." He sat informally and told me, "When we are alone together, don't call me 'sir.'" I had been thinking about him as I had told you, and from the beginning was completely taken by him. We drank and talked about those things for about two hours, and then we went to bed. For the first time in a long while we were able to make love slowly, and I thought that Ishida was pretty skilled.

In fact, of all the men I had known, Ishida was the best, the most skilled in bed. After making love and just playing around with each other, while we were still in bed we decided to make the twenty-third our anniversary and call a geisha in to celebrate. We both thought it was a good idea and quickly had a geisha called.

I'm not sure what Ishida was thinking, but I thought that if things stayed as they were we would always have more opportunities [to call a geisha]. So after the geisha had performed for about two hours it was close to mealtime, being six o'clock, and I thought it was a good time to go home. I prepared to take a bath and went to the second floor guest room. We had had a geisha and a meal, and I thought that that had been quite enough. When I went back to the bedroom I asked Ishida, who was in bed, "It's six o'clock. What shall we do?" Then I gave him a little pinch on the face. He started to pull me under the covers, and I couldn't continue to get things together. He pulled me into the futon with him and we slept together again. We stayed there until the evening of the twenty-seventh with the futon out the whole time. Day and night we made love. We had a geisha join us in the bedroom, where we drank saké and got totally absorbed in having an uproariously good time.

On the twenty-eighth we had a geisha come to Tagawa again. From the evening of the twenty-seventh until the morning of the twenty-ninth we had kept the futon out. We hardly slept all night and did every kind of erotic play that we could think of. When I told Ishida that I was very tired, he would let me sleep while we were still making love, and gently caress my body and do other kind things. He was the first man I had ever met who made a woman feel important and who would do things to make her happy, and I fell completely in love with him. It became increasingly difficult to part from him, but our money was running out and we couldn't stay as we were. I thought I would go visit Professor Ômiya and get some money from him. So I told Ishida that I would go and raise some money and since I couldn't do it in Tokyo, I would have to go to Nagoya. I asked him if he would wait for me while I went to Nagoya, where I could get at least fifty yen, and he said that he would be waiting.

What would he do if his wife, Otoku, came to get him? I asked. And because he said that he would say something to her, I thought it would be all right. I asked the woman who ran the place not to let Ishida leave before I returned. At around seven in the morning on the twenty-ninth of April I left Tagawa and went to a geisha parlor run by a friend in Yanagibashi, Asakusa, called Utanoie and visited someone named Yamako. There, I borrowed ten yen for travel expenses and then went to Nagoya. From Kiyokoma Inn, located in front of Nagoya Station, I called Professor Ômiya, but since I couldn't see him that day I stayed there under the name Kurokawa Kayo. I sent a letter special delivery to Ishida so he would know what I was doing. The next day, the thirtieth, at about one in the afternoon, I met Professor Ômiya at Nan'yôkan. We talked for about an hour and a half and I soon returned to Tokyo.

I told Professor Ômiya some real nonsense about how I had a no-good lover that I had kept secret until then, and that he had forced himself into Yoshidaya demanding a reconciliation with me. The owner of Yoshidaya had done what he could to help, I added, but this no-good said that if he received two hundred yen he would go to Talien. I used this to ask for two hundred yen from Professor Ômiya.

He said that he would give me the money, but that since he had only one hundred yen with him at the time he would have to give me the rest when he came to Tokyo, which he was planning to do five days later. He gave me the one hundred yen and travel expenses and added that if I really loved that man I should not restrain myself and go with him, but I replied that if I planned to run off with him I wouldn't be asking for money.

Actually, I could only think about Ishida, but I didn't want to get rid of Professor Ômiya. I wanted to stay with Professor Ômiya but was also very much in love with Ishida.

While on the train back to Tokyo from Nagoya at about five in the afternoon on the thirtieth, I sent Ishida a telegram from Shizuoka saying, "Will arrive at Tokyo at eight." We arrived at about eight-thirty and I called Ishida on the telephone, saying that I was tired and would like for him to meet me at Kanda Station. He got there after about thirty minutes. From the time I had left for Nagoya I had not been able to get Ishida out of my mind for even a moment. And while I was staying at Kiyokoma Inn in Nagoya I debated whether to send Ishida a letter, but decided that if he were the kind of man who would leave me just because I hadn't written him then I wouldn't find it very interesting to chase after him either. But in the end, I missed him so much that I did send him a letter. Even when I was staying alone at the inn I felt so lonely for Ishida that I went so far as to drink two bottles of beer to put me to sleep.

While I was with Professor Ômiya I couldn't help but think about Ishida and want to return to him, even though I thought there was no excuse for my behavior. If I didn't get on the three o'clock express I would have to take the six o'clock local. I felt hurried and so was discouraged when Professor Ômiya said he was going to take a bath. But since he took me to the station in a taxicab, I was able to make the three o'clock train. On the train I could hardly wait to get back and to sink my teeth into Ishida. At the same time I felt that I had gone overboard with my feelings and thought it would be better if Ishida were to go back to his home while I was away. If he did that, I would have been disappointed but I would have gotten over it. But when the train pulled into Shizuoka Station I couldn't hold back my feelings and sent Ishida a telegram. I was still thinking things over when we got to Tokyo Station and I called him on the telephone from there. Ishida was still at Tagawa, and when I remembered that he had really been patient waiting for me while I was away my own feelings instantly changed, and all I could think about was Ishida.

When I say I missed Ishida, it was fine to miss him, but then the proprietress came . . . and made things complicated. I guessed that she had come to see about our bill and so suggested that we leave. Ishida had a friend in Ogu in Arakawa and said we could go there. We took a taxi to Ogu, but we then realized that it was possible that Mitsuwa had sent a bill to Yoshidaya and they had gone to look for us at his friend's place, so the two of us went from one place to another. A place at 82–1 Ogu-chô called Masaki looked good to us, so we went in.

That was at about ten-thirty. At Masaki I asked Ishida what he had said at Tagawa so that he could leave. He said that he had told them that he had to go and meet me because I wasn't feeling well and then left. Thinking that it would cause trouble if the people at Tagawa called Yoshidaya, he then called Tagawa and told them that we might not return to Tagawa that night and that they absolutely should not call Yoshidaya, and they told us to come back. On the night of the thirtieth we had been apart for two days and a night, so once we went to bed we had sex twice. While I was away Ishida had slept the whole time at Tagawa, so he wasn't sleepy. When I got sleepy and dozed off he would tease me, so as a joke I tied Ishida's hands and feet with the cord to my sash. That delighted Ishida to no end, and when I fell asleep he would pinch me with his tied hands. In the end I wasn't able to sleep and we just fooled around together, and on the first of May from dawn to late at night we continued to drink sake and have sex without even eating anything.

During that time, Ishida said, "If I stay together with you, I'll end up a skeleton," but we didn't discuss the matter.

Because we had left Tagawa without paying our bill, we paid our bill of twenty yen and left Masaki after ten on the night of the first of May. We then took a taxi to Futago Tamagawa and went to Tagawa. On the way we picked up some sweets at Fujiya in Ginza as a gift for the people at Tagawa and arrived there at about eleven. We had a bill of eighty yen there but paid only fifty yen and a three-yen tip, and stayed there from that night until the evening of the third. But because Ishida had been a dependable patron of the proprietress when she had been a geisha in Arai-chô, we knew that she had a close relationship with Yoshidaya and we couldn't relax, thinking that [Ishida's wife] might telephone at any time. We figured that our bill would come to fifty or sixty yen, so we told her that we would be back on the sixth to pay up and left at about seven in the evening on May third.

At that time we only had about twenty yen, but by no means did we want to split up. I had promised to meet Professor Ômiya on the fifth and thought I could get some money then. I said to Ishida that we should got to Ogu again. On the way, we had a drink at a crab restaurant in Shinjuku and then at about ten that night took a taxi to Masaki. Since they didn't know Ishida there they wouldn't let us stay on credit, and we had to think about what to do. I said that in a day or two I would go somewhere and borrow the money, and he said, "Okay." On the night of the third we called in a geisha, and from then until the evening of the fifth we stayed in bed without even taking a bath, making love the whole time.

It was during that time that I cut Ishida's nails with my scissors and he said things like, "I want to cut off one of your fingers and eat it." I cut off a few of his pubic hairs and grabbed his penis, pretending that I would cut it off. He said, "Don't do something stupid," but was laughing the whole time. Whenever I teased Ishida like that, it made him happy.

I had promised to meet Professor Ômiya at Meijiya in Shinjuku at around noon on the fifth of May. He said, "We were supposed to meet at noon and I waited four hours for you. But since you didn't come, I decided to eat." He was never one to drink much, but this time he was a little drunk. Because he asked whether I was seeing a man, I told him some nonsense about being with a man that I had left, with a social welfare commissioner named Takahashi in Ogu. He said that it was very strange that I was together with a man who wanted to break things off, but that if I was having a relationship with a man it would be best if we didn't have sex that night.

I said, "Yeah," and that I didn't feel much in the mood. So he said, "Then let me give you some money," and gave me 120 yen.

Since I had been hanging out with Ishida for some time, my cheeks had become sunken. Professor Ômiya said that I looked tired and suggested that I go to Kusatsu again. Then he said that we should go to Ginza for dinner together, and we went out. While we were walking along he said that he would give me one thousand yen that year, and that I could either start a small business or quit seeing him altogether. I told him that I didn't want to stop seeing him.

We had dinner at the Olympic Restaurant in Ginza, and he kept saying that I should drink some coffee and some stomach medicine that he had, and other kind things. He seemed to want to take his time with me, but all I could think about was Ishida, so I told him that I would have to go soon. I said that I would be leaving but that I would take care of the man by the fifteenth, and we promised to meet again that day at Tokyo Station. We left without even shaking hands that day.

Somehow, I felt sorry for Professor Ômiya. I returned to Masaki at about ten at night on the fifth. Ishida was in bed, reading a magazine. I had been away only two or three hours, but Ishida had gotten really horny during that time, and that night we had sex without sleeping and I completely forgot about Professor Ômiya.

We telephoned Inaba from Masaki, and he said that the phone had been ringing off the hook with calls from Yoshidaya asking where we had gone. That didn't bother either Ishida or myself, and decided there was nothing we could do about it. We decided that if we where going to catch hell we might as well have a real good time, and so we enjoyed ourselves until the evening of the sixth of May. We knew that if we kept this up we never would want to separate, but that our money wouldn't last forever. So I decided to talk with Ishida about how to end things.

By that time I had gone out twice to get money, and Ishida seemed to be thinking that I had gotten it from a man and was a little bit down about it, and thought it was a pity that it should have to be that way. He said that after going home he would make do somehow and pay me back. We talked it over and he said that he didn't want to take any more money from me, and that even if he had to have me pay for our room he would have to go home and put things in order. So with that we decided to go back.

That night it was drizzling. I was upset that we had decided to separate for a while. When I thought that I would have to send him back to his wife, it made me sad and lonely and I couldn't stop crying. Even Ishida started to cry. It was a really pathetic scene.

I thought that if I had to send him back to his wife that night I wouldn't let her enjoy it, and so I made him come twice.

Then I paid seventy yen to cover our bill, including the tip, at Masaki. We had them buy us an umbrella and I borrowed some clogs from Masaki. Ishida wore rubber boots and we left Masaki at about ten on the night of the sixth. We made a really strange sight together.

Even after we had left Masaki the pain of leaving each other was too much, so we walked around together. We still didn't feel like leaving each other and so we hired a taxi to take us to Asakusa, where we walked around the park. We decided to have a drink together before parting and went into a crab restaurant. They chased us out when they closed at midnight. I told Ishida that since we had to part, I would go to Inaba's place and he should go home. But we still couldn't part and went on walking around together. We went to a sweets shop called Umezono and drank a soda and continued to walk around, going in the direction of Yanagibashi. At the foot of the bridge we went into a small restaurant and had another drink. We were drinking there until two in the morning, when we got chased out again when the place closed. After that we wandered all around Yanagibashi looking pretty pitiful.

No matter how late it got, I couldn't get in the mood to part, so I offered to go with him to Nakano, and Ishida said that would be nice. We hired a taxi and set off, and at about three in the morning, while we were on our way, we were scolded by a police officer.

We got in the neighborhood of Ishida's house and I said that I didn't want to go back alone since I would be scolded again. Ishida said, "In that case, you should stay at a place in Shinjuku." He saw me to a place called Sekiya in Nakano-chô.

We drank beer together for about an hour on the second floor. When it came time for Ishida to leave, we started to kiss and touch each other. He told me, "I'll tell the people at Tama Sushi what is happening, so in two or three days call there and we can meet again when it is convenient." Then he left, but came right back again. I got up and removed his kimono, and we had sex and played around until morning.

At about nine the next morning I told him that if we kept it up he never would go home, and gave him ten yen. I took a car to Shirokiya where I gave them a remembrance, and then went to Inaba's place.

### Fifth Interrogation of Abe Sada

**Q:** You and Ishida parted, but you enticed him out again and stayed at a teahouse called Masaki from May eleventh.

**AS:** That's right. After parting with Ishida at the teahouse called Sekiya at Nakano-chô in Shinjuku, at around noon on May seventh I went back to the residence of Inaba Masatake, at 51 Shitaya-chô in Shitaya Ward. All of the sudden I felt really hungry, and so I got out the sushi that I had brought as a present and ate it together with the people in the house. We also had Chinese noodles brought to the house, and drank tea. After that we all decided to go to bed. Then, all of the sudden, I thought that Ishida was probably in the thick of it with his wife, and I couldn't stand it. I shouldn't have let him go back. Thinking how I had let him go back, I began to doubt myself. I had become so attached to Ishida that no matter what, the next time we met I would do whatever it took to keep him from going back. There was nothing I could do about it, so to make myself feel better I drank three bottles of beer at the Inaba residence.

After going to bed all I could do was think of Ishida and I couldn't fall asleep. For a while I thought that I would go to Nakano and see what was happening there, but then I thought that I shouldn't be jealous and so I went downstairs and smoked cigarettes and read magazines. On the eighth I felt the same way the entire day. During the afternoon I listened to Kiyomoto's broadcast on the radio and that made me even lonelier for Ishida than before. I thought about telephoning Nakano and about going to the movies, but just stayed upstairs reading magazines and lying around. Since I knew the circumstances around Yoshidaya pretty well, all I had to do was to look at my watch and I could imagine what Ishida would be doing just then. From around this time I started to suffer from jealousy.

On the night of the eighth I couldn't sleep again. The later it got, the more irritated I felt. I went downstairs and did some sewing on my undergarments.

While I was sewing, all I could do was think about Ishida. Becoming his mistress and sharing him with somebody else didn't interest me, and so all that there was left to do was to get married. The only way we would be able to get married would be to run off together. But then I thought that Ishida wasn't the type to run off, and I even thought about killing him. Jealousy can make a person think like that, and so I thought there was nothing I could do to stop it.

On the ninth, the Inaba family went to Narita Shrine, and they asked me to watch over the house. But I couldn't even read a book. All I could do was think about Ishida.

I didn't sleep well that night, and since on the tenth they were cleaning the house, I went to a coffee shop nearby and drank beer. When I went back late in the afternoon, I found out that a jacket I had ordered on the seventh had arrived, so I went to Asakusa to look around for a sash for it. I went to a play at Meijiza, but the whole time I was thinking about Ishida.

In that play there was a scene in which there appeared a large vegetable knife, and it made me want to go buy a large knife like that and to tease Ishida with it. I went back to the Inaba residence at about eleven that evening. When Ishida and I had parted we had talked about getting together again after five or six days, but it was impossible for me to wait that long. I decided to call Tama Sushi. Mr. and Mrs. Inaba were out, so I had their son telephone Tama Sushi to see if there had been a message from Ishida. He had asked the people there to get my phone number so that he could call and said that he would telephone again and hung up. That was all, but it was enough to make me swoon.

I immediately put my things in a suitcase and left the Inabas'. After having a beer at Meijiya in Shinjuku, I stayed there for the night. On the eleventh, I realized that I was short of cash and so went to a used clothing shop in Ueno to sell a kimono and a jacket. Since only a little boy was there at that time, I left the goods and went to a movie, had a coffee laced with whiskey at Meiji Confectionery, and went back to the used clothing shop, where I sold my things for four yen. After that I bought some sushi at Sachi Sushi, and called Tama Sushi to leave the telephone number of Meijiya Inn. About three doors down from Sachi Sushi was a hardware store called Kikuhide. There, I bought a kitchen knife for ninety *sen*. I thought I would borrow some money from my older sister Teruko in Ôtsuka, but I got busy and didn't have time to go, and so returned to Meijiya.

Because I had stayed at Meijiya with Professor Ômiya, the proprietor and his wife both came out to greet me. They called me "Mrs. Ômiya" and gave me special service. Until then I had always been with Professor Ômiya and I had always acted very elegantly to please him. But that evening I was so happy that I was going to see Ishida before long that I couldn't stand it. The professor wasn't a problem, and so I smoked cigarettes and drank beer. That must have surprised the people at the inn.

While I was drinking beer at about seven-thirty that night, I got a call from Ishida. Since the phone was on the desk, the people at the inn could hear what I was saying. But I was both drunk and thrilled, and right there in front of everybody I got really mushy with Ishida on the phone. When I think about it now, it must have been a pretty ugly sight. Anyhow, Ishida was saying that I should wait until the fourteenth, but I told him that I couldn't wait that long and had to meet him soon. I said that I would go to Nakano Station and call him from there. We got cut off, and I was very disappointed. But then he called back, and that made me happy again. We decided to meet at about half-past eight on the evening of the eleventh of May, and to stay together at a teahouse.

**Q:** Why is it that you fell so deeply in love with Ishida?

**AS:** It is hard to say exactly what was so good about Ishida. But it was impossible to say anything bad about his looks, his attitude, his skill as a lover, the way he expressed his feelings. I had never met such a sexy man. He didn't seem to be forty-two years old. He had the skin and looks of someone in his twenties, twenty-seven or eight at the most. Emotionally he was a very simple man. Even little things would make him happy. He tended to show his emotions and was as innocent as a little baby. He was happy about anything that I did, and he adored me. Once, I had him put on my red under-kimono, and he wore it to sleep. While we were staying together he never once talked about his family.

Ishida was very skilled in bed. When it came to sex, he understood a woman's feelings. He was very patient and did a lot to give pleasure. Even just after having sex he could get an erection again.

Once, I tested Ishida to see if he was just using me to have a good time or if he made love to me because he was in love with me. Talking about it makes it sound rude or hateful, but on the twenty-third of April, when we ran away from Yoshidaya, I was a little dirty because of my period. But even that didn't bother Ishida, and he touched me and licked me. Around the twenty-eighth of April, while we were staying at Tagawa, I had ordered a broth with shiitake mushrooms in it. I said to him that if he really loved me he would put shiitake and sashimi on my front and eat them from there. He said that of course he would do that, and took a shiitake out of the broth with a pair of chopsticks and put it inside of me. After putting it back in the broth and putting it on the tea table and teasing me with it, he ate half of it and I ate the other half. While he was squeezing me so hard in his arms that I could hardly breathe, I told him that so he couldn't have fun with anybody else maybe I should kill him. Ishida said that if it were for me, he wouldn't mind dying. Around the fourth or fifth of May, while we were staying at Masaki, and talking about how our money wouldn't last and how we would have to part, I said that maybe I should cut off his organ. He said that even if he went home there was no way he would do it with his wife, that I was all he needed. Ishida was a great lover even when it came to making jokes. As I have been telling you, Ishida was always very kind to me, and after the first time we had sex I fell more and more in love with him. From the twenty-third of April until the seventh of May we went from one teahouse to the next for two whole weeks. After that you would usually expect to get tired of someone after all that, but with Ishida it just got better and better. Nothing has been so painful in all my life as the time between the eighth and the tenth, when I felt incredibly jealous and irritable. At about half past eight on the evening of the eleventh of May I took a taxi to Nakano Station. Ishida was there wearing a serge kimono. I was so happy to see him that I almost fell out of the taxi.

We went to a place where it was dark, where Ishida said, "I'm so in love I'll always call back if we get disconnected." I pulled the kitchen knife out of my bag and threatened him as it had been done in the play I had seen, saying, "Kichi, you wore that kimono just to please one of your favorite customers. You bastard, I'll kill you for that." Ishida was startled and drew away a little, but he seemed delighted with it all, and said that I had better put that thing away or somebody might see it, which would get us in real trouble. He said that Otoku had carped at him about money and wouldn't let him have any. But I told him that I wouldn't let him go home that night and, saying that it was all that I had, gave him twenty yen. He took it and we went to an *oden* shop near Nakano Station, where we drank three bottles of sake. Later, I heard that I had made quite a scene, kissing him and hugging him. At the time I was drunk and didn't remember any of it. After that I asked Ishida to stay the night at Masaki, and we took a taxi to Ogu, where we arrived at about nine in the evening.

**Q:** After that, what kind of things did you do at the teahouse?

**AS:** Once we got to Masaki, whether the maid or anybody else came to the room, I wouldn't let go of Ishida. I was sad and crying. During the three days that we had been apart, I knew I shouldn't be jealous when I imagined what he had done with his wife. I felt incredibly confused. I was happy and hurt at the same time; I loved Ishida and hated him. When I asked him, Ishida said that on the morning of the seventh he had been ticked off because I had left before him, and so he went to Togetsuen in Itabashi and spent a night there. The next day he called his house and had some money sent over, and then went home himself. His wife made more of a fuss than he had thought she would. He told her that he had been out with Okayo, but not because he had fallen in love with me. I was the one who pulled him around, he said, and added that no matter what he wouldn't have any more relations with Okayo, but his wife didn't believe him. She told him that at that time they didn't have two or three hundred yen to fool around with and that he should just be patient. Also, Ishida didn't have sex with his wife. He said that if she came up to him he shoved her away. I had made him wear a sash that I had bought for him while we were together, and he had on another under-sash. I thought it would be impossible for him to be home for three days and not have sex with his wife. No matter what he said, he couldn't make me feel differently. So after we had sex I pinched and hit and bit him all over his body in a really violent way. No matter what I did, he didn't get angry. He only asked me to forgive him, saying that since we had parted he had been consumed with jealousy. I didn't understand what he meant by that and thought that he was trying to cover up something with sweet words. So I dove under the covers and continued to torture him, and he said, "Don't kill me."

In any event, on the evening of the eleventh I was so happy that I felt as though I were seeing the man of my dreams for the first time in a hundred years. I could hardly speak, and went the whole night without sleeping, crying and teasing him the entire time.

And that night I pulled out the kitchen knife and held it, saying, "Hey, Kichi." When I pretended to cut him with it, he said that little knife wouldn't do the job, that I had to hold the edge against him, that it wouldn't cut to the cutting board, and that it wasn't enough to kill him. But he was happy and excited the whole time. When I put the edge against the base of his penis and said that I would make sure he wouldn't fool around with other women, he just laughed and said that I was being stupid. On the next day, the twelfth, I thought that it would be a bad idea if the maid were to see the knife, so I hid it behind a picture. On the thirteenth we had a geisha come and entertain us for about an hour and a half. From early in the evening until about eleven on the fifteenth I was out with Professor Ômiya. Except for the time when Ishida went to get a haircut on the evening of the sixteenth, until I killed him on the evening of the eighteenth, we spent the entire time with each other naked in bed.

As I had promised Professor Ômiya on the seventh of May, I met him at about five in the afternoon at Ginza. We had dinner at a small restaurant and then went to Yumenosato in Shinagawa where we played around for about an hour and a half. At that time I had sex as an obligation to him. I was thinking of Ishida the whole time and had no interest in it.

Professor Ômiya paid me fifty yen and we got in a taxi. He got out in Yotsuya and I went back to Ogu. At about eleven at night we changed our room to the "Cherry Blossom Room" and Ishida went to sleep. . . . He said, "Why is it you are always telling me about what I do?" I told him, "I didn't go out with a man." But he said, "Next time, I'll have to go buy a big knife."

I had drunk some beer with Professor Ômiya and it showed on my face, so I had another beer in our room and then went and took a bath. Ishida said that I had taken a bath because there was something suspicious that I wanted to wash off, and pinched me and pulled my hair. It pleased me that he was torturing me so. Of course I told Ishida that I had received fifty yen, and I'm sure that he knew I had gotten it from a man, so he pretended to be jealous and made a good time of it.

**Q:** Tell us about the events on the night of the sixteenth, when you almost strangled Ishida while having sex with him.

**AS:** Before that, on around the twelfth or thirteenth, when I was teasing Ishida in the way I was telling you about earlier, I had put my hands around his throat so that I was almost strangling him and he said, "I hear it is good when you squeeze the neck at the same time," so I said, "Do it to me." We then had sex and he squeezed my neck but he didn't seem to like it, and said that he sort of felt sorry for me. Then I got on top of him and squeezed his neck with my hands, but he said that it tickled and told me to stop.

On the night of the sixteenth while Ishida was embracing me, I thought it might be good to be squeezed so hard it cut off the breath. So I told him, "This time, I'll wrap a cord around your neck." I grabbed the sash cord and wound it around Ishida's neck and held both ends of it in my hands. Then I got on top of him, and while we were having sex I pulled them so that it squeezed his neck and then got loose again. At first, Ishida enjoyed it. He made sport of hitting his forehead and sticking out his tongue, and when I would squeeze the cord he joked by sticking out his tongue in the same way. While we were doing this I left the cord wrapped around his neck and we drank some sake. We then continued to have sex while I would pull the cord around his neck and we started to get the hang of it. When I pulled on the cord his hips would raise up and his penis would get larger. It felt really good. When I told this to Ishida, he said that if it was good for me he didn't mind suffering a little, and I said that I would do as I pleased. Around this time Ishida was getting pretty tired and his eyes were glazing over, and I said, "You don't like that, and since you don't like it I'm going to pull even harder." Ishida said, "I don't mind. Do whatever you want with my body."

We went on having sex while I pulled on the cord and loosened it for about two hours. At about two o'clock on the morning of the seventeenth, I was looking at what was happening down below while I gave the cord a strong pull when Ishida groaned and his penis suddenly became limp. That startled me and I took the cord off his neck. He raised up a little, put his arms around me, and said, "Okayo." He seemed to be crying. I massaged his chest.

After a short time, Ishida said, "What happened? My face is hot." His face was red, his eyes were a little swollen, and there was a mark around his neck where the cord had been. I immediately took him to the bath and washed his face, put him to bed, and continued to wipe his face and to cool him off until it got light.

While I was doing that I got bored and touched his penis. It immediately got hard, and I put it in my mouth and played with it. Ishida's face looked pretty bad. When he saw it in the mirror he said, "You are really cruel," but he didn't get angry.

On the morning of the seventeenth we had a fish stew and pickles. I fed Ishida, and drank sake by myself. Ishida didn't want to be seen and so he didn't even go downstairs to wash his face, so I did everything I could to be nice and brought him some water.

At around eleven o'clock, I was drinking sake alone and started to feel horny again and started to play with his thing. He said that maybe he couldn't do it but said that he would try, and told me to come over to him. We had sex and then fell asleep for a short time. At around one o'clock Ishida's face still hadn't gotten back to normal. I said that he couldn't go out looking like that and that I would call a doctor. When he had called a doctor while at Mitsuwa the doctor had just asked him if he had drunk something. This time, if a doctor came to see him he would tell the police, so we decided not to call one.

After we decided not to call a doctor I wiped his face and massaged his body, but it didn't do any good. Early that evening I told him that I would go to a pharmacy for some medicine and would consult the pharmacist about what could be done, and that he should wait for me. Ishida said that I should tell the pharmacist that a customer had gotten into an argument and was almost strangled and that his face was red. I went to Shiseidô in Ginza and told that to the pharmacist there. He said that the blood vessels were swollen and that there was nothing that could be done about it except to rest quietly until they went back to normal. He added that it would take a month or two for that to happen. I bought some powdered eye medicine to take the red out and went to a coffee shop called Monami, where I ate "chicken rice" and drank some coffee for dinner and bought some vegetable soup and sweets to take back to Ishida. I went back to Shiseidô and asked them to mix the eye medicine. There, they also showed me a box of thirty tablets of Calmotin [a sleeping medicine] and said not to take more than three tablets at a time. It cost seventy *sen*, which I paid. Then I went to Senbikiya and bought a watermelon for one yen, forty *sen* and returned to Masaki at around nine that night.

Ishida was asleep, but he soon got up. When he heard what the pharmacist had told me, he said he was really in trouble. Because we didn't have much money, we couldn't stay very long where we were. He looked slightly despondent and I felt sorry for him. At that time I had forgotten about the knife and I borrowed a knife from the maid so that I could cut the watermelon, and I gave some to Ishida. I also had the maid heat the soup and had him take three tablets of Calmotin with it.

But because Ishida had only eaten the fish stew since morning, he was hungry, so I had wheat noodles brought to him and I ordered some sushi rolls and ate them. Ishida said that three tablets of Calmotin wouldn't have any effect on him. I told him that he didn't need to have any more, that it would be enough.

At that time I was holding Ishida in my arms and my hand naturally started to fondle his penis. As soon as I touched him he started to get big, but he didn't have the energy to have sex.

As it got late, I ordered one serving of rice gruel and Ishida took five or six tablets of Calmotin. From around that time his eyes glazed over, but he still didn't fall asleep. He said that there was nothing we could do but to leave, and that we didn't have enough money even to pay the bill. When I said, "I don't want to leave," he told me, "If I don't leave, the maid will see me and with this face it will be extremely troublesome. In any event we will have to leave sometime. There is nothing that can be done about it, and if it is difficult for you to be at the house in Shitaya, make arrangements to go someplace else." What he said was completely heartless.

I told him, "I still don't want to leave." With that, he said, "Then I'll borrow the money to pay the bill here and we can go to a friend's place in Yugawara. After we stay two or three nights there I'll have Otoku come and we can leave after that." I told him that I didn't like that idea either. Then he said, "You don't like anything. But you knew from the very beginning that I have children and that we couldn't stick together forever."

Then he told me that if we were to be able to enjoy each other for a long time, I would have to be patient. At that time I started to think that Ishida wanted to leave me, but when I started to cry tears came to his eyes and he said nice things to me.

But the more he said nice things to me, the more irritated I got. I didn't listen to the words he was saying and could only think about how to stay together with Ishida. I probably heard only about half of what he said. But I know that he said, "My wife is nothing but a house ornament, so don't be jealous of her. We have to think of ways we can do business together. If all we do is sit around the house quarreling with each other, we just lose money."

Just then, the maid brought some chicken soup that we had ordered and I had Ishida eat it. There were still twelve or thirteen tablets of Calmotin left and I gave all of them to him with the soup. We went to bed at midnight.

Ishida wasn't feeling too well but I was feeling a bit randy, so he fondled and licked me to try to make me feel better. Then he got on top of me and we had sex.

After having sex, Ishida said that he was sleepy. He said that if I got up first I should look at his face. I told him that I would, so that he should sleep as long as he could. I put my cheek against his face and could hear him breathing deeply.

During the seventh to the tenth of May, while Ishida had gone home and I was staying at the Inabas', I had suffered a great deal thinking about Ishida and I even thought about killing him. But that feeling was soon overcome by another. That night, I had listened to him talk, saying that for his face to get better and for us eventually to stay together, we would have to separate for a time. While I looked at his face as he slept, I thought that he would embrace his wife in the same way he had embraced me, and that if we parted this time it would be at least a month or two before we could see each other again. If it had been so painful last time, I thought that there was no way I could stand it this time. So I didn't want to let him leave me.

When I suggested that we commit a double suicide or run off together, Ishida said that he wanted to go on meeting me at teahouses. When we met, Ishida had already made a success of himself and his business. There was no reason for him to think of committing suicide or of running off. I knew all too well that he would refuse my suggestions and didn't even think of double suicide or of running off as serious options. So in the end, I decided that there was nothing I could do but kill him and make him mine forever.

**Q:** Tell us how you strangled Ishida with your sash cord while he was sound asleep.

**AS:** While Ishida was dozing, I lay down next to him. His pillow was to the south, and I put his right hand under my hips and stretched out toward my back as though he was holding me. I placed his left hand next to his left shoulder and looked at his sleeping face. Now and then Ishida would open his eyes and see that I was next to him and then relax, knowing that I was there. Once, he said, "Okayo, you'll put the cord around my neck and squeeze it again while I'm sleeping, won't you." I said that I would and smiled. Then he said, "If you start to strangle me, don't stop, because it is so painful afterward." At that time I wondered if he wanted me to kill him, but after thinking it over I knew all too well that wasn't possible and that he must have been joking. After a while Ishida was sound asleep, and with my right hand I took my peach-colored sash cord that was next to his pillow and with my left hand pulled the end of it under his neck, wrapped it twice around his neck, adjusted the ends, and pulled on them. He opened his eyes and said, "Okayo." His body raised up a little and moved as though he was going to give me a hug. I put my face against his chest and cried, "Forgive me," and pulled on the ends of my sash cord with all my might. Ishida moaned once and his hands shook violently. When he went limp I released the ends of the cord. My whole body was trembling and I went over to the tea table where there was a bottle of sake. I gulped down everything that was in it and then, so that he wouldn't come back to life, I tightly tied my sash cord in a knot across his throat and wrapped the rest of it around his neck and placed the ends under his pillow. After that I went downstairs to see if there was anybody around. The clock at the desk said that it was about two in the morning.

**Q:** Explain how you cut off his penis and scrotum, carved your name in his left arm, left some writing in blood on the body and bedding, and then ran away from Masaki.

**AS:** After I had killed Ishida I felt totally at ease, as though a heavy burden had been lifted from my shoulders, and I felt a sense of clarity. I drank a bottle of beer that I had brought back with me from downstairs and then lay down next to Ishida. His throat rattled as though it was getting dry, so I wetted his tongue with my own and then wiped off his face. It didn't seem as though I was next to a corpse. He seemed dearer to me than when he was alive, and until dawn I slept next to him, played with his penis, and once I pressed it up against me. All the while I thought about things, and thought that Ishida really was dead. Because at around noon on the sixteenth I had had the maid at Masaki take a letter to Professor Ômiya, who was staying at Manseikan in Kanda, I realized that the police would investigate him. I thought I should see him and apologize.

While I was playing with Ishida's penis I thought of cutting it off and taking it with me and got out the knife that I had hidden behind the picture frame. I put the knife against the base of his penis, but it was hard to cut off and it took a long time. Once the knife slipped and cut his thigh while I was doing that. After that I put the knife against the base of his scrotum so that I could cut off his testicles, but that was hard to cut too, and I think I left some of the scrotum behind.

I placed his penis and testicles on a piece of tissue, but there was a lot of blood coming out of the wound and I pressed the tissue against it. Then I put some of the blood that was coming out on my right index finger and wiped it on my undergarments, sleeves, and collar. After that, I wrote, "Sada, Kichi together," on Ishida's left thigh in blood, and then wrote the same on the bedding.

Next, I carved the character for my name in him and then washed my hands in the basin at the window. I then tore off the cover of the magazine *Fuji* that was next to his pillow and wrapped his penis and testicles in it. I took Ishida's under-kimono that was in the clothes basket and put it on so that it was against the skin on my stomach, and then put his wrapped-up penis inside of it so that it pressed against me. After that I put on his underpants and then put my kimono on over it and closed my sash. Once I had gotten dressed and ready to go, I cleaned up the room. I wiped the blood off the knife and wrapped everything that was soiled in newspaper, threw it down the toilet, and washed it down with the water in the wash bucket. That still didn't get everything, so I got a bucket of water from downstairs and cleaned up the toilet with it. While I was doing that in the toilet I had turned the wash bucket upside down and dropped the lid down the toilet. That finished all my preparations. I wrapped the knife in newspaper and took it with me, kissed Ishida good-bye, covered the body with a blanket and a quilt, wiped his face, and placed a magazine next to his pillow so that it looked as though he was reading. At eight in the morning I went downstairs and told the maid that I was going out to buy some sweets and that she shouldn't get Ishida up until around noon. Then I called the taxi company that Masaki usually patronized. Before long a taxi came and I escaped in it.

**Q:** Why did you cut off Ishida's penis and scrotum?

**AS:** They were the dearest and most important part of him. His wife would have touched it when she washed the body, and I didn't want anybody else touching it. In any event, I had to flee from that place, but if I had Ishida's penis I thought I wouldn't get lonely. It would be as though he were with me. I wrote "Sada, Kichi together" on his thigh and on the bedding because after I had killed him it seemed that he had become a part of myself and I felt relieved. So when I wrote "Sada, Kichi together" twice on him, it meant that he was completely a part of me.

**Q:** Why did you carve the character for your name in his left arm?

**AS:** I carved my name in him because I wanted to put myself onto his body.

**Q:** Why did you put on his under-kimono and underpants?

**AS:** His under-kimono and underpants had his manly smell, and by putting them on my own body it was as though through Ishida's smell I was with him in person.

### Sixth Interrogation of Abe Sada

**Q:** While you were at Masaki on the night of the sixteenth of May of this year, when you gave all that Calmotin to Ishida, didn't you hope he would die from it?

**AS:** No, I didn't think he would die even if he were to take the whole thirty tablets. If it was something that could kill a person, they wouldn't be selling it at a pharmacy. I knew from reading in a newspaper that to die from Calmotin a person would have to take over eight hundred tablets.

**Q:** We have heard that while you were at Masaki you hid Ishida's clothes. Why did you do that?

**AS:** I didn't think that he would leave without telling me, but I was so crazy about him that I hid his clothes to keep him from leaving. Besides, it was a joke.

**Q:** Wasn't Ishida wanting to go home?

**AS:** Of course, I don't really know what he was thinking, but he didn't act that way around me.

If he really had wanted to leave he had any number of opportunities to do so. I was away on the fifteenth, and on the sixteenth I gave him five yen to go to the barber. I might have hidden his clothes, but if he had looked for them he would have found them. That was no reason for him not to leave. He talked about going home for the first time on the evening of the seventeenth.

**Q:** We were told that you made numerous telephone calls while you were staying at Masaki from May eleventh. Why?

**AS:** On the twelfth I called three places: Kuroda Hana, who was staying at the Inabas'; Tama Sushi in Nakano; and Meijiya in Shinjuku. I called Kurota to say that I had left without calling but that I would be back by the fifteenth. I called Tama Sushi to get the telephone number of Meijiya. And I called Meijiya to explain why I had left without paying my bill. On the sixteenth I called Kurota because it seemed like I might be staying a long time at Masaki and I was afraid that things might not end so well, so I did it on purpose so that they could hear me at the desk and I could smooth things over. Also, I wanted to find out if there had been any calls from Yoshidaya to Kurokawa.

Just for the record, I would like to say that at that time I was not making calls because I was planning to kill Ishida and wanted to think of ways to fool people after the killing. Had I been planning to kill Ishida at that time, I wouldn't have been making phone calls all over the place.

**Q:** What did the letter say that you sent to Ômiya Gorô on the fifteenth of May?

**AS:** I asked him to give fifty yen to the person who brought him the letter.

**Q:** What did you plan to do with the money once you got it?

**AS:** At the time I only had about forty-five yen, and I knew that it wouldn't be enough to pay the bill. I thought it would be possible to have a good time with Ishida if I knew we had some money, so I asked Professor Ômiya to give me some. But the maid came back and said that he was out at a party and left the letter for him. Even so, I hadn't been counting on getting the money I asked for in the letter and just let it go at that. I hadn't thought about using it to pay for my escape after killing Ishida. And when I think about it now, I know that if I hadn't sent this letter to Professor Ômiya, everyone wouldn't be looking at me now as though I am insane, so I very much regret having sent it.

**Q:** Why is that?

**AS:** In any event I had no choice but to kill Ishida, but until I actually killed him, I didn't think too much about my behavior. But after I killed Ishida and realized what I had done, I felt there was no way I could go on living. I thought that I had to die and didn't fear dying in the least. But when I thought of Professor Ômiya and that the letter I had sent on the previous day didn't get to him, I realized that just because of that letter, even though he might not be called forward as a witness, the police would be sure to investigate him and it would all be quite an inconvenience. I had done a terrible thing for which there was no excuse. If I hadn't thought about Professor Ômiya in that way, I am certain that I would have hanged myself on the clothes-drying rack on the second floor of Masaki. But when I thought of Professor Ômiya I felt like going out. Because I knew I would miss Ishida, I decided to put on his under-kimono, cut off his penis, and do other insane things.

Now, I find it extremely regrettable that because of all this everybody thinks I am a pervert.

**Q:** Tell us about the escape route you took after the crime.

**AS:** When I left Masaki at about eight in the morning on the eighteenth of May I had about fifty yen on me. I took a taxi to the corner of Isetan in Shinjuku, then got another at Shinjuku Station and went to Matsuzakaya in Ueno. At about nine o'clock in the morning I went to Ono's used clothing shop. There, I sold a white kimono and a quail-patterned gray jacket for thirteen yen, fifty *sen*, and bought an octopus-patterned gray kimono for five yen. I changed clothes there and had a boy go buy me a cotton wrapping cloth, in which I wrapped the knife that I had wrapped in newspaper. After leaving that store I went to a footwear shop on the street in front of Matsuzakaya, and there I bought a pair of clogs made of paulownia wood for one yen, forty *sen* and left the clogs that I had been wearing at that shop. Thanks to the people at the footwear shop, I was able to use the telephone next door. I called the maid at Masaki and said that I would be back at about noon and asked her to let Ishida sleep until I got back. She replied that she understood. That told me that they still had not discovered his body, and I relaxed. After that I telephoned Professor Ômiya at Man'yokan in Kanda. He was just about to go out, and I asked him to meet me for only five or ten minutes; we agreed to meet in front of Bansô Fruitery and I took a taxi there. I met with him, and we took a taxi together to Kimuraya Coffee Shop in Nihonbashi. We had coffee and toast and chatted for a while. When I looked at Professor Ômiya tears came to my eyes and I couldn't stop crying. The shop was noisy and I couldn't tell him very much in detail, but I apologized for having sent him such a rude letter. After that I ate a bowl of tempura on rice in a noodle shop on Shôwa Avenue. When I told Professor Ômiya that by all means I wanted an hour or so of his time, he suggested that we go to Yumenosato, but I said that we should go someplace we hadn't been before. We then took a taxi in the direction of Ôtsuka and went to Midoriya Inn, close to the trolley stop.

Once we got to Midoriya Inn, all I could was cry, but I couldn't tell him that I had killed Ishida. I told him that no matter what came to pass, I wanted him to feel nothing more than that he had bought me with money. While crying the whole time, I told him repeatedly that there was no way I could apologize to him but that I didn't want him to hate me. But I could see that he didn't understand my feelings and seemed to think that I was apologizing for having a lover. He said that he knew about that, and there was nothing to apologize for at this point. During the previous few days he had been looking for an apartment, he said, but couldn't find anyplace suitable. As of that day he had resigned from his position as head of his school, and added that he wanted to go on seeing me since I had given him the most pleasure in life until then.

When I realized how forgiving he had been with me and that even at this time he didn't know anything, I only cried all the more. He said that since we hadn't seen each other for a long time it would comfort him if we went to bed together. The maid put out the bedding, and I took off the men's underclothes I had on so that he wouldn't see them. Then, I put the penis wrapped in paper under the futon and went to bed with Professor Ōmiya.

At that time, he said that he was sorry to bring up such a thing, but that I smelled odd. I wasn't at all in the mood and had sex with him only out of a feeling of obligation. Afterward, while Professor Ōmiya was taking a bath, I dressed as I had before, paid [for the room with] the ten yen that he had given me, and at about one o'clock that afternoon we left Midoriya. We got a taxi and went in it to Shinjuku. While on the way there, Professor Ōmiya suggested that we meet again on the twenty-fifth at Tokyo Station. He got out at Ikizaka in Koishikawa, and I left the taxi at Shinjuku 6-*chōme*.

At first, after I had seen Professor Ōmiya, I had been thinking of dying, but after I had left him I just had vague thoughts that in any case I would have to die. Because I had Ishida's penis on me, it was hard for me to be at ease. I felt that I wanted to spend more time with Ishida, that I wanted to do something fun in his memory, so that I would stay for a while in Tokyo and then go to Osaka.

Because the summer kimono that I was wearing at the time was not quite in season yet and the clogs that I had just bought were hurting my feet, I went to Azumaya, a used clothing shop on Shinbashi Nakadōri, where I bought an unlined serge kimono and Nagoya sash for twelve yen, twenty *sen*, changed my clothes, and had the kimono that I had taken off wrapped in paper. At a footwear shop close by I bought a pair of leather sandals for two yen, eighty *sen*, put them on, had my clogs put in a cardboard box, and left the store. Then, at another store close by I bought a pair of glasses for two yen, fifty *sen*, and put them on so that people wouldn't recognize me. At about four o'clock that afternoon I went to a sushi shop at Shinbashi 6-*chōme* and ordered about fifty *sen* worth of sushi and ate a little. The rest I had wrapped up and started to walk around. I went to Columbin, a coffee shop in Ginza, and from there started to walk down Shōwa Avenue. I then got a taxi and went to the park in Hama-chō, where I sat on a bench and thought about things for about an hour. No matter how much I thought, I could only come to the same conclusion. If I had to die, I thought that I would throw myself into the bottom of a valley off Mount Ikoma in Osaka and die that way. I had heard about Mount Mihara and other places but didn't know how to get there. But I had been to Mount Ikoma and knew the way and so decided that I would die there. In any event, I didn't want to die soon. I wasn't brave enough to do it and felt that I wanted to think more about Ishida. So I decided to spend that night in Tokyo and had a cup of coffee at a coffee shop in front of the park. There, I read the newspaper and didn't see anything unusual, so I thought that I was still safe. At about seven o'clock that evening I went to a place called Uenoya, where I had stayed before. As soon as I got there I took a bath and I took my treasure wrapped in paper with me to the bath. I slept alone in a room on the second floor, but I spread out the paper package on top of the futon and stared at Ishida's penis and testicles. For a few moments I put his penis in my mouth and pressed it against me. While thinking about things I cried a little and didn't sleep very well.

Early the next morning I went to the desk and got the newspaper. It had a picture of me when I was young and told about my life in Ogu. I thought that if the people at the inn saw the newspaper I would be in trouble, so I hid it under the futon. Later, at around ten o'clock, I paid the bill, and because it was raining I borrowed some clogs and an umbrella and went out.

Even if I were to go to Osaka, it would still be raining. Because I didn't look good, I thought I would take the night train and so went to Asakusa. There, I went to Shôchikukan and watched a film starring Onatsu Seijûrô. Around two o'clock in the afternoon I took a blue bus to Ginza, thinking I would have something to eat. There, I walked around for some time but quit doing that, thinking it didn't look too good. Then I took a taxi to Shinagawa Station and at about four o'clock that afternoon I bought a third-class ticket for Osaka. Because the train didn't leave until six-nineteen, I still had about two hours, so I bought five newspapers at a station shop, planning to read them on the train. I put them together with my luggage and went to a coffee shop in front of the station, and drank a bottle of sake. Because I drank it on an empty stomach, I soon got drunk and sleepy. At around five in the afternoon I went to a place called Shinagawa Inn, which was close to the station, where I took a bath, drank a bottle of beer, and had a masseuse called for me.

While the masseuse was giving me a massage I started to fall asleep and dreamed about Ishida and spoke in my sleep. The masseuse heard me say something, but nothing came of it.

After the masseuse left, I ate dinner and looked at the evening edition of a newspaper. Until then I didn't think that the whole affair amounted to much, but the paper compared me to Takahashi Oden and wrote it up as though it had been a major incident. The article said that police had been put on alert to look for me at every railway station. Because things had gotten out of hand, I knew that I couldn't go on living and that there was no way I could go to Osaka. So I decided that it was a pity, but I had to die in that inn, and had the clerk in the inn get a refund for my ticket. If I were to stay in that inn the police would come looking for me and I would be arrested that night, so I wanted to die as soon as I could. But because my feet reached the floor from the lintel in the room it was too low for me to hang myself there. I stayed up until one that morning knowing that I would be arrested. But that evening the police never came around, so thinking I would die there, in the morning I paid the maid what I owed and had myself moved to another room.

If I hanged myself in that room, my feet would hang out over the garden so I would be sure to die. I borrowed some stationery and a fountain pen from the inn and wrote suicide notes addressed to Professor Ômiya, Kurokawa, and Ishida, even though he was dead. Planning to die that night, I ordered three bottles of beer and went to sleep after drinking them. At about four o'clock that afternoon a policeman came to my room. I told him that I am Abe Sada and he arrested me.

**Q:** Do you remember any of these articles?

**AS:** [She is obviously pointing out numbered articles.]

Number one is my sash cord, the one I used in Masaki to strangle Ishida.

Numbers two and three are tissue paper that I was using at Masaki. If it was in the "Cherry Blossom Room," it is probably some paper that I forgot to clean up.

Number four is Ishida's pubic hair. I cut it off when I cut off his genitals, and probably left it in the room.

Number five is a magazine I had bought for me at Masaki and that I read while I was there. It is the one that I left next to Ishida's pillow after I killed him.

Number six is the eye medicine that I bought for Ishida at Shiseidô after I had choked him and his face had turned red.

Numbers seven and nine are jackets that Ishida had used, having borrowed at Masaki. Because he was naked when I killed him, I put them on his body after I had killed him.

Number eight is a sheet that was over Ishida on which I had written "Sada, Kichi together."

Number ten is the Japanese playing cards we had borrowed at Masaki. Ishida and I had played cards with them.

Number eleven is part of a newspaper I had borrowed at Masaki and had put in the "Cherry Blossom Room." I had used one or two sheets of it to wrap dirty things and throw them down the toilet.

As for number twelve, I do not remember ever using this piece of gauze.

Numbers thirteen through fifteen are dirty things that I had thrown down the toilet, so if they are things that came out of the toilet at Masaki they are things that I had thrown out.

Number sixteen is the lid to the wash bucket that I dropped down the toilet while I was washing things.

I am certain that numbers seventeen and eighteen are the penis and testicles that I cut off Ishida and carried with me until the time of my arrest.

Number nineteen is the butcher knife that I bought and that I used when I cut off Ishida's genitals and carved my name in his arm.

Numbers twenty, twenty-one, and twenty-two are Ishida's clothes.

[Number twenty-three is not mentioned in the transcript.]

Number twenty-four is the summer kimono that I bought at Ono's used clothing shop and that I wore for a short time while I saw Professor Ômiya.

Number twenty-five is the serge summer kimono that I bought at Azumaya in Shinbashi and that I wore as far as Shinagawakan.

Number twenty-six is the Nagoya sash and number twenty-seven is the sash cord that I wore to the same place.

Number twenty-eight is the eyeglasses that I bought in Shinbashi and wore to Shinagawakan.

Number twenty-nine is the newspapers that I bought at Shinagawa Station.

**Q:** According to the suicide note that you wrote to Ishida, at the time you strangled Ishida on the night of the sixteenth you said that you had intended to kill him. Is that right?

**AS:** When I had choked him on the previous night I didn't decide for certain that I wanted to kill him, but when we were having sex while I was choking him I really adored him. I adored him so much that I wanted to kill him, so I pulled really hard on the cord. But when I saw how painful it was for him, I let go.

**Q:** What do you think about this incident?

**AS:** While I was at Metropolitan Police Headquarters I still felt at peace and happy. Whenever I talked about Ishida I felt happy, and at night I wanted to go to sleep so that I could dream about him. When I arrived at the prison and I saw Ishida in my dreams I still adored him and felt happy, but little by little my feelings have changed, and now I think it would have been better not to have done that. I regret having done something so very stupid.

For certain, I shouldn't have killed him, but once the deed was done, I don't think I should have cut off his penis and put on his clothes. The thing I regret most is that if I hadn't done that, I would be happy with Professor Ômiya right now. When I think that I was foolish to be with Ishida when I had Professor Ômiya, I feel very sorry for Ishida. Now, I am doing everything in my power to forget Ishida. As a result, I don't want to talk or even to think about this incident. Because I don't want a public hearing or trial where I will be asked a lot of things in front of many people, I hope that it will be possible for justice to be served just with a consultation among the judges. I will not object to anything that the court decides. Because of this I'm not sure I need a lawyer. My greatest regret is that people will misunderstand me and think I'm a lunatic, and because I want someone to argue my side, I think that perhaps I do need a lawyer. Finally, I would like to be allowed to say a few words on this point. With regard to the question of my being a sexual pervert, I think that if you investigate my past you will find a clear answer. In the past I have had sex with men to the point that

I almost forget about myself. But I never do forget myself and always keep time and place clearly in mind.

For instance, I had a good time while I was sleeping with Nakagawa Asajirô. But I knew that he was ugly and didn't cut a good figure. When he left me while I was asleep after we had had sex, it didn't bother me to imagine that he was then in his wife's arms. A man named Yagi Kôjirô, whom I met while I was working as a prostitute in Osaka, was good-looking and seemed quick to part with his money. We had real crushes on each other, but when I realized that he was just putting on a show and didn't really have any money, I didn't think twice about leaving him.

Until now, I have always been given over to my rational side, to the point where it has really surprised some men. It was only with Ishida that I let things get out of control. He didn't really have the goods, but he had a suave side that swallowed me up body and soul.

People have made an incredible fuss since they found out what I did, but there are lots of women who fall hopelessly in love with a man. Even if a wife doesn't like sashimi, if her husband likes it she will naturally start to like it, too. And there are lots of wives who sleep with their husband's pillow in their arms while he is away.

For some women the smell of the quilted kimono of the man they love might make them feel ill. But there are lots of women who think that the tea left behind by the man they love or the food that he has already had in his mouth are delicious.

Just as when men redeem a geisha so that they can keep her all to themselves, there are women who are so enraptured with a man that they think of doing what I did. They just don't act it out. There are all kinds of women. There are women who decide that it just is not possible for love to be the standard by which they measure men, and so they measure them by their material possessions. But there are women who just can't stop loving a man. So people need to understand that when an incident like mine happens, it isn't just because a woman is crazy about sex.

The End

## Introduction

1. "Lizzie Borden took an ax, and gave her mother forty whacks. / When she saw what she had done, she gave her father forty-one."

2. For a macroscopic study that describes the intersection of science, politics, and changing social values in female-male sexuality in modern Japan, see the groundbreaking work by Sabine Frühstück, *Colonizing Sex: Sexology and Social Control in Modern Japan* (Berkeley: University of California Press, 2003).

3. An early exception was the psychoanalyst Takahashi Tetsu, who had a number of Edo-period primary sources republished and had penned works relevant to the history of sexuality. See his *Tokugawa seiten taikan* [Sexual classics of the Tokugawa period], 2 vols.

(Tokyo: Nihon Seishinbunseki Gakkai & Nihon Seikatsu Shinrigakkai, 1953), and *Nihon seiten taikan* [Sexual classics of Japan], 2 vols. (Tokyo: Nihon Seikatsu Shinrigakkai, 1954); the former reprints eleven premodern texts and the latter, ten. All are primarily manuals of sexual techniques. He also published a study of historical and contemporary sexual customs, including a loose survey of practices in different parts of the country; see Takahashi Tetsu, *Kôkei hikô* (Tokyo: Daiichi Shuppansha, 1952) and the three-volume *Kôza Nihon fûzoku shi, sei fûzoku* [Studies on the history of Japanese customs, sexual customs] (Tokyo: Yûzankaku, 1959). An annotated bibliography of erotic books and books containing explicitly erotic passages appeared in the next decade; see Enbon Kenkyû Kankôkai, ed., *Nihon enbon daishûsei* [Collected Japanese erotica] (Tokyo: Uozumi Shoten, 1965). This was followed by books such as Higuchi Kiyoyuki, *Edo sei fûzoku yawa* [A night's talk on the sexual customs of the Edo period] (Tokyo: Haga Shoten, 1976), which raised issues including both male and female prostitution and exhibitionism during this period. During the 1980s, books on the history of sexuality in Japan started to appear from major publishing houses, yet the subject remained the purview of amateur historians and professional writers. See, for example, Fukuda Kazuhiko's *Edo no seiaigaku* [The sexology of the Edo period] (Tokyo: Kawade Shobô, 1988). With this book, Fukuda and Kawade challenged the standing taboo on the publication of explicit images of genitalia. Fukuda followed this small volume with large-size books that included images of genitalia. Fûzoku Genten Kenkyûkai, ed., *Nihon no seigaku kotohajime* [The beginning of Japanese sexology] (Tokyo: Kawade Shobô, 1989), although published a year later, reverted to the police censorship–pleasing insertion of blank white spaces over the genitalia in the illustrations. Also see Teruoka Yasutaka, *Nihonjin no ai to sei* [Love and sex of the Japanese people] (Tokyo: Iwanami Shoten, 1989) and Nakae Katsumi, *Sei no Nihon shi* [Sex in Japanese history] (Tokyo: Kawade Shobô, 1995) for two scholarly essays on the history of sex in Japan. Most of these works focus on sexual practices depicted in various texts, problems surrounding love suicides, women and sexual customs of the pleasure quarters, the women of the *shogun* and various *daimyo*, and similar topics. Since the mid-1990s, professional historians of Japan, both Japanese and foreign, have published a growing number of works on the history of sex and sexuality in Japan. In addition to the diverse range of sources that professionally trained historians examine, a major shift between these earlier works and those by more recent scholars such as Narita Ryûichi, Greg Pflugfelder, Furukawa Makoto, Sabine Frühstück, Kawamura Kunimitsu, Sheldon Garon, Saitô Hikaru, Gaye Rowley, Timon Screech, and Akagawa Manabu, among others, is a growing emphasis on integrating the history of sexuality into parallel developments in the historical discourse. Topics they have explored include changes in gender boundaries, the emergence of virginity as an issue at the time of marriage, same-sex love and eroticism, the introduction of ideas that masturbation was somehow harmful, issues concerning the state and prostitution, sexuality as expressed in visual images, and the cultural history of sex among various groups and classes.

4. At a research seminar held at an Ivy League university in 2001, most of the twelve or fifteen middle-aged Japanese historians in the room snickered when I explained that I was researching Abe Sada from the perspective of cultural history. On another occasion, a leading American historian of Japan suggested that it would be better were Abe Sada to disappear completely from historical memory, implying that I should drop the project.

5. That group, which called itself the Sôtai Kenkyû Kai in homage to Ogura Seizaburô's Sôtaikai, included Inoue Shôichi, Furukawa Makoto, Sabine Frühstück, Saitô Hikaru, Akagawa Manabu, and myself, among others.

6. *Sôtaikai kenkyû hôkoku*, Vol. 1 (Tokyo: Ginza Shokan, 1986), 42–74.

7. Gregory M. Pflugfelder, *Cartographies of Desire: Male-Male Sexuality in Japanese Discourse, 1600–1950* (Berkeley: University of California Press, 1999), 8–9. Of course, it is possible to approach these women and their practices only through the discourse of documentary evidence. In the following chapters I examine some of the issues inherent in the interrogation and police investigation documents of Abe Sada.

8. Exceptions include Wada Yoshiko, "Yûjo nikki" [The diary of a prostitute] in Tanikawa Ken'ichi, ed., *Kindai minshû no kiroku, 3, shôfu* [Records of modern commoners, vol. 3., prostitutes] (Tokyo: Shinjinbutsu Ôrai Sha, 1971), 204–238; and Masuda Sayo, *Autobiography of a Geisha*, trans. G. G. Rowley (New York: Columbia University Press, 2003). Mineko Isasaki with Rande Brown's *Geisha, A Life* (New York: Atria, 2002) is an insightful story of the life of a *geisha* in contemporary Kyoto. This book is especially useful for its explanation of relationships between the geisha, their managers, and the rest of the Kyoto environment. There are a number of other significant works, mostly by more affluent Japanese women, that open a window on their lives. Two that have been translated into English are Yamakawa Kikue, *Women of the Mito Domain: Recollections of Samurai Family Life*, trans. Kate Wildman Nakai (Tokyo: Tokyo University Press, 1992) and Nakano Makiko, *Makiko's Diary: A Merchant Wife in 1910 Kyoto*, trans. Kazuko Smith (Stanford: Stanford University Press, 1995). The folklorist Yanagita Kunio urged Yamakawa to write her book in 1943, based on a combination of oral and documentary sources, primarily about her mother's generation of women. Despite his broad interests, Yanagita shunned references to sexual topics; Yamakawa discusses sexuality primarily to condemn the moral hierarchy of the samurai class. Similarly, Nakano's diary tells much about many facets of quotidian life in early twentieth-century Kyoto—except sex. Its absence reflects the moral values of wealthy townspeople and former samurai; as in "proper" American society at the same time, issues of sex tended to fall from discourse, both oral and written. Peasant women, however, discussed it openly. See Robert J. Smith and Ella Lurie Wiswell, *The Women of Sue Mura* (Chicago: University of Chicago Press, 1982), especially 61–110.

9. Alternative strategies for interpretation are compelling. A psychoanalytical approach to Abe Sada is easy to imagine. The concepts of *jouissance*, lack, castration, love, phallus, desire for unattainable unity, the absence of natural, innate characteristics of feminine and masculine: all are central both to the story of Abe Sada and to Lacanian analysis. An example of Lacanian analysis used on Japanese literary texts that deal with issues in many respects parallel to those in the story of Abe Sada can be found in Nina Cornyetz, *Dangerous Women, Deadly Words: Phallic Fantasy and Modernity in Three Japanese Writers* (Stanford: Stanford University Press, 1999). Cornyetz uses a Lacanian perspective to establish the "dangerous woman," discussed below, as a locus of *jouissance*. However, from a historical perspective I must disagree with some facets of her argument, such as her depiction of a "grossly misogynist, Neo-Confucian–rooted homosociality that dominated the Edo period" (11). This might have been true for the samurai class, as I argue below, yet was hardly the case for most commoners: the farmers, merchants, craftspeople, and others who made up most of the population. For an introduction to the ideas of Jacques Lacan, see Madan Sarup, *Jacques Lacan* (Toronto: University of Toronto Press, 1992) and Elizabeth Wright, ed., *Feminism and Psychoanalysis: A Critical Dictionary* (Oxford: Blackwell, 1992). The ideas of Lacan, Michel Foucault, Joan Scott, and Natalie Davis, among others, are present throughout this work, especially with regard to the themes in the life of Abe Sada on which it is focused.

10. These works include Natalie Davis's *The Return of Martin Guerre* (Cambridge: Harvard University Press, 1983), Carlo Ginzburg's *The Cheese and the Worms* (New York: Penguin, 1982), and Simon Schama's *Dead Certainties* (New York: Knopf, 1991).

11. For this meaning of "gender" see the entry in the second edition of the *Oxford English Dictionary*. This is not to obviate the need to be conscious of how perceived differences between the sexes relate to the distribution of power. It is, rather, to raise the possibility that "gender" can be used with very broad limits. See Joan Scott, *Gender and the Politics of History*, rev. ed. (New York: Columbia University Press, 1999), 42. A survey of ideas concerning gender appears in Donna J. Haraway, "'Gender' for a Marxist Dictionary: The Sexual Politics of a Word," in *Simians, Cyborgs, and Women* (New York: Routledge, 1991), 127–148.

12. In addition to the work by Joan Scott cited above, two key studies that make this observation are Judith Butler, *Gender Trouble: Feminism and the Subversion of Identity* (London: Routledge, 1990) and Denise Riley, "*Am I that Name?": Feminism and the Category of "Women" in History* (Minneapolis: University of Minnesota Press, 1988).

13. Georges Bataille extends this argument into the realm of the sexual itself, writing, "Erotic experience will commit us to silence." See Georges Bataille, *Erotism: Death & Sensuality* (San Francisco: City Lights, 1986), 252.

14. Oda Makoto, *Ichi go no jiten: sei* [A single-term dictionary: Sex] (Tokyo: Sanseidô, 1996), 5–6.

15. Both were coined by the specialist in military hygiene and writer Mori Rintarô, better known by his pen name, Mori Ôgai. See ibid., 39, 42.

16. See Cynthia Eagle Russett, *Sexual Science: The Victorian Construction of Womanhood* (Cambridge: Harvard University Press, 1989), especially 54–57, for the scientific depiction of women as closer to savages and children than were men.

## Prologue: A Murder Grips the Nation

1. Numerous writers describe the humorous responses to this incident. See, for examples, Setouchi Jakuchô, "Kaisetsu," in Nanakita Kazuto, ed., *Abe Sada densetsu* [The legend of Abe Sada] (Tokyo: Chikuma Bunko, 1998), 296; Horinouchi Masakazu, *Abe Sada shô den* [The true biography of Abe Sada] (Tokyo: Jôhô Sentaa Shuppan Kyoku, 1998), 186.

2. The first reads "Sada Kichi *futari kiri*"; literally, this means "Sada and Kichi, cut two persons" but is better translated "all alone." On his thigh she had written, "Sada Kichi *futari*," literally, "Sada, Kichi, two persons."

3. A discussion of the "dangerous woman" in contemporary literary discourse appears in Nina Cornyetz, *Dangerous Women, Deadly Words: Phallic Fantasy and Modernity in Three Japanese Writers* (Stanford: Stanford University Press, 1999), especially 9–12.

4. An excellent study of the early history of "evil women" and their penchant for expressing their sexuality independently is Tanaka Takako, "*Akujo" ron* [An essay on "evil women"] (Tokyo: Kinokunia, 1992). Discussions of seventeen women from the Edo and Meiji periods, most of whose fame was reinforced by their treatment in theatrical and other literary works, can be found in Watatani Kiyoshi, *Kinsei akujo kibun* [Tales of evil women from the early modern period] (Tokyo: Seiabô, 1979). A brief discussion on "evil women" of the early modern period appears in Seki Tamiko, *Edo kôki no josei tachi* [Women of the late Edo period] (Tokyo: Aki Shobô, 1980), 55–84. A study of Abe Sada in the context of other "evil women" of the twentieth century appears in Koike Mariko, *Akujo to yobareta onna tachi* [Women who have been called "evil women"] (Tokyo: Shufu to Seikatsu Sha, 1982), 12–38. A similar study of Abe, this time in the context of other "poisonous women," appears in Asakura Kyôji, *Dokufu den* [Biographies of poisonous women] (Tokyo: Heibonsha, 1999), 247–381, although the author does not develop a theoretical basis for the "poisonous woman" in this work. The previously cited book by Nina Cornyetz is an important discussion of the "dangerous woman" in modern literary discourse. Also see Christine Marran, "'Poison woman': Takahashi Oden and the Spectacle of Female Deviancy in Early Meiji," in *US–Japan Women's Journal* (English supplement) 9 (1995): 93–110.

5. Sheldon Garon, "The World's Oldest Debate?: Regulating Prostitution and Illicit Sexuality," in *Molding Japanese Minds: The State in Everyday Life* (Princeton: Princeton University Press, 1997), 95. This essay provides an excellent short history of the evolution of

prostitution in modern Japan. Also see Fujime Yuki, "The Licensed Prostitution System and the Prostitution Abolition Movement in Modern Japan," *Positions* 5 (1997): 135–170. In Japanese, see Fujime Yuki, *Sei no rekishi gaku: kôshô seido dataizai taisei kara baishium bôshi hô yûsei hogo hô taisei e* [The history of sex: From the system of legal prostitution and criminalized abortion to the system of the law forbidding prostitution and the Eugenics Protection Law] (Tokyo: Fuji Shuppan, 1999), 89–115.

## 1. An Unremarkable Family History

1. Ogura Seizaburô, ed., "Abe Sada no chôsho," in Dai 2 Kumiai Sôtai kai, ed., *Sôtaikai kenkyû hôkoku*, vol. 1 (Tokyo: Ginza Shokan, 1986), 61.

## 2. Early Childhood

1. The term "Low City" appears in Edward Seidensticker, *Low City, High City: Tokyo from Edo to the Earthquake* (Rutland, Vt.: Tuttle, 1984). Seidensticker quotes the poet Takahama Kyoshi's description of the Marunouchi district as home to foxes and badgers; see 76.

2. See, for example, Mori Arinori, "On Wives and Concubines, Part Two," in *Meiroku Zasshi: Journal of the Japanese Enlightenment*, trans. William R. Braisted (Cambridge: Harvard University Press, 1976), 143–145.

3. For examples of *yûjo* (women of the "pleasure quarter") who became fashion leaders from the Edo through the Meiji periods, see J. E. de Becker, *The Nightless City, or the History of the Yoshiwara Yûkaku* (New York: ICG Muse, 2000) (a facsimile of the version published in 1905), 330–351.

4. Ogura Seizaburô, ed., "Abe Sada no chôsho," in Dai 2 Kumiai Sôtai kai, ed., *Sôtaikai kenkyû hôkoku* (Tokyo: Ginza Shokan, 1986), 1:62.

5. For a description of Abe Sada's childhood and early cultural environment, see Kubo Kumi and Kubo Senko, "Tatamiya no Osada chan" [The tatami maker's little Osada], in Nanakita Kazuto, ed., *Abe Sada densetsu* (Tokyo: Chikuma Bunko, 1998); this description of Abe's childhood was published originally in the July 1936 issue of *Fujin kôron*.

6. Ibid., 98–100.

## 3. Maidens or Harlots Only

1. This development paralleled a similar one in the West. Michel Foucault notes that "the working classes managed for a long time to escape the deployment of 'sexuality,'" by which he meant the ideological and cultural restraints on sexual behavior and ideas first accepted by the wealthier part of society. See Michel Foucault, *The History of Sexuality: An Introduction* (New York: Penguin, 1978), 121–122. An excellent study of the emergence of the "Japanese family" in modern times and the transformation of sexual values

that accompanied its emergence appears in Ueno Chizuko, "Kaisetsu" [Analysis], in Ogi Shinzô, Kumakura Isao, and Ueno Chizuko, *Fûzoku sei* [Ethnography sex], *Nihon kindai shisô taikei*, vol. 23 (Tokyo: Iwanami Shoten, 1990), 505–550. In this essay, Ueno examines the construction of the modern household model of the family, the emerging discourse of scientific sexology, and the crystallization of gender categories during the late nineteenth century.

2. An essay critical of the standard depiction of the Japanese household centered on the *ie* appears in Ueno Chizuko, "Modern Patriarchy and the Formation of the Japanese Nation State," in Donald Denoon, Mark Hudson, Gavan McCormack, and Tessa Morris-Suzuki, eds., *Multicultural Japan: Paleolithic to Postmodern* (Cambridge: Cambridge University Press, 2001), 213–223. A more thorough critique appears in Muta Kazue, *Senryaku toshite no kazoku: Kindai Nihon no kokumin kokka keisei to josei* [The family as strategy: Women and the formation of the national state in modern Japan] (Tokyo: Shin'yôsha, 1996).

3. Ogura Seizaburô, "Shojo to shôfu" [Virgins and prostitutes], *Sôtaikai kenkyû hôkoku*, vol. 1 (Tokyo: Ginza Shokan, 1986), 473.

4. At the time of Toyotomi Hideyoshi's cadastral surveys during the late sixteenth century, substantial numbers of women were listed as property owners. See Miyashita Michiko, "Kinsei zenki ni okeru ie to josei no seikatsu" [The household and women's lives during the first years of the early modern period], in Josei shi Sôgô Kenkyûkai, ed., *Nihon josei seikatsu shi*, vol. 3 (Tokyo: Tokyo University Press, 1990), 1–34. For a study of women and property in early modern Kyoto, see Yasukuni Ryôichi, "Kinsei Kyôto no shomin josei" [Commoner women in early modern Kyoto], in Josei Shi Sôgô Kenkyûkai, ed., *Nihon josei seikatsu shi*, vol. 3, 93–109. For a study that focuses on women's inheritance rights in three specific villages during the nineteenth century, see Ôguchi Yûjirô, "Kinsei kôki ni okeru nôson kazoku no keisei: josei sôzoku nin o chûshin ni" [Family formation in rural villages during the late early modern period, centered on women who inherited property], in Josei Shi Sôgô Kenkyûkai, ed., *Nihon josei shi*, vol. 3 , 193–225. In the northeastern part of Japan, "female primogeniture" (*ane katoku*) had been practiced from the Edo period (1600–1868); it did not, however, last into the twentieth century. See Yamamoto Jun, "A Case Study of Female Primogeniture in Pre-modern Japan: Ariga Village, 1739–1868," in Ochiai Emiko, ed., *The Logic of Female Succession: Rethinking Patriarchy and Patrilineality in Global and Historical Perspective* (Kyoto: International Research Center for Japanese Studies, 2003), 299–319. Although by no means common, women did become heads of households in early modern Kyoto. See Mary Louise Nagata, "Headship and Succession in Early Modern Kyoto: The Role of Women," in Ochiai Emiko, ed., *The Logic of Female Succession*, 269–298.

5. A succinct but insightful explanation of the effects of the Civil Code of 1898 on

women's lives appears in Ueno Chizuko, "Modern Patriarchy and the Formation of the Japanese Nation State," 213–214.

6. In the *Meiroku zasshi*, Sakatani Shiroshi took note of the "common custom in the back streets of Tokyo for the wives to dominate their husbands." See Sakatani Shiroshi, "On Concubines," in *Meiroku Zasshi: Journal of the Japanese Enlightenment*, trans. William R. Braisted (Cambridge: Harvard University Press, 1976), 395.

7. See ibid., 392–399; it is Sakatani who advocates "no more than one" concubine per man should the practice continue. Also see Katô Hiroyuki, "Abuses of Equal Rights for Men and Women," 376–379; Tsuda Mamichi, "Distinguishing the Equal Rights of Husbands and Wives," 435–436. Tsuda is incredulous at the equation of "equal rights of men and women" with "equal rights of husbands and wives." In the latter, he sees some merit; the former is mistaken.

8. A compilation of numerous texts of this kind along with a historical essay examining their evolution is Ishikawa Matsutarô, *Onna daigaku shû* [A collection of the Greater Learning for Women] (Tokyo: Heibonsha, 1977). Edo-period editions of *Onna daigaku*, *Onna Imagawa*, and similar texts are not unusual in antiquarian bookstores. Books of a similar nature included *Onna chôhô ki*, which contained practical information concerning numerous topics in addition to moral strictures.

9. For discussions regarding these changes, see Kawamura Kunimitsu, *Otome no karada: josei no kindai to sekushuariti* [The maiden's body: Women, modernity, and sexuality] (Tokyo: Kinokuniya, 1994).

10. Ibid., 184–208.

11. There had existed the terms *kimusume* and *oboko* that signified a young woman who had not had any sexual experience but neither carried any connotation of "purity." The more modern term *shojo* came to mean "virgin" with the connotation of purity only in the late nineteenth century. See Kawamura Kunimitsu, "'Shojo' no kindai—hôin sareta nikutai" [Virginity's modernity—the sealed body] in Inoue Shun, Ueno Chizuko, Ôzawa Mayuki, Mita Shûsuke, and Yoshimi Shuniya, eds., *Sekushuariti no shakaigaku* [The sociology of sexuality], *Gendai shakaigaku* [Contemporary sociology], vol. 10 (Tokyo: Iwanami Shoten, 1996), 131. A more extended discussion of the evolution of concepts of virginity in modern Japan appears in Kawamura Kunimitsu, *Otome no karada*, especially 184–208, and Muta Kazue, *Senryaku toshite no kazoku*, 138–144. Also see Oda Makoto, *Ichi go no jiten: sei* [A single-term dictionary: Sex] (Tokyo: Sanseidô, 1996), 68–72. Oda points out that the term *shojomaku*, literally "young girl's membrane," had appeared as a translation of the word "hymen" by the early nineteenth century, yet the word *shojo* did not come to mean "virgin" until decades later. See 24–26. Sugita Genpaku, in the *Kaitai shinsho* [New book of anatomy] (1774) does not use the single term *shojomaku* but makes that statement that "maidens always have a membrane" (*shojo wa kanarazu maku ari*);

see Sugita Genpaku, *Kaitai shinsho* [New book of anatomy] (1774), section 26. A comparison of the terms for female virgin, or *shojo*, and for male virgin, or *dôtei*, appears in Koyano Atsushi, *Sei to ai no Nihongo kôza* [Studies on sex and love in the Japanese language] (Tokyo: Chikuma Shôbô, 2003), 115–144. For a useful essay on gender, sexuality, politics, and society, see Narita Ryûichi, "Eisei kankyô no henka no naka no josei to josei kan" [Women and images of women in the changing hygienic environment], in *Nihon josei seikatsu shi* (Tokyo: Tokyo University Press, 1990), 89–124. A general survey of women and sexuality in modern Japan can be found in Sôgô Josei Shi Kenkyûkai, ed., *Nihon josei no rekishi sei ai kazoku*, 168–209.

12. For a tour de force on the advocacy of virgin marriage, see Ikeda Kinsui, "Shojo to kekkon," chapter 4 of his *Fujin no zekkyô* [Women's shouts] (1902), in Yuzawa Motohiko, ed., *Nihon fujin mondai shiryô shûsei* [Collected documents concerning women's issues in Japan], vol. 5 (Tokyo: Domesu Shuppan, 1976), 387–393.

13. Ueno Chizuko, *Seiairon* [On sex and love] (Tokyo: Kawade Shobô, 1991), 10–11.

14. Oda Makoto, *Ichi go no jiten: sei*, 68, makes the argument that there were only "virgins" and "prostitutes" under the twentieth-century regime of sexual morals. Concubines and mistresses arguably created a kind of middle ground, but not if the discussion is focused on the status of young women at the time of their marriage. Also see Ueno Chizuko, *Seiairon*, 10–11.

15. Ethnographic evidence concerning this custom, based on conversations with informants across Kyushu, Shikoku, and Honshu, appears in Segawa Kiyoko, *Wakamono to musume o meguru minzoku* [Folklore surrounding young men and women] (Tokyo: Miraisha, 1972). Other important works on this custom are Akamatsu Keisuke, *Hijômin no minzoku bunka* [The cultural ethnology of the uncommon people] (Tokyo: Akashi Shobô, 1986); Akamatsu Keisuke, *Hijômin no sei minzoku* [The sexual ethnology of the uncommon people] (Tokyo: Akashi Shobô, 1991); Akamatsu Keisuke, *Yobai no seiai ron* [Sex and love in *yobai*] (Tokyo: Akashi Shobô, 1994); Akamatsu Keisuke, *Yobai no minzokugaku* [Ethnography of *yobai*] (Tokyo: Akashi Shobô, 1994). Akamatsu emphasizes his differences with Yanagita Kunio and his concept of *jômin*, and consequently examines many of the issues that Yanagita avoided, including sexuality and discriminatory practices.

16. Segawa Kiyoko, *Wakamono to musume o meguru minzoku*, 430–431.

17. Ogura Seizaburô, "Shojo to shôfu," 473.

18. Regarding frank talk in a rural village in Kyushu, see Robert J. Smith and Ella Lurie Wiswell, *The Women of Sue Mura* (Chicago: University of Chicago Press, 1982), 61–62 and 61–84 *passim*.

19. An extensive discussion of matters concerning sexuality in a rural village in Kyushu can be found in ibid., 61–139. Numerous examples of the varied attitudes toward sexuality in rural villages throughout Japan appear in Segawa Kiyoko, *Wakamono to*

*musume o meguru minzoku,* especially 359–556. For an example of women who were attacked for having sex with a person from outside their village, see 537.

20. Segawa Kiyoko, *Wakamono to musume o meguru minzoku,* 330.

21. Segawa Kiyoko, *Wakamono to musume o meguru minzoku,* 536, 539.

22. Sheldon Garon, "The World's Oldest Debate?: Regulating Prostitution and Illicit Sexuality," in *Molding Japanese Minds: The State in Everyday Life* (Princeton: Princeton University Press, 1997), 94–95.

### 4. Geisha and Prostitute

1. For an anthropological examination of the world of the geisha, which includes informative historical information, see Liza Dalby's *Geisha* (New York: Vintage, 1985). A more detailed historical study of early geisha appears in Cecilia Segawa Seigle's *Yoshiwara* (Honolulu: University of Hawai'i Press, 1993). Another history of the geisha appears in Lesley Downer, *Women of the Pleasure Quarters: The Secret History of the Geisha* (New York: Broadway Books, 2001).

2. A detailed examination of the history and customs of Edo-period prostitution appears in Nakano Eizô, *Yûjo no seikatsu* [The life of prostitutes] (Tokyo: Yûzankaku, 1982). Nakano includes an extensive bibliography of both primary and secondary sources.

3. A succinct history of the regulations governing prostitution in modern Japan appears in Sheldon Garon, "The World's Oldest Debate?: Regulating Prostitution and Illicit Sexuality," in *Molding Japanese Minds: The State in Everyday Life* (Princeton: Princeton University Press, 1997); see especially 91–92. Also see G. G. Rowley, "Prostitutes and the Prostitution Prevention Act of 1956," *U.S.–Japan Women's Journal,* English Supplement no. 23, 39–56.

4. Remarkably, there exists at least one firsthand account written by a prostitute, generally contemporary to Abe, about her stay in a syphilis hospital. See Wada Yoshiko, "Yûjo nikki" [The diary of a prostitute], in Tanikawa Ken'ichi, ed., *Kindai minshû no kiroku, 3, shôfu* [Records of modern commoners, vol. 3., prostitutes] (Tokyo: Shinjinbutsu Ôraisha, 1971), 204–210. Wada also gives a vivid account of what it was like working in the brothels, with descriptions of her clients and working conditions.

5. Garon, "The World's Oldest Debate?," 96. Garon bases these figures on several surveys conducted during the 1920s and 1930s.

6. Garon, "The World's Oldest Debate?," 95–97 presents statistics for redemption and health issues among women in the sex industry. Also see Yokota Fuyuhiko, *Shôgi to yûkaku—kindai Kyoto no yûkaku* [Prostitutes and their customers: The brothels of modern Kyoto] in Kyoto Tachibana Joshi Daigaku Josei Shi Bunka Kenkyûkai, eds., *Kyoto no josei shi* [History of Kyoto women] (Kyoto: Shibunkaku, 2002). Yokota calculates numbers

of customers for a small group of prostitutes, whose averages range between 0.86 and 1.16 per day over the course of one year.

## 5. Acquaintance Rape

1. Kubo Kumi and Kubo Senko, "Tatamiya no Osada chan" [The tatami maker's little Osada], in Nanakita Kazuto, ed., *Abe Sada densetsu* (Tokyo: Chikuma Bunko, 1998), 94.

2. Ogura Seizaburô, ed., "Abe Sada jinmon kikô," in Dai 2 Kumiai Sôtai kai, ed., *Sôtaikai kenkyû hôkoku* (Tokyo: Ginza Shokan, 1986), 1:44.

3. For Abe's testimony in her trial, see Horinouchi Masakazu, *Abe Sada shô den* [The true biography of Abe Sada] (Tokyo: Jôhô Sentaa Shuppan Kyoku, 1998), 244.

4. Martha C. Nussbaum, *Sex and Social Justice* (Oxford: Oxford University Press, 1999), 137.

5. Ogura Seizaburô, ed., "Abe Sada no chôsho," in Dai 2 Kumiai Sôtai kai, ed., *Sôtaikai kenkyû hôkoku* (Tokyo: Ginza Shokan, 1986), 1:62.

6. For an excellent, if short, study (with bibliography) of rape and its health consequences, particularly as a source of post traumatic stress disorder (PTSD), see Solveig Dahl, *Rape—A Hazard to Health* (Oslo: Scandinavian University Press, 1993). While it is impossible to diagnose Abe *in absentia*, evidence suggests that she suffered from some degree of PTSD as a result of this incident. Her later reflections indicate that soon after it occurred she had recurrent and intrusive distressing recollections of the event; felt estranged from others, unable to have loving feelings; had a strong sense of a foreshortened future (seeing marriage as impossible); and had outbursts of anger. All of these are listed in the *DSM-IV* as symptomatic of PTSD. A complete set of criteria for Abe would require the addition of one of the following: insomnia, difficulty concentrating, hypervigilance, an exaggerated startle response, or physiological reaction to events that symbolize the incident. It is easy to imagine that she experienced at least one of these symptoms soon after her rape but did not discuss them in her police interrogation, which was over fifteen years later.

## 6. Acting Up

1. Ogura Seizaburô, ed., "Abe Sada jinmon kikô," in Dai 2 Kumiai Sôtai kai, ed., *Sôtaikai kenkyû hôkoku* (Tokyo: Ginza Shokan, 1986), 1:44–45.

2. Ogura Seizaburô, ed., "Abe Sada no chôsho," in Dai 2 Kumiai Sôtai kai, ed., *Sôtaikai kenkyû hôkoku* (Tokyo: Ginza Shokan, 1986), 1:62.

3. "Abe Sada jinmon kikô," 45.

4. "Abe Sada no chôsho," 62.

5. "Abe Sada no chôsho," 62.

## 7. Becoming Professional

1. Ôkubo Hasetsu, *Kagai fûzoku shi* (1906; reprint, Tokyo: Nihon Tosho Sentaa, 1983), 47.

2. Ôkubo Hasetsu, *Kagai fûzoku shi*, 230–231. The evidence Sheldon Garon presents makes this seem a rather high estimate, however. See Sheldon Garon, "The World's Oldest Debate?: Regulating Prostitution and Illicit Sexuality," in *Molding Japanese Minds: The State in Everyday Life* (Princeton: Princeton University Press, 1997), 94–95.

3. For one example, see Robert J. Smith and Ella Lurie Wiswell, *The Women of Sue Mura* (Chicago: University of Chicago Press, 1982), 139.

4. Ogura Seizaburô, ed., "Abe Sada no chôsho," in Dai 2 Kumiai Sôtai kai, ed., *Sôtaikai kenkyû hôkoku* (Tokyo: Ginza Shokan, 1986), 1:62.

5. Ogura Seizaburô, ed., "Abe Sada jinmon kikô," in Dai 2 Kumiai Sôtai kai, ed., *Sôtaikai kenkyû hôkoku* (Tokyo: Ginza Shokan, 1986), 1:45.

## 8. Changing Saddles

1. Ogura Seizaburô, ed., "Abe Sada jinmon kikô," in Dai 2 Kumiai Sôtai kai, ed., *Sôtaikai kenkyû hôkoku* (Tokyo: Ginza Shokan, 1986), 1:45.

2. Ibid.

3. Ogura Seizaburô, ed., "Abe Sada no chôsho," in Dai 2 Kumiai Sôtai kai, ed., *Sôtaikai kenkyû hôkoku* (Tokyo: Ginza Shokan, 1986), 1:63.

4. Ibid.

## 9. Legal Prostitution and Escape

1. Ogura Seizaburô, ed., "Abe Sada jinmon kikô," in Dai 2 Kumiai Sôtai kai, ed., *Sôtaikai kenkyû hôkoku* (Tokyo: Ginza Shokan, 1986), 1:46.

2. Ogura Seizaburô, ed., "Abe Sada no chôsho," in Dai 2 Kumiai Sôtai kai, ed., *Sôtaikai kenkyû hôkoku* (Tokyo: Ginza Shokan, 1986), 1:63.

3. "Abe Sada jinmon kikô," 46.

4. "Abe Sada jinmon kikô," 47.

## 10. From Prostitute on the Lam to Mistress

1. Ogura Seizaburô, ed., "Abe Sada jinmon kikô," in Dai 2 Kumiai Sôtai kai, ed., *Sôtaikai kenkyû hôkoku* (Tokyo: Ginza Shokan, 1986), 1:47.

2. Ibid.

## 11. A Search for Stability

1. Ogura Seizaburô, ed., "Abe Sada jinmon kikô," in Dai 2 Kumiai Sôtai kai, ed., *Sôtaikai kenkyû hôkoku* (Tokyo: Ginza Shokan, 1986), 1:48.

2. Ibid., 49.

3. Ibid.

## 12. Discovering Love

1. Ogura Seizaburô, ed., "Abe Sada jinmon kikô," in Dai 2 Kumiai Sôtai kai, ed., *Sôtaikai kenkyû hôkoku* (Tokyo: Ginza Shokan, 1986), 1:49.

2. Ibid., 50.

3. Ibid.

4. Ibid., 51.

5. Ibid.

## 13. Love's Intoxication

1. These include a spectrum of meanings for the Chinese term *ai* that range from carnal lust to compassion for all sentient beings. See the *Zuochan sanmeijing* (Jap. *Zazen sanmai kyô*), translated from Sanskrit by Kumarajiva (344–413); see Takakusu Junjirô and Watanabe Kaigyoku, eds., *Taishôshinshû daizôkyô* [The Buddhist canon newly compiled during the Taishô era] (Tokyo: Taishô Issaikyô Kankôkai, 1924–1935), vol. 15, no. 614, 271.

2. Ujie Mikito, "*Ai no yukue—Date Tsunamura no yuigon o yomu*" [What's love got to do with it?: Reading the last will and testament of Date Tsunamura], in Kuroda Hiroko and Nagano Hiroko, eds., *Esunishiti•jenda-kara miru Nihon no rekishi* [Japanese history as seen from the perspectives of ethnicity and gender] (Tokyo: Yoshikawa Kôbunkan, 2002), 292–312.

3. The literature on "love" in Japanese is, as one might expect, immense. An informative collection of literary essays on the topic written during the twentieth century appears in Hasegawa Shuntarô, ed., *Koi* [Love] (Tokyo: Sakuhinsha, 1985). This volume includes a bibliography of works on love in Japanese, most of which date from the 1960s and 1970s. For a history of "love" in Japan, see Nakanishi Susumu, *Nihonjin no ai no rekishi* [A history of love among the Japanese] (Tokyo: Kadokawa Shoten, 1978). The extent to which western concepts of love are integral to the Japanese concepts in modern discourse can be seen in Imamichi Tomonobu, *Ai ni tsuite* [On love] (Tokyo: Kodansha, 1972). Imamichi moves seamlessly between discussions of Christian love and *koi* in, for example, the works of Ihara Saikaku.

4. See Mark Schreiber, "O-sada Serves a Grateful Nation," in *The Dark Side: Infamous Japanese Crimes and Criminals* (Tokyo: Kodansha, 2001).

5. "Abe Sada jinmon kikô," 54.

6. Ibid., 51.

## 14. Murder

1. Ogura Seizaburô, ed., "Abe Sada no chôsho," in Dai 2 Kumiai Sôtai kai, ed., *Sôtaikai kenkyû hôkoku* (Tokyo: Ginza Shokan, 1986), 1:64.

2. Ogura Seizaburô, ed., "Abe Sada jinmon kikô," in Dai 2 Kumiai Sôtai kai, ed., *Sôtaikai kenkyû hôkoku* (Tokyo: Ginza Shokan, 1986), 1:54.

3. "Abe Sada no chôsho," 64.

4. Ibid.

5. "Abe Sada jinmon kikô," 54.

6. Ibid.

7. Ibid.

8. Ibid., 55.

9. Ibid.

10. Ibid., 57.

11. Ibid.

12. Ibid.

13. "Abe Sada no chôsho," 69.

14. Julia Kristeva, *Tales of Love*, trans. Leon S. Roudiez (New York: Columbia University Press, 1987), 1.

15. Ibid., 4–5.

16. A paradigmatic example is Tokutomi Roka, *Hototogisu.* in Satô Zen'ya and Satô Masaru, eds., *Kitamura Tôgoku-Tokutomi Roka shû* [Collected works of Kitamura Tôgoku and Tokutomi Roka] (Tokyo: Kadokawa Shoten, 1972). For further examples, see William Johnston, *The Modern Epidemic: A History of Tuberculosis in Japan* (Cambridge: Council on East Asian Studies Publications, Harvard University, 1995), 124–159.

## 15. No Longer Private

1. Ogura Seizaburô, ed., "Abe Sada no chôsho," in Dai 2 Kumiai Sôtai kai, ed., *Sôtaikai kenkyû hôkoku* (Tokyo: Ginza Shokan, 1986), 1:69.

2. *Tokyo Asahi shinbun*, 19 May 1936, 11.

3. *Yomiuri shinbun*, 20 May 1936, 7.

4. Ibid.

5. *Yomiuri shinbun*, 21 May 1936, 7.

6. "Abe Sada no chôsho," 67.

7. Ibid.

8. *Tokyo Asahi shinbun*, 21 May 1936, 11.

9. Ibid.

10. *Yomiuri shinbun*, 21 May 1936, 7.

11. *Tokyo Asahi shinbun*, 21 May 1936, 11.

12. Ibid.

13. *Yomiuri shinbun*, 21 May 1936, 7.

14. *Tokyo Asahi shinbun*, 22 May 1936, 11.

15. *Tokyo Asahi shinbun*, 10 June 1936, 11.

16. Horinouchi Masakazu, *Abe Sada shô den* [The true biography of Abe Sada] (Tokyo: Jôhô Sentaa Shuppan Kyoku, 1998), 213.

17. Ibid., 209.

## 16. Interrogation and Investigation

1. Abe described her first days in jail and subsequent events in Abe Sada, *Abe Sada shuki* (Tokyo: Chûôkôronsha, 1998), 245. This is a reprint of the original work, published under the same title in 1948. The reprint also contains a number of other documents relevant to this case, including a number of reactions to it.

2. Kokura Michiyo, "Kôsei tojô ni aru dokubô no Abe Sada rinshitsu kansatsu tôkakan" [Ten days of observing Abe Sada while on the way to a new life in a prison cell], in Dai 2 Kumiai Sôtai kai, ed., *Sôtaikai kenkyû hôkoku* (Tokyo: Ginza Shokan, 1986), 1:370. Despite the promising title, this short piece reveals little about Abe herself.

3. Ogura Seizaburô, ed., "Abe Sada no chôsho," in Dai 2 Kumiai Sôtai kai, ed., *Sôtaikai kenkyû hôkoku* (Tokyo: Ginza Shokan, 1986), 1:69.

4. Quoted in Masakazu Horinouchi, *Abe Sada shô den* [The true biography of Abe Sada] (Tokyo: Jôhô Sentaa Shuppan Kyoku, 1998), 207. Originally published in *Shûkan gendai*, 14 May 1961.

5. Titles for these two documents are based on those used in *Sôtaikai kenkyû hôkoku*, vol. 1. Later printings of the interrogation record present it under different titles, including some that imply that it was the record of the preliminary investigation. However, the titles in *Sôtaikai kenkyû hôkoku*, vol. 1 were published soon after the documents' use in court. The "Notes from the Interrogations of Abe Sada" appear at the end of this book.

6. This was Abe Sada, *Abe Sada shuki*, originally published in 1948, as noted above.

7. Ogura Seizaburô, ed., "Abe Sada jinmon kikô," in Dai 2 Kumiai Sôtai kai, ed., *Sôtaikai kenkyû hôkoku* (Tokyo: Ginza Shokan, 1986), 1:43.

8. Ibid., 47.

9. "Abe Sada no chôsho," 67.

10. Ibid., 68.

11. See Carol Groneman, *Nymphomania: A History* (New York: Norton, 2000) for a history of the concept in western discourse.

12. "Abe Sada no chôsho," 73, 74.

13. Ibid., 69.

14. Ibid., 73–74.

15. Relevant passages appear in the *Tokyo Asahi shinbun* on the days noted.

16. *Abe Sada shuki*, 246–247.

## 17. Judgment

1. Hosoya Keijirô, *Dotera saiban* [Judge in the quilted robe] (Tokyo: Moriwaki Bunko, 1956), 69–120. Most of the following is based on three essays in this collection, "Osada jiken to sono saiban" [The Sada incident and her trial] 69–106, "Kyokubu to sono shoyûken no kizoku" [Notes on the extremity and rights of its possession], 107–115, and "Interi kaikyû to sei seikatsu" [The intellectual class and sexual life], 116–120.

2. In English, an excellent description of the *kafe* appears in Miriam Silverberg, "The Cafe Waitress Serving Modern Japan," in Stephen Vlastos, ed., *Mirror of Modernity: Invented Traditions of Modern Japan* (Berkeley: University of California Press, 1998), 208–225.

3. Hosoya Keijirô, *Dotera saiban*, 81–83.

4. Ibid., 80–81.

5. Ibid., 83–86.

6. In both cases, the *Yomiuri* used Japanese transliterations of the English-language terms, literally "Osada *mania*" and "Osada *fuan.*" *Yomiuri shinbun*, evening edition, 26 November 1936, 2.

7. *Tokyo Asahi shinbun*, evening edition, 26 November 1936, 2; *Yomiuri shinbun*, evening edition, 26 November 1936, 2; Horinouchi Masakazu, *Abe Sada shô den* [The true biography of Abe Sada] (Tokyo: Jôhô Sentaa Shuppan Kyoku, 1998), 238, 240.

8. In court, Abe used the term *muri* in Japanese, generally translated as "forced" or "coerced," to describe how she lost her virginity. Horiuchi Masakazu, *Abe Sada shô den*, 244.

9. *Tokyo Asahi shinbun*, 22 December 1936, 2.

10. Hosoya Keijirô, *Dotera saiban*, 98.

11. The literature in Japanese in this field is rich. Early twentieth-century books on forensic medicine, and especially on sexuality and crime, develop this theme at length. See, for examples, Kawai Ken'ichi and Sawada Junjirô, *Shikijô no hanzai* [Crimes of passion] (Tokyo: Seibunsha, 1913), 1; Sugie Kaoru, *Hanzai seishinbyô gairon* [A general theory of psychopathological crime] (Tokyo: Hakuhôdô, 1924); Terada Seiichi, *Fujin to hanzai* [Women and crime] (1928; reprint, Tokyo: Nihon Tosho Sentaa, 1982); Nozoe Atsumi, *Josei to hanzai* [Women and crime] (Tokyo: Bunkyûsha, 1930), 290; Miyake Kôichi, *Sekinin nôryoku—seishin byôgaku yori mitaru* [Capacity for responsibility, as seen from the perspective of psychopathology] (Tokyo: Nankôdô, 1930). All of these works preceded the Abe Sada incident and could easily have influenced Hosoya's thinking in this case.

12. Hosoya Keijirô, *Dotera saiban*, 100.

13. Ibid., 102.

14. The entire text of the admonition appears both in ibid., 100–103 and in contemporary newspaper reports. See *Tokyo Asahi shinbun*, 22 December 1936, 2.

15. Hosoya Keijirô, *Dotera saiban*, 117–118.

## 18. Imprisonment and Release

1. Abe Sada, *Abe Sada shuki* [Memoirs of Abe Sada] (Tokyo: Chûôkôron Sha, 1998), 253.

2. Ibid., 255–256.

3. Ibid., 260.

4. Ibid., 261–262. The documents related to Abe Sada reveal much about life in Japan at the time that is not described elsewhere; life in a women's prison as she describes it here is yet another instance.

5. Ibid., 269.

6. Abe described this entire episode in ibid., 265–271.

7. Ibid., 271–272.

8. Ibid., 275.

9. Ibid., 276.

10. Ibid., 278.

11. Ibid., 280.

## 19. Celebrity, Hardship, and Escape

1. The best account of Abe at this time appears in Horinouchi Masakazu, *Abe Sada shô den* [The true biography of Abe Sada] (Tokyo: Jôhô Sentaa Shuppan Kyoku, 1998), 296–299.

2. See Sakaguchi Ango, "Abe Sada san no inshô" [My impression of Abe Sada], in *Sakaguchi Ango zenshû, vol. 15* (Tokyo: Chikuma Shobô, 1991), pp. 238–243, and Sakaguchi Ango, "Abe Sada to iu onna" [A woman named Abe Sada] in *Sakaguchi Ango zenshû*, vol. 15, 278–281.

3. Donald Richie, *Different People: Pictures of Some Japanese* (Tokyo: Kodansha, 1987), 27.

4. Stated in a personal conversation with the author.

5. The most detailed and comprehensive account of Abe in the last period during which anything was known about her appears in Horinouchi Masakazu, *Abe Sada shô den*, 389–423.

## Epilogue

1. Both works appear in Nanakita Kazuto, ed., *Abe Sada densetsu* [The legend of Abe Sada] (Tokyo: Chikuma Bunko, 1998).

2. Kawaguchi Shûshi, "Toki no wadai: jikken shin kagagu wa danshi fuyôron ni sono no mesu o togu" [Talk of the times: New experimental science sharpens its scalpel on the theory that men are not necessary], *Tsûzoku igaku* 14 (7) (1936): 86–90.

3. Ôtsuki Kenji, Kaneko Junji, Nagasaki Bunji, Takahashi Tetsu, and Morooka Zon, *Abe Sada no seishin bunseki teki shindan* [A psychoanalytic diagnosis of Abe Sada] (Tokyo: Tokyo Seishin Bunsekigaku Kenkyûjo Shuppan Bu, 1937).

4. These three works all appear in Abe Sada, *Abe Sada shuki* [Memoirs of Abe Sada] (Tokyo: Chûôkôron Sha, 1998), 56–69.

5. Dai 2 Kumiai Sôtai kai, ed., *Sôtaikai kenkyû hôkoku*, vols. 1 & 2 (Tokyo: Ginza Shokan, 1986).

6. Oda Sakunosuke, *Yôfu* [A bewitching woman] (Tokyo: Fûsetsusha, 1947). This also appeared in the March 1947 edition of the magazine *Fûsetsu*.

7. This book was reprinted in 1998, with an extensive interpretive essay by Suzuki Toshifumi. See Kimura Ichirô, *Osada iro zange* [The erotic confessions of Abe Sada] (Tokyo: Kawade Shobô, 1998).

8. Kuwahara Inatoshi, *19 nin no Abe Sada* [19 Abe Sadas] (Tokyo: Gendai Shorin, 1981).

9. A recent novel based on the story of Abe Sada is Nishizawa Hiroko, *SADA* (Tokyo: Chûôkôronsha, 1998). Nishizawa presents a perspective of Abe much more sympathetic to her position as a woman in Japanese society. Her novel was released at the same time as the film *SADA* by Ôbayashi Yoshihiko.

10. For example, see Mori Kei, *Natsukashiku omoimasu* [Remembered fondly] (Tokyo: Gendai Shokan, 1996).

11. Of these three films, Ôshima Nagisa's is the most significant and the most accessible. For Ôshima's own thoughts concerning this film, see Nagisa Ôshima, *Cinema, Censorship, and the State: The Writings of Nagisa Oshima* (Cambridge: MIT Press, 1992), 251–286.

# BIBLIOGRAPHY

Abe Sada. *Abe Sada shuki* [Memoirs of Abe Sada]. Tokyo: Chûôkôron Sha, 1998.

Akamatsu Keisuke. *Hijômin no minzoku bunka* [The cultural ethnology of the uncommon people]. Tokyo: Akashi Shobô, 1986.

——. *Hijômin no sei minzoku* [The sexual ethnology of the uncommon people]. Tokyo: Akashi Shobô, 1991.

——. *Yobai no minzokugaku* [Ethnography of *yobai*]. Tokyo: Akashi Shobô, 1994.

——. *Yobai no seiai ron* [Sex and love in *yobai*]. Tokyo: Akashi Shobô, 1994.

Asakura Kyôji. *Dokufu den* [Biographies of poisonous women]. Tokyo: Heibonsha, 1999.

Bataille, Georges. *Erotism: Death & Sensuality*. San Francisco: City Lights, 1986.

Braisted, William R., trans. *Meiroku Zasshi: Journal of the Japanese Enlightenment*. Cambridge: Harvard University Press, 1976.

Butler, Judith. *Gender Trouble: Feminism and the Subversion of Identity*. London: Routledge, 1990.

Cornyetz, Nina. *Dangerous Women, Deadly Words: Phallic Fantasy and Modernity in Three Japanese Writers*. Stanford: Stanford University Press, 1999.

Dahl, Solveig. *Rape—A Hazard to Health*. Oslo: Scandinavian University Press, 1993.

Dai 2 Kumiai Sôtai Kai, ed. *Sôtaikai kenkyû hôkoku*, vols. 1 & 2. Tokyo: Ginza Shokan, 1986.

Dalby, Liza. *Geisha*. New York: Vintage, 1985.

Davis, Natalie. *The Return of Martin Guerre*. Cambridge: Harvard University Press, 1983.

de Becker, J. E. *The Nightless City, or the History of the Yoshiwara Yûkaku*. New York: ICG Muse, 2000 (a facsimile of the version published in 1905).

Downer, Lesley. *Women of the Pleasure Quarters: The Secret History of the Geisha*. New York: Broadway Books, 2001.

Enbon Kenkyû Kankôkai, ed. *Nihon enbon daishûsei* [Collected Japanese erotica]. Tokyo: Uozumi Shoten, 1965.

Foucault, Michel. *The History of Sexuality: An Introduction*. New York: Penguin, 1978.

Frühstück, Sabine. *Colonizing Sex: Sexology and Social Control in Modern Japan*. Berkeley: University of California Press, 2003.

Fujime Yuki. "The Licensed Prostitution System and the Prostitution Abolition Movement in Modern Japan." *Positions* 5 (1997): 135–170.

———. *Sei no rekishi gaku: kôshô seido dataizai taisei kara baishium bôshihô yûsei hogohô taisei e* [The history of sex: From the system of legal prostitution and criminalized abortion to the system of the law forbidding prostitution and the Eugenics Protection Law]. Tokyo: Fuji Shuppan, 1999.

Fukuda Kazuhiko. *Edo no seiaigaku* [The sexology of the Edo period]. Tokyo: Kawade Shobô, 1988.

Fûzoku Genten Kenkyûkai, ed. *Nihon no seigaku kotohajime* [The beginning of Japanese sexology]. Tokyo: Kawade Shobô, 1989.

Garon, Sheldon. "The World's Oldest Debate?: Regulating Prostitution and Illicit Sexuality." In *Molding Japanese Minds: The State in Everyday Life* (Princeton: Princeton University Press, 1997).

Ginzburg, Carlo. *The Cheese and the Worms*. New York: Penguin, 1982.

Groneman, Carol. *Nymphomania: A History*. New York: Norton, 2000.

Haraway, Donna J. "'Gender' for a Marxist Dictionary: The Sexual Politics of a Word." In *Simians, Cyborgs, and Women* (New York: Routledge, 1991).

Hasegawa Shuntarô, ed. *Koi* [Love]. Tokyo: Sakuhinsha, 1985.

Higuchi Kiyoyuki, *Edo sei fûzoku yawa* [A night's talk on the sexual customs of the Edo period]. Tokyo: Haga Shoten, 1976.

Horinouchi Masakazu. *Abe Sada shô den* [The true biography of Abe Sada]. Tokyo: Jôhô Sentaa Shuppan Kyoku, 1998.

Hosoya Keijirô. *Dotera saiban* [Judge in the quilted robe]. Tokyo: Moriwaki Bunko, 1956.

Ikeda Kinsui. "Shojo to kekkon" [Virgins and marriage] (1902). In Yuzawa Motohiko, ed., *Nihon fujin mondai shiryô shûsei* [Collected documents concerning women's issues in Japan], vol. 5 (Tokyo: Domesu Shuppan, 1976).

Imamichi Tomonobu. *Ai ni tsuite* [On love]. Tokyo: Kodansha, 1972.

Ishikawa Matsutarô. *Onna daigaku shû* [A collection of the Greater Learning for Women]. Tokyo: Heibonsha, 1977.

Johnston, William. *The Modern Epidemic: A History of Tuberculosis in Japan*. Cambridge: Council on East Asian Studies Publications, Harvard University, 1995.

Katô Hiroyuki. "Abuses of Equal Rights for Men and Women." In *Meiroku Zasshi: Journal of the Japanese Enlightenment*, trans. William R. Braisted (Cambridge: Harvard University Press, 1976).

Kawaguchi Shûshi. "Toki no wadai: jikken shin kagagu wa danshi fuyôron ni sono no mesu o togu" [Talk of the times: New experimental science sharpens its scalpel on the theory that men are not necessary]. *Tsûzoku igaku* 14 (7) (1936): 86–90.

Kawai Ken'ichi and Sawada Junjirô. *Shikijô no hanzai* [Crimes of passion]. Tokyo: Seibunsha, 1913.

Kawamura Kunimitsu. *Otome no shintai: josei no kindai to sekushuariti* [The maiden's body: Women, modernity, and sexuality]. Tokyo: Kiinokuniya, 1994.

——. "'Shojo' no kindai—hôin sareta nikutai" [Virginity's modernity—the sealed body]. In Inoue Shun, Ueno Chizuko, Ôzawa Mayuki, Mita Shûnsuke, and Yoshimi Shuniya, eds., *Sekushuariti no shakaigaku* [The sociology of sexuality], *Gendai shakaigaku* [Contemporary sociology], vol. 10 (Tokyo: Iwanami Shoten, 1996).

Kimura Ichirô. *Osada iro zange* [The erotic confessions of Abe Sada]. Tokyo: Kawade Shobô, 1998.

Koike Mariko. *Akujo to yobareta onna tachi* [Women who have been called "evil women"]. Tokyo: Shufu to Seikatsu Sha, 1982.

Koyano Atsushi. *Sei to ai no Nihongo kôza* [Studies on sex and love in the Japanese language]. Tokyo: Chikuma Shôbô, 2003.

Kristeva, Julia. *Tales of Love*. Trans. Leon S. Roudiez. New York: Columbia University Press, 1987.

Kubo Kumi and Kubo Senko. "Tatamiya no Osada chan" [The tatami maker's little Osada]. In Nanakita Kazuto, ed., *Abe Sada densetsu* (Tokyo: Chikuma Bunko, 1998).

Kuwahara Inatoshi. *19 nin no Abe Sada* [19 Abe Sadas]. Tokyo: Gendai Shorin, 1981.

Marran, Christine. "'Poison woman': Takahashi Oden and the Spectacle of Female Deviancy in Early Meiji." *US–Japan Women's Journal* (English supplement) 9 (1995): 93–110.

Masuda Sayo. *Autobiography of a Geisha*. Trans. G. G. Rowley. New York: Columbia University Press, 2003.

Miyake Kôichi. *Sekinin nôryoku—seishin byôgaku yori mitaru* [Capacity for responsibility, as seen from the perspective of psychopathology]. Tokyo: Nankôdô, 1930.

Miyashita Michiko. "Kinsei zenki ni okeru *ie* to josei no seikatsu" [The household and women's lives during the first years of the early modern period]. In Josei shi Sôgô Kenkyûkai, ed., *Nihon josei seikatsu shi*, vol. 3 (Tokyo: Tokyo University Press, 1990).

Mori Arinori. "On Wives and Concubines, Part Two." In *Meiroku Zasshi: Journal of the Japanese Enlightenment*, trans. William R. Braisted (Cambridge: Harvard University Press, 1976).

Mori Kei. *Natsukashiku omoimasu* [Remembered fondly]. Tokyo: Gendai Shokan, 1996.

Muta Kazue. *Senryaku toshite no kazoku: Kindai Nihon no kokumin kokka keisei to josei* [The family as strategy: Women and the formation of the national state in modern Japan]. Tokyo: Shin'yô Sha, 1996.

Nagata, Mary Louise. "Headship and Succession in Early Modern Kyoto: The Role of Women." In Ochiai Emiko, ed., *The Logic of Female Succession: Rethinking Patriarchy and Patrilineality in Global and Historical Perspective* (Kyoto: International Research Center for Japanese Studies, 2003), 269–298.

Nakae Katsumi. *Sei no Nihon shi* [Sex in Japanese history]. Tokyo: Kawade Shobô, 1995.

Nakanishi Susumu. *Nihonjin no ai no rekishi* [A history of love among the Japanese]. Tokyo: Kadokawa Shoten, 1978.

Nakano Eizô. *Yûjo no seikatsu* [The life of prostitutes]. Tokyo: Yuzankaku, 1982.

Nakano Makiko. *Makiko's Diary: A Merchant Wife in 1910 Kyoto*. Trans. Kazuko Smith. Stanford: Stanford University Press, 1995.

Nanakita Kazuto, ed. *Abe Sada densetsu* [The legend of Abe Sada]. Tokyo: Chikuma Bunko, 1998.

Narita Ryûichi. "Eisei kankyô no henka no naka no josei to josei kan" [Women and images of women in the changing hygienic environment]. In *Nihon josei seikatsu shi* (Tokyo: Tokyo University Press, 1990).

Nishizawa Hiroko. *SADA*. Tokyo: Chûôkôronsha, 1988.

Nozoe Atsumi. *Josei to hanzai* [Women and crime]. Tokyo: Bukyûsha, 1930.

Nussbaum, Martha C. *Sex and Social Justice*. Oxford: Oxford University Press, 1999.

Ochiai Emiko, ed. *The Logic of Female Succession: Rethinking Patriarchy and Patrilineality in Global and Historical Perspective*. Kyoto: International Research Center for Japanese Studies, 2003.

Oda Makoto. *Ichi go no jiten: sei* [A single-term dictionary: Sex]. Tokyo: Sanseidô, 1996.

Oda Sakunosuke. *Yôfu* [A bewitching woman]. Tokyo: Fûsetsusha, 1947.

Ôguchi Yûjirô. "Kinsei kôki ni okeru nôson kazoku no keisei: josei sôzoku nin o chûshin ni" [Family formation in rural villages during the late early modern period, centered on women who inherited property]. In Josei Shi Sôgô Kenkyûkai, ed., *Nihon josei shi*, vol. 3 (Tokyo: Tokyo University Press, 1982).

Ogura Michiyo. "Kôsei tojô ni aru dokubô no Abe Sada rinshitsu kansatsu tôkakan" [Ten days of observing Abe Sada while on the way to a new life in a prison cell]. In Dai 2 Kumiai Sôtai kai, ed., *Sôtaikai kenkyû hôkoku* (Tokyo: Ginza Shokan, 1986), 1:370.

Ogura Seizaburô. "Shojo to shôfu" [Virgins and prostitutes]. In Dai 2 Kumiai Sôtai kai, ed., *Sôtaikai kenkyû hôkoku* (Tokyo: Ginza Shokan, 1986), vol. 1.

——, ed. "Abe Sada jinmon kikô" [Notes from the police interrogation of Abe Sada]. In Dai 2 Kumiai Sôtai kai, ed., *Sôtaikai kenkyû hôkoku* (Tokyo: Ginza Shokan, 1986), vol. 1.

——, ed. "Abe Sada no chôsho" [Police interrogation of Abe Sada]. In Dai 2 Kumiai Sôtai kai, ed., *Sôtaikai kenkyû hôkoku* (Tokyo: Ginza Shokan, 1986), vol. 1.

Ôkubo Hasetsu. *Kagai fûzoku shi* [Customs of the pleasure quarters]. 1906; reprint, Tokyo: Nihon Tosho Sentaa, 1983.

Ôshima, Nagisa. *Cinema, Censorship, and the State: The Writings of Nagisa Oshima*. Cambridge: MIT Press, 1992.

Ôtsuki Kenji, Kaneko Junji, Nagasaki Bunji, Takahashi Tetsu, and Morooka Zon. *Abe Sada no seishin bunseki teki shindan* [A psychoanalytic diagnosis of Abe Sada]. Tokyo: Tokyo Seishin Bunsekigaku Kenkyûjo Shuppan Bu, 1937.

Pflugfelder, Gregory M. *Cartographies of Desire: Male-Male Sexuality in Japanese Discourse, 1600–1950*. Berkeley: University of California Press, 1999.

Richie, Donald. *Different People: Pictures of Some Japanese*. Tokyo: Kodansha, 1987.

Riley, Denise. *"Am I that Name?": Feminism and the Category of "Women" in History*. Minneapolis: University of Minnesota Press, 1988.

Rowley, G. G. "Prostitutes and the Prostitution Protection Act of 1956." *U.S.–Japan Women's Journal*, English Supplement, no. 23, 39–56.

Russett, Cynthia Eagle. *Sexual Science: The Victorian Construction of Womanhood*. Cambridge: Harvard University Press, 1989.

Sakaguchi Ango. "Abe Sada san no inshô" [My impression of Abe Sada]. In *Sakaguchi Ango zenshû*, vol. 15 (Tokyo: Chikuma Shobô, 1991).

——. "Abe Sada to iu onna" [A woman named Abe Sada]. In *Sakaguchi Ango zenshû*, vol. 15 (Tokyo: Chikuma Shobô, 1991).

Sakatani Shiroshi. "On Concubines." In *Meiroku Zasshi: Journal of the Japanese Enlighten-ment*, trans. William R. Braisted (Cambridge: Harvard University Press, 1976).

Sarup, Madan. *Jacques Lacan*. Toronto: University of Toronto Press, 1992.

Schama, Simon. *Dead Certainties*. New York: Knopf, 1991.

Schreiber, Mark. "O-sada Serves a Grateful Nation." In *The Dark Side: Infamous Japanese Crimes and Criminals* (Tokyo: Kodansha, 2001).

Scott, Joan. *Gender and the Politics of History*, rev. ed. New York: Columbia University Press, 1999.

Segawa Kiyoko. *Wakamono to musume o meguru minzoku* [Folklore surrounding young men and women]. Tokyo: Miraisha, 1972.

Seidensticker, Edward. *Low City, High City: Tokyo from Edo to the Earthquake*. Rutland, Vt.: Tuttle, 1984.

Seigle, Cecilia Segawa. *Yoshiwara*. Honolulu: University of Hawai'i Press, 1993.

Seki Tamiko. *Edo kôki no josei tachi* [Women of the late Edo period]. Tokyo: Aki Shobô, 1980.

Setouchi Jakuchô. "Kaisetsu." In Nanakita Kazuto, ed., *Abe Sada densetsu* [The legend of Abe Sada] (Tokyo: Chikuma Bunko, 1998).

Silverberg, Miriam. "The Cafe Waitress Serving Modern Japan." In Stephen Vlastos, ed., *Mirror of Modernity: Invented Traditions of Modern Japan* (Berkeley: University of California Press, 1998).

Smith, Robert J. and Ella Lurie Wiswell. *The Women of Sue Mura*. Chicago: University of Chicago Press, 1982.

Sôgô Josei Shi Kenkyûkai, ed. *Nihon josei no rekishi sei ai kazoku* [The history of Japanese women: Sex, love, family]. Tokyo: Kadokawa Shoten, 1992.

Sugie Kaoru. *Hanzai seishinbyô gairon* [A general theory of psychopathological crime]. Tokyo: Hakuhôdô, 1924.

Sugita Genpaku. *Kaitai shinsho* [New book of anatomy]. 1774.

Takahashi Tetsu. *Kôkei hikô* [The box of secret pleasures]. Tokyo: Daiichi Shuppansha, 1952.

———. *Kôza Nihon fûzoku shi, sei fûzoku* [Studies on the history of Japanese customs, sexual customs]. Tokyo: Yûzankaku, 1959.

———. *Nihon seiten taikan* [Sexual classics of Japan], 2 vols. Tokyo: Nihon Seikatsu Shinri-gakkai, 1954.

———. *Tokugawa seiten taikan* [Sexual classics of the Tokugawa period], 2 vols. Tokyo: Nihon Seishinbunseki Gakkai & Nihon Seikatsu Shinrigakkai, 1953.

Tanaka Takako. <*Akujo*> *ron* [An essay on "evil women"]. Tokyo: Kiinokunia, 1992.

Terada Seiichi. *Fujin to hanzai* [Women and crime]. 1928; reprint, Tokyo: Nihon Tosho Sen-taa, 1982.

Teruoka Yasutaka. *Nihonjin no ai to sei* [Love and sex of the Japanese people]. Tokyo: Iwanami Shoten, 1989.

Tokutomi Roka. *Hototogisu*. In Satô Zen'ya and Satô Masaru, eds., *Kitamura Tôgoku-Tokutomi Roka shû* [Collected works of Kitamura Tôgoku and Tokutomi Roka] (Tokyo: Kadokawa Shoten, 1972).

*Tokyo Asahi shinbun*, 1936.

Tonomura, Hitomi. "Black Hair and Red Trousers: Gendering the Flesh in Medieval Japan." *American Historical Review* 99 (1994): 129–254.

Tsuda Mamichi. "Distinguishing the Equal Rights of Husbands and Wives." In *Meiroku Zasshi: Journal of the Japanese Enlightenment*, trans. William R. Braisted (Cambridge: Harvard University Press, 1976).

Ueno Chizuko. "Modern Patriarchy and the Formation of the Japanese Nation State." In Donald Denoon, Mark Hudson, Gavan McCormack, and Tessa Morris-Suzuki, eds., *Multicultural Japan: Paleolithic to Postmodern* (Cambridge: Cambridge University Press, 2001).

——. *Seiairon* [On sex and love]. Tokyo: Kawade Shobô, 1991.

Wada Yoshiko. "Yûjo nikki" [The diary of a prostitute]. In Tanikawa Ken'ichi, ed., *Kindai minshû no kiroku, 3, shôfu* [Records of modern commoners, vol. 3., prostitutes] (Tokyo: Shinjinbutsu Ôrai Sha, 1971).

Watatani Kiyoshi. *Kinsei akujo kibun* [Tales of evil women from the early modern period]. Tokyo: Seiabô, 1979.

Wright, Elizabeth, ed. *Feminism and Psychoanalysis: A Critical Dictionary*. Oxford: Blackwell, 1992.

Yamakawa Kikue. *Women of the Mito Domain: Recollections of Samurai Family Life*. Trans. Kate Wildman Nakai. Tokyo: Tokyo University Press, 1992.

Yamamoto Jun. "A Case Study of Femal Primogeniture in Pre-modern Japan: Ariga Village, 1739–1868." In Ochiai Emiko, ed., *The Logic of Female Succession: Rethinking Patriarchy and Patrilineality in Global and Historical Perspective* (Kyoto: International Research Center for Japanese Studies, 2003), 299–319.

Yasukuni Ryôichi. "Kinsei Kyôto no shomin josei" [Commoner women in early modern Kyoto]. In Josei Shi Sôgô Kenkyûkai, ed., *Nihon josei seikatsu shi*, vol. 3 (Tokyo: Tokyo University Press, 1990).

*Yomiuri shinbun*, 1936.

Yuzawa Motohiko, ed. *Nihon fujin mondai shiryô shûsei* [Collected documents concerning women's issues in Japan], vol. 5. Tokyo: Domesu Shuppan, 1976.

*Italic* page numbers refer to photographs.